C000000833

NOTHING

TRI◎S

*Each TRIOS book
addresses an important
theme in critical theory,
philosophy, or cultural
studies through three
extended essays written
in close collaboration by
leading scholars.*

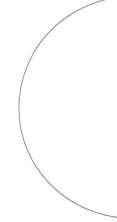

NOTHING

THREE INQUIRIES
IN BUDDHISM

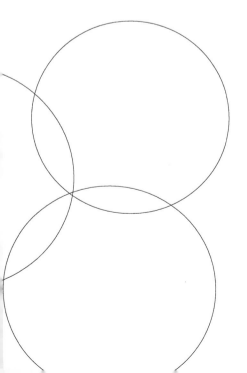

MARCUS
Boon

ERIC
Cazdyn

TIMOTHY
Morton

The University of Chicago Press
Chicago and London

MARCUS BOON is professor of English at York University in Toronto.
ERIC CAZDYN is Distiguished Professor of Aesthetics and Politics at the University of Toronto. TIMOTHY MORTON is the Rita Shea Guffey Chair in English at Rice University in Houston, Texas.

The University of Chicago Press, Chicago 60637
The University of Chicago Press, Ltd., London
© 2015 by The University of Chicago
All rights reserved. Published 2015.
Printed in the United States of America

24 23 22 21 20 19 18 17 16 15   1 2 3 4 5
ISBN-13: 978-0-226-23312-3 (cloth)
ISBN-13: 978-0-226-23326-0 (paper)
ISBN-13: 978-0-226-23343-7 (e-book)
DOI: 10.7208/chicago/9780226233437.001.0001

Library of Congress Cataloging-in-Publication Data
Nothing : three inquiries in Buddhism / Marcus Boon, Eric Cazdyn, and
Timothy Morton.
     pages cm
  ISBN 978-0-226-23312-3 (cloth : alkaline paper) — ISBN 978-0-226-23326-0
(paperback : alkaline paper) — ISBN 978-0-226-23343-7 (e-book) 1. Buddhism.
2. Buddhism and philosophy. 3. Critical theory. I. Boon, Marcus, author.
II. Cazdyn, Eric M., author. III. Morton, Timothy, 1968– author.
  BQ4040.N68 2015
  294.3'42—dc23

                                                                    2015003606

♾ This paper meets the requirements of ANSI/NISO Z39.48-1992
(Permanence of Paper).

CONTENTS

INTRODUCTION

Marcus Boon, Eric Cazdyn,
and Timothy Morton

1

So much nothing, so little time. This is a book made of nothings:
with a smile and a quizzical frown, let us talk about nothing. Ours
is a moment replete with theoretical and philosophical nothings: Alain Badiou with his zero, Slavoj Žižek with his *Less than
Nothing*, and nihilist forms of speculative realism (Ray Brassier,
Nihil Unbound) to name but a few. In this book, the reader will
encounter all kinds of nothing. There are the epistemological
gaps between Buddhism and critical theory—for instance, their
misalignments and misunderstandings. Then there are gaps
and voids that might be ontological: gaps between and within
things themselves, within what the many forms of Buddhism
and theory take to be reality: nothingness, gap, no-thing, emptiness, annihilation; event, revolution, void. There are indeed
cracks and spaces within the very concepts of *nothing* and *nothingness* that pervade Buddhism, theory, and Western philosophical appropriations of Buddhism more generally.

Beyond and behind all these, we hope that *Nothing: Three Inquiries in Buddhism* will engage the void between Buddhism and
critical theory—precisely by opening up these nothings, gaps,
and zeroes. The purpose of this introduction is to outline the
contours of the nothings that make up this book.

Perhaps one could sum up the story of Buddhism and theory

by remarking that there are two kinds of bridges between them: totally nonexistent bridges, and burned bridges. In 1978, during a dialogue with a Zen monk in Japan, Michel Foucault asserted that this was "the end of the era of Western philosophy. Thus if philosophy of the future exists, it must be born outside of Europe or equally born in consequence of meetings and impacts between Europe and non-Europe."[1] Thirty-four years later, there are some signs of the "birth" Foucault predicts, as philosophers and other humanities scholars make use of Buddhism, not simply as an object of study. The enactive AI theory of Francisco Varela, Evan Thompson, and Eleanor Rosch; Raul Moncayo's careful mapping of the shared territories of Lacanian psychoanalysis and Zen; the dialetheias of Graham Priest; the controversies surrounding the Speculative Non-Buddhism and Critical Buddhism projects; the existence of bodies such as the Comparative and Continental Philosophy Circle; currents within ecological philosophy—all indicate that something is gestating.[2] Yet will there emerge a true fusion of "Europe and non-Europe" from these swirls and information transfers? And what might the thinking that Foucault sees might be born have to do with contemporary "theory" and indeed with political practice? Will what is born even look like philosophy, at the moment of its appearance?

Or we can come at this from the other direction and ask if the fusion has already played itself out, if the fantasy of the non-West as buried treasure, in the form of exotic desire or career opportunism coming from the West or of incorrigible nativism and self-orientalism from the East, has now died a merciful death like so many other cross-cultural utopias—from the failed projects of world literature and global philosophy to the neoliberal appropriation of multiculturalism. Either way, as beginning or end, birth or death, the meetings and nonmeetings of Europe and non-Europe persist and must persist, even if the integrity of these geographical and philosophical categories might not.

Plato's *Theaetetus* asserts that philosophy begins in astonishment.[3] This feeling of wonder or astonishment is akin to Buddhist experiences of realization, enlightenment, *kenshō* or *satori*. To this extent, Buddhism is itself a kind of theory: there is an inner affinity between the two terms. The Tibetan for *Buddhist* is *nangpa*: literally this means "internalist" someone with a passion for exploring inner space, someone who has decided that external solutions always come up short. Why? Because the very notion of external solutions presupposes some kind of inner disposition that seeks out certain kinds of things in the outer world. Pushed by an inner compulsion, the murderer looks for a suitably sharp knife. Even though the point of philosophy may be to change the world rather than to interpret it, this very point is itself an interpretation, as Heidegger argues. The point implies an inner disposition, a disposition that one hesitates to call *subjectivity*—even the term *inner* is itself suspect.

What is called *theory*, then—critical theory, literary theory, and so on—seems at first glance to be remarkably like what is called Buddhism. Both these terms are Western. There is no Buddhism as such, and there is no one Buddhism, although the multiplicity of "Buddhisms" now popular in modern religious studies scholarship might obscure the commonalities between different sects of Buddhism, commonalities that are familiar enough to a practitioner of Buddhism. The notion of *practice* is precisely at issue. To practice Buddhism is to be involved in a deeply theoretical, reflective exercise that in Theravadin traditions and elsewhere is formalized as *hearing, contemplating*, and *meditating*. Hearing implies not simply reading and hearkening to discourse, but fully absorbing and understanding. Contemplating is making the Buddhadharma personal: to "read, mark, learn and inwardly digest" it (*The Book of Common Prayer*). This phase can involve intense debate, such as the ritualized, intense debating promulgated in the Gelugpa sect of Tibetan Buddhism, where monks and nuns will debate for days concerning the finer points of dharma, down to the last one standing. The historical Buddha himself was said to require his students to test the metal of the teachings themselves by subjecting them to rigorous intellectual and practical scrutiny. Meditating is the practical part—in Tibetan, meditation is called *gom*, which means "getting used to." To become deeply familiar with a set of meditation techniques is to realize the dharma on an existential level. Theory then becomes a kind of practice and practice in turn is a form of theoretical reflection, a radical hesitation in the face of one's confusion.

As for praxis, the inescapable and irresolvable problem of the relation between theory and practice, in which each term can never be fully incorporated into the other and the ultimate unevenness of the two terms is precisely what enriches the problem, it is the key component that Buddhism shares with the various subgenres of critical theory. From the radical feminisms of Luxemburg and hooks to the revolutionary psychoanalyses of Lacan and Guattari, the implacable problem of praxis, of rigorous reflection and go-for-broke action, is the hallmark. Or we might, however counterintuitively, turn to the Frankfurt School, where despite Marcuse's and Adorno's suspicion of Buddhism not to mention Eric Fromm's overzealous attraction to it, we can locate the shared priority of turning to the superstructure, to the complexity of subject formation and un-formation as well as to the process of ideological interpellation, without turning away from infrastructural realities.

Indeed, it is the question of desire itself that runs like a red thread through Buddhism and critical theory. Why would someone desire their own oppression, the Frankfurt School thinkers asked when challenging the false consciousness models of the orthodox Marxisms. Likewise any radical Buddhist, either on the cushion or in the library, must necessarily struggle with the question of how to make a desirable revolution, of the self and of the social, without desiring it.

To borrow again from the language of the early Theravadin schools of Buddhism, in meditation one severs a link in the chain of causation (the twelve *nidānas*), the link between *craving* and *grasping.* In one popular contemporary meditation instruction, this consists of an injunction to, as it were, drop the storyline and feel the feeling.[4] What is happening here? In terms of Hegelian philosophy or Althusserian ideology theory, what happens is that the content of a thought is ignored and the subject position, or phenomenological attitude, that thinks the thought is stripped naked and studied. Thinking to the second power is the way Fredric Jameson put it. If this isn't theoretical reflection, it's hard to know what is. Moreover, the foregoing processes— contemplation, debate, testing of hypotheses—must surely strike a chord in the mind of anyone attuned to philosophical and theoretical work in the humanities in a Western context.

What it means, therefore, to practice today, and what possible relations there could be between theory and practice are open questions, and one of the principal focuses of this volume. Theory itself—beginning with Marx, Nietzsche, Freud, Wittgenstein, you choose—emerged as a decisive problematizing of the relationship between philosophy and practice: think of the famous line of Marx's "Theses on Feuerbach" "the philosophers have only interpreted the world, in various ways; the point, however, is to change it."[5] What if, despite everything that has happened over the last 170 years, an adequate response to Marx's assertion required the opening up of something like a Buddhist understanding of the relationship of theory and practice, of praxis? Even of a new kind of Buddhist modernity, that, although grounded in the vast archive of historical teachings of Asian Buddhism, nonetheless reciprocally asserted a reformulation of what Buddhism means, and the recognition that hitherto existing Buddhist societies have themselves failed to realize completely that centerpiece of Mahāyāna Buddhist ethical practice, the bodhisattva's vow to bring to liberation all sentient beings. In other words, and appropriating Habermas: for us, both Buddhism and modernity remain incomplete projects. What if, in their incompletions, theory and Buddhism shared something?

2

It is thus somewhat surprising that there has not yet been very much of a rapprochement between Buddhism and theory. Our book is a contribution to critical theory, and to the recent religious turn in critical thought, which has been felt in fields such as political philosophy, aesthetics, science studies, psychoanalysis, postcolonial theory, and globalization studies. It is striking that Buddhist thought has not so far played a significant role in this religious turn. While there are Buddhist thinkers who have things to say about these fields, they are usually bracketed as symptoms of liberal utopian projections (thus the Dalai Lama is ridiculed as a Hollywood figure despite having made the claim that he considers himself "half-Marxist, half-Buddhist").

For reasons that remain unclear, but which are worth thinking about, the most vocal Buddhist academics have not engaged critical theory or its thinkers. Despite the fact that throughout history, Buddhism has had a necessary and rigorous philosophical dimension, most contemporary Buddhist thinkers seem to become populists when they talk ideas, a position that places them firmly in the hands of the powers that be, for the most part. Or they espouse an anti-intellectual and antiseptic "Buddhism without beliefs" as in the case of Stephen Batchelor, in which a crude insistence on practice negates the possibility of meaningful intervention in the modern world. Dōgen, the renowned thirteenth-century Zen Buddhist, might have become famous for saying "just sit" (shikan taza), an admonition to the overthinkers and spiritual instrumentalists, but he also wrote rigorously and voluminously about the finer points of Buddhist philosophy, reminding the meditator to think about what it means not to think.

Or the Buddhist academics attempt to suture Buddhism to prevailing academic fashions, whether it be neuroscience, a return to Kantianism, the new relational turn in psychoanalysis, and so on. The recent Donald Lopez edited volume, *Critical*

Terms for the Study of Buddhism, part of the University of Chicago's Buddhism and Modernity series, an excellent collection of essays that does occasionally cite Foucault and others, is nonetheless not critical in the sense of a demanding critique of the conditions of contemporary thought, but focuses firmly on the historical and scholarly apparatus of Buddhist studies, maintaining a partition between "Buddhist studies" on the one hand and modernity on the other, even when discussing modern Buddhist communities and thinkers.

As for other volumes which cover similar materials as this one: while there are many volumes of essays on Buddhism and everything from ecology to politics (though not political theory), very little has been published on Buddhism and theory, and the majority of those texts that do exist focus on the connections between Buddhism and deconstruction. These books include Robert Magliola's *Derrida on the Mend* (1984), Youxuan Wang's *Buddhism and Deconstruction* (2001), Jin Park's edited volume of essays *Buddhisms and Deconstructions* (2006), and several books by David Loy, including *Nonduality: A Study in Comparative Philosophy* (1988), *Lack and Transcendence: The Problem of Death and Life in Psychotherapy, Existentialism, and Buddhism* (1996), and *The Great Awakening: A Buddhist Social Theory* (2003). Loy is an interesting case because his earlier work responding to Derrida is rigorously theoretical, but his later work on Buddhism and psychoanalysis or politics is strikingly populist in tone: the book on psychoanalysis, for example, does not mention Lacan.

In general, these books might be considered part of an attempt to formulate a "postmodern" Buddhism built around a perception of a shared agenda of critiquing foundationalist thought. Fair enough. The anti-postmodern turn of critical thought in the last decade brackets Buddhism as another postmodern phenomenon, superficially committed to a lack of foundations while ideologically integrated into a late capitalist economy. According to this account, Buddhist practice allows the practitioner to imagine that he or she is beyond ideology when meditating, and to disavow his or her participation in capitalist social relations. Or it urges the practitioner to adapt to and accept dominant power structures, in either the cynical mode captured by Sloterdijk, in a stupid mode parodied by Žižek, or in a hyper-empathic and hysterically compassionate mode practiced by so many bleeding hearts. Caring precious little for the political unconscious or the utopian dreams flashing radically different futures, these naive Buddhist desires cannot help but resemble the toothless ego psychologies that Freud feared would mean the death of psychoanalysis. The same could, of course, be said of critical theory itself, postmodern or anti-postmodern.

As this volume indicates, there are other histories that could be spoken of. For example, there has been a serious engagement with Buddhism by Heideggerians, for obvious reasons. Heidegger befriended D.T. Suzuki, who published many of the earliest books in English on Zen; he was also engaged in a dialogue with the Kyoto School philosophers that spanned several decades, even if, as we know from Reinhold May's recent book *Heidegger's Hidden Sources*, his presentation of this relationship in his work was at best highly circumspect. It's unsurprising, therefore, that the Heideggerian philosopher Joan Stambaugh would be capable of writing sensitive and profound studies that link Buddhism and Western philosophy. And, of course, there are notable exceptions among Buddhists, in particular the aforementioned Kyoto School of philosophers such as Nishida, Miki, and Nishitani. And exceptions among those most taught in the intro to theory class (most notably, Sedgwick and Bataille).

But what constitutes serious engagement with Buddhism in the first place? Does one need to practice Buddhism in order to have something legitimate to say about it? Does one need to be intimate with all forms of Buddhist scholarship? And, if so, for how long and to what degree? No doubt, the academic Buddhologist will answer these questions differently than the dedicated monk. Or maybe not. At any rate, for us, who are invested in both Buddhism and critical theory, we want to begin to answer these questions in the following way: a serious engagement with Buddhism can take many forms, from obvious ones (such as scrupulous historical research or daily meditation practice) to ones that look nothing like Buddhism at all. The threshold of "seriousness," therefore, is whether or not such thinking and practices open up to Buddhist principles, and can productively push and be pushed by them. Just as the most direct Buddhist act might have no feel for Buddhism at all, so too might a non-Buddhist intervention shoot straight to the heart of Buddhist matters. That being said, there is still a conspicuous lack of critical theorists who engage Buddhism (either directly or indirectly) compared to those who examine other spiritual or religious traditions. And this gap, we believe, is symptomatic of something more than just being raised or trained in a different tradition.

3

What explains this gap? Is it hostility? Is it the institutional structures of the modern university and the Taylorization of knowledge? Is it plain ignorance? Is it some structural ideological blockage—the resistance of those in Religious Studies or Asian Studies to participate in what they are examining, the enforcement of extraversion everywhere in social space, some sclerotic orientalism or even racism that prevents even progressive scholarship from employing Buddhism honestly and with passion? Or is it the recognition that such a connection is false, incommensurable and, therefore, not worth the heavy lifting and theoretical effort required? Now that we have reached the second decade of the twenty-first century, some answers seem to be in order.

Critical theorists and radical philosophers are not unwilling to think religion. Yet the decidedly Christian turn taken by a number of contemporary European philosophers (Žižek, Badiou, Agamben) has not been matched by anything like a Buddhist turn. This is perhaps surprising, given affinities between

Buddhism and contemporary Western thinking in general, along with the fact that Buddhism has now been practiced in the West for over one hundred years. To an innocent onlooker it might seem strange, then, that not one of the philosophers has turned to Buddhism rather than to Christianity. How can we account for this?

First we should consider the stated reasons for the turn to Christianity. They are different, but they share certain core features. Each philosopher, for instance, is fascinated by St. Paul. For Žižek, Christianity provides a way to think historical materialism without recourse to anything like a beyond.[6] What Christianity announces is the death of God—though this might come as news to an orthodox Christian, and perhaps even to Jesus himself, who does on occasion talk about prayer. St. Paul becomes for Žižek the Lenin of Christianity, ruthlessly establishing an actually existing community based on the death of God. For Badiou, it is St. Paul who exemplifies a faithful adherence to what he calls "truth process," an emptying or kenosis of the subject in the face of some real event: the term *event* denotes a habit-shattering rupture in the continuity of things. For Agamben, Christianity provides a model for thinking political coexistence as an economy as well as providing the paradigm of sovereignty (God as heavenly king). St. Paul exemplifies the political ambiguity in Christianity, for according to Agamben he is concerned with a "messianic" abolition of Jewish law.

While it seems true that each philosopher is in no sense supporting orthodox forms of Christianity, the overall effect to an outsider is of an underwriting of Christianity, and of Abrahamic theism in general. What doesn't kill you makes you stronger, and protestations of atheism notwithstanding, none of these philosophers is happy with run of the mill "new" atheism (Dawkins, Hitchens, Dennett, Harris). It seems significant that Agamben has called himself a Christian philosopher, and that the subtitle of one of Žižek's books on Christianity can at the very least be misinterpreted to mean that Christianity is "worth fighting for": "for" rather than "against" protestations again notwithstanding.[7]

In the case of these philosophers' treatment of Buddhism, things are complex. There is the fact of simple omission. Badiou could easily have chosen Dōgen rather than St. Paul, or Milarepa for that matter—Siddhārtha Gautama himself would have made an even better example yet. There is no earthly reason why a Buddhist would not have done as well or better than St. Paul to exemplify adherence to a world-disrupting truth process. Legends of Buddhist teachers abound with Pauline conversion experiences. Personal accounts of *kenshō* and *satori* in Zen are crammed with blinding flashes, feelings of losing the ground under one's feet, a sudden sense of devotion to a purpose that is far higher or deeper than the ego. Why not use these narratives?

Agamben's neglect of Buddhism is not as strange as Badiou's. Agamben is explicitly reframing a tradition of Christianity to reflect his larger work on sovereignty and the state of exception. Working within Christianity to accomplish this work seems like a coherent strategy. There are, however, moments at which Agamben's embrace of Heidegger leads him to say things that Buddhists would certainly agree with. For instance, the discussion of boredom as a gateway to a mystical coexistence in what Rilke calls the "Open" would ring bells with a Buddhist meditator.[8]

The case of Žižek is a little easier. This is because throughout Žižek's work there are countless direct statements of active hostility toward Buddhism. So much is this the case that one of the essays in this volume (Morton) explores this hostility in the light of Jacques Lacan's actually rather generous and nuanced assessment of Buddhism in the tenth seminar (on anxiety). It is perhaps the case that Lacan, attuned to Heidegger's exploration of anxiety, was at least sympathetic to quasi-Buddhist lines of thinking, since Heidegger appears at points in *Being and Time* to be "channeling" something like Buddhism, and later remarked favorably that his work resembled that of D.T. Suzuki.

Moreover, the lineage Heidegger–Lacan–Derrida seems at several points actively hospitable to Buddhism. Despite some obvious affinities, Frankfurt School Marxism (in particular, Adorno) has been more hostile than friendly. This school's inheritance of Hegel might begin to explain this, as Žižek's Hegelianism might well explain his own explicit anti-Buddhism, since it was Hegel who established Buddhism as a cult of nothingness (in the memorable phrase of Roger Pol Droit).[9] Likewise, Badiou's adherence to Hegel and Marx might also explain his omission of Buddhism. It's less clear why Agamben, working in the tradition of Heidegger, remains silent on Buddhism.

Or, and as usual, we can turn all of this around, and see the hostility of the Heidegger–Lacan–Derrida line and the affinity to Buddhism in the Frankfurt School–Hegel–Lacan line, in which it is the dialectic itself that binds these thinkers to Buddhism— even a Hegelian dialectic insofar that absolute spirit is not a destination or a prophecy, an out-of-date teleology, but something more akin to Lacanian drive as Jameson and Žižek would have it. This also accounts for why Lacan can occupy a central position in both trajectories. In short, how hard is it to imagine a brilliant book written by Žižek arguing for the revolutionary core of Buddhism?

In sum, what we have in the case of Badiou, Žižek, and Agamben is a twofold reluctance to engage Buddhism. First, there is lack of engagement born from the sheer compulsion inherent in Western traditions that makes it difficult for any scholar to realize how entangled in them she is, critical as she may be of those traditions. Secondly, we should consider the influence of Hegel: a highly Eurocentric two-centuries-old philosophy of religion, whose approach to Buddhism is based on rather sketchy Jesuit reports from Tibet—in short, the work of Hegel—is taken at its word, without so much as a nod to Schopenhauer, who to all intents and purposes became a Buddhist, or even to Nietzsche, who explored Buddhism in illuminating ways; or to Heidegger, whose work reads so much like proto-Buddhism that

his translator Joan Stambaugh was effortlessly able to integrate his thinking into her work on Nishitani and other Buddhist philosophers. Buddhism is taken as an inconsistent symptom of consumerist passivity, nihilism, Japanese fascism, and
Nazism.

Irony of ironies—these fearful projections are justified.
Buddhism may indeed be a religion of disturbing passivity,
what one philosopher calls *radical passivity*, an unconditional
being-with.[10] Whether this is the case is one of the areas of debate between us. Against most forms of theism Buddhism does
indeed appear nihilistic, with its doctrines of no-self (*anātman*)
and emptiness (*śūnyatā*). And Buddhist cults of devotion to the
guru and adherence to discipline might strike non-Buddhists as
proto-Nazi, and there is always the case of actual appropriations
of Zen for fascism in Japan (implicating even the patron saint
of Western Buddhism, D.T. Suzuki, and his erstwhile comrade
in ideas, Nishida), or indeed the often highly problematic theocratic Buddhist traditions found in premodern Tibet. Or, for
that matter, Italian fascist Julius Evola's valorization of the Zen
warrior during World War II. We don't want to dispel the idea
that Buddhism is frightening. To a Buddhist herself, Buddhism
is rather frightening. It is somewhat accurate to be afraid of a set
of techniques ruthlessly designed to root out the ego and burn
it on the spot; let alone the historical uses to which Buddhism
has been put.

Again, what this points to is the unfinished nature of historical and existing Buddhist societies. But it also means recognizing that far from being a static entity even in a traditional society
in which Buddhism is hegemonic, there were important debates
and dissents within Buddhist traditions, prior to the historical
ruptures that have impacted Asian Buddhist societies, such as
the Chinese invasion of Tibet in 1950, or the end of the Japanese
imperialist project in 1945. We are interested in relatively marginal voices that did attempt "theoretical" critiques of existing
Buddhist society, such as Tibetan modernist Gendun Chopel,

as well as emerging Buddhisms such as the Critical Buddhism movement in Japan today.

4

Arranged in alphabetical order, the three essays in this book move in different directions and make different arguments, sometimes in direct opposition to each other. Indeed, it should already be clear from this introduction that depending on which theoretical problems and lines are pursued, distinct groups of allies and opponents are formed. What is shared by all three of us, nevertheless, is a commitment to making the connections between Buddhism and critical theory in the first place. And why pursue the connections? Because at the contemporary moment Buddhism and critical theory share the same historical situation of global capitalism and, therefore, are struggling with the same material limits—from ecological peril to so much psycho-social violence. Buddhism and critical theory also share the same utopian possibilities, or at least the same radically negative critique of the present that itself is life-nourishing and terrifyingly beautiful. This shared double jeopardy is also to understand critical theory less as a twentieth- and twenty-first-century theory of the subject or as so much European idealist and social philosophy, and to understand Buddhism less as a traditional Asian spiritual movement or even as a failed political experiment, but to approach and understand both as problematics—as modes of engagement that prioritize the inextricable relation between their very forms of thought and action (and the relation between thought and action) on the one hand and the historical situation on the other hand.[11]

Boon's essay explores the politics of *śūnyatā* or emptiness as they emerged circa 1936–76 in the wake of particular moments of political crisis in which both Buddhism and Marxism are implicated, through a crisis in the relation of ideology to practice. He explores the extensive reference to Buddhism in the work of the key French theoretical thinker Georges Bataille (1897–1962) after the failure of the French Surrealists' involvement in the leftist Popular Front in the 1930s, and his use of ideas from Buddhism and yoga in initiating a new kind of politico-theological practice, which involved specific techniques of breathing, meditation, and visualization. Although Bataille quickly gave up his own yoga practice (though not before writing some remarkable texts on it), Boon argues that Buddhist concepts and practices (about which Bataille was remarkably well informed, for the era) are decisive in Bataille's later work on general economy in texts such as *The Accursed Share*, and offer provocative ways of rethinking the relationship between "emptiness," "excess," and "nothing" as a political problem—specifically one resonant to the question of "nonalignment" as it manifested in Asian societies at the moment of decolonization after World War II, and the hitherto unacknowledged importance of Buddhist ideas—Buddhist socialist ideas even—in the development of a politics of nonalignment.

Boon then explores several articulations of a Buddhist politics from the period of the Cold War: one, the work of Tibetan modernist writer Gendun Chopel (1903–51), who undertook an unprecedented questioning of Buddhist philosophy and practice as it existed in Tibet at the moment of the Chinese invasion—a questioning that arguably resulted in his untimely death. In Chopel's work too, notably the remarkable theoretical text "Adornment of Nagarjuna's Thought" recently translated by Donald Lopez, Jr. in his book *Madman's Middle Way*, Boon identifies a certain crisis in how human beings relate, as individuals but also as collectives, to a constitutive emptiness, and specifically how unenlightened beings might ever recognize enlightenment and find their way toward it: in other words, Chopel poses the problem of the politics of practice from within a Buddhist tradition, and finding no answer there, is exposed to a certain abyss that is called theory. The second is Gary Snyder's remarkable short essay "Buddhist Anarchism" from 1961, in which

Snyder condenses a detailed vision of what a nonaligned global Buddhist anarchist movement might or should look like. The third is Christian monk Thomas Merton's last speech, made the day before his untimely death in a hotel room in Bangkok. Merton had recently spent time with exiled Tibetan monks in the Indian Himalayas, and tries to reconcile this experience with his readings of Herbert Marcuse. In doing so, he struggles to articulate a new kind of gift economy, impossible within the framework of the Cold War, but on the very edge of articulability.

In the final sections of his essay, Boon takes up the problem of a contemporary Buddhist politics, using Giorgio Agamben's work on bare life, Karatani Kōjin's recent proposals concerning gift economies in *The Structure of World History*, and the post-Bataillean corpus of work on non-identitarian forms of community—a community exposed to what we can variably call nothingness, emptiness, the void. Boon explores various iterations of this politics of nothingness in the work of Alain Badiou, and a recent group of theorists associated with the Speculative Non-Buddhism blog, and shows the way that in the appropriation of the Common, both Buddhists and non-Buddhists, theorists and practitioners are exposed to what Tibetan modernist Gendun Chopel calls the "Great Contradiction."

Cazdyn's essay begins by claiming that there is a shared function between the Buddhist category of "enlightenment," the Marxist category of "revolution," and the psychoanalytic category of "cure." Although oftentimes mobilized in sloppy and counterproductive ways, Cazdyn argues that enlightenment, revolution, and cure need to be reclaimed today or else Buddhism, Marxism, and psychoanalysis risk losing their radical force and turning into revisionist farces of themselves. This reclamation project turns on re-theorizing praxis and then tracking it within the three fields, for it is praxis (as the implacable problem of the relation between theory and practice) that pressurizes the coming-into-being of Buddhism, Marxism, and psychoanalysis as well as their most radical transformations.

Cazdyn proceeds by returning to the original production of the problem of praxis in the histories of Buddhism, Marxism, and psychoanalysis (beginning with the Zen Buddhism of Dōgen in the early to mid-thirteenth century and his monumental text on practice, *Shōbōgenzō*, before moving to Marx and an analysis of *Capital* and then to Freud and his writings on clinical practice and his *The Interpretation of Dreams*). Cazdyn then studies the historical transformations in each problematic by focusing on key *moments of return* to the problem of praxis, all the while accumulating a series of connections among the three problematics. After tracking these shifts Cazdyn arrives at the contemporary moment of global capitalism and claims that some of the most radical interventions today are staged as reengagements with the problem of praxis and are occurring off the cushion, off the factory floor, and off the couch . . . but ineluctably based on the fundamental logics of these three practices and inextricably tied to the categories of enlightenment, revolution, and cure.

One of these impressive interventions is by Isozaki Arata, the great architect who has incorporated into his diverse work over the past fifty years the concept of *ma* (a kind of negative time-space) that flashes a new way into the problems of enlightenment, revolution, and cure. Isozaki's *ma* also serves as a way to mobilize the category of *nothing* that links the three problematics of Buddhism, Marxism, and psychoanalysis, for *ma* turns out to be a materialist nothing (or the nothing of materiality) that Isozaki spectacularly activates in his most recent project ("Ark Nova") in connection to the 2011 Japanese disasters (earthquake, tsunami, nuclear meltdown). "Ark Nova" is a portable art-community space that can hold up to five hundred people before being deflated and transported to the next disaster, a disaster that has yet to occur but that is built right inside of our present. "Ark Nova" is an architecture of the future, not a model for a future architecture but an architectural figure for a radically different future, one that is—at once—different than our present, different than our wildest speculations on the future, and different than our very concept of the future itself. Isozaki's work, moreover, provides the opportunity to link the shared problems of enlightenment, revolution, and cure, and to argue that each problematic (Buddhism, Marxism, and psychoanalysis) flashes the blind spots of the others and comprises critical theoretical acts of the highest order.

Morton's essay is an exploration of a phenomenon he calls *Buddhaphobia*, a "fear of Buddhism" that he equates with anxieties generated within modernity as such. These anxieties pertain to *nothingness*, which can be defined not as the "absolutely nothing at all" of *oukontic* nothing, but rather as the *meontic* nothing of a spectral flickering that cannot be posited as constantly present in a metaphysical sense. It was Immanuel Kant who opened the Pandora's box of meontic nothingness, and since the publication of *The Critique of Pure Reason*, European philosophers have assumed various stances toward it. Most notable for the purposes of this book is Hegel's attempt to ascribe such a view to a primitive form of consciousness—primitive in his sense: he calls this *Buddhism*. Yet this nothingness is palpably present within the philosophical history of "the West." Buddhaphobia thus looks like a disavowal of something within thought, with which thought is already intimate: a disavowal that maps onto homophobia, a fear of intimacy with the same.

What provokes anxiety about Buddhism is not total void, but the weird presence of nothingness, which Morton reads as a queer proximity of the uncanny within one's experience. From this arises the critique of Buddhism as a form of automation, which is roughly how Žižek interprets it. There is a lineage of such interpretations, going back through Monier Monier-Williams, whose criticism of Tibetan prayer wheels and other technologies sounds exactly the same as Žižek's. Such criticism exposes fault lines in leftist thought concerning industrial automation, despite the ostensible disavowal of a fully present subject in the work of Hegelians such as Žižek. The anxiety about

Buddhism is also an anxiety about industrial and consumer capitalism. Yet the game was already afoot, within Western philosophy as such. To study Buddhaphobia is to reveal tensions within Hegelian-Marxist thought that can be traced to the difficult and ongoing engagement of modern philosophers with Kant, whose phenomenon-thing gap opens up nothingness within reason. Thus despite "subjective destitution" and other forms of quasi-Buddhist ideas in Žižek, what this Hegelian lineage resists is precisely modernity, in which the fundamental philosophical question is how to dispose oneself toward (or against) nothingness. If Marxism is to survive into a postmodern—that is, ecological—age, Morton argues, then it would be best for it to engage with nothingness and the concomitant nihilisms of consumerism and industry; and this would involve a deeper and less phobic engagement with Buddhism.

5

You will find an introductory glossary of Buddhist terms at the back of this volume, expertly compiled by Claire Villareal. We debated the necessity of including a glossary—which could be interpreted as a reinstatement of Buddhological disciplinary knowledge as being the ultimate guarantor of our attempts to open up an interdisciplinary space in which both Buddhism and critical theory are interdependent actants. Why not have a glossary of critical theoretical terms—or an interdisciplinary glossary of all of the various disciplinary terms that we use? But the contestation and exploration of both Buddhist and critical theory lexicons is already one of the responsibilities we have taken on in our individual chapters. In the end we have pragmatically assumed that most readers of this text will already have some familiarity with the critical theory lexicon, and that a glossary of Buddhist terms will allow those who are unfamiliar with this lexicon to follow the arguments being made with increased focus and clarity.

This conversation is not intended to end, but rather to begin or, at any rate, to make explicit what has been ongoing in Western thought since the skeptical engagement with Buddhism in Greek philosophy. In particular, we see our work in direct relation to this urgent moment within the global transition from modernity to whatever comes next. We seek to restore to (Western) theory its repressed underside, in the name of increasing that phenomenon variously called consciousness, critique, and struggle.

NOTES

1. Michel Foucault, *Religion and Culture*, ed. Jeremy Carette (New York: Routledge, 1999), 113.

2. Space does not permit a full account. But see Simon P. James, *Zen Buddhism and Environmental Ethics* (Aldershot: Ashgate, 2004); Mary Evelyn Tucker and Duncan Williams, eds., *Buddhism and Ecology: The Interconnection of Dharma and Deeds* and *Environmental Ethics: An Interdisciplinary Journal Dedicated to the Philosophical Aspects of Environmental Problems* 22, no. 2 (Summer 2000): 207–10; Jacquelynn Baas and Mary Jane Jacob, eds., *Buddha Mind in Contemporary Art* (Berkeley: University of California Press, 2004). For more general histories of Buddhism in the West, see Lawrence Sutin, *All Is Change: The Two-Thousand-Year Journey of Buddhism to the West* (New York: Little Brown, 2006); Rick Fields, *How the Swans Came to the Lake: A Narrative History of Buddhism in America* (Boston: Shambhala, 1992). For neuroscience, see Francisco Varela, Evan Thompson, and Eleanor Rosch, *The Embodied Mind: Cognitive Science and Human Experience* (Cambridge, MA: MIT Press, 1992); Bernhard Poerksen and Francisco J. Varela, "Truth Is What Works: Francisco J. Varela on Cognitive Science, Buddhism, the Inseparability of Subject and Object, and the Exaggerations of Constructivism—A Conversation," *Journal of Aesthetic Education* 40, no. 1 (Spring 2006): 35–53. Other important resources include: *Encyclo-*

pedia of Buddhism, ed. Robert E. Buswell Jr. (New York: Thomson Gale, 2004); *The Princeton Dictionary of Buddhism*, ed. Robert E. Buswell Jr. and Donald S. Lopez Jr. (Princeton, NJ: Princeton University Press, 2014); and John Powers, *A Concise Encyclopedia of Buddhism* (Boston: Oneworld, 2000).

3. Plato, *Theaetetus*, trans. Benjamin Jowett, http://classics.mit.edu/Plato/theatu.html, accessed November 29, 2012.

4. Pema Chödron, *The Wisdom of No Escape and the Path of Loving-Kindness* (Boston: Shambhala, 2010), 15–26.

5. Karl Marx, "Theses on Feuerbach," in *The Marx-Engels Reader* (New York: Norton, 1972), 145.

6. Slavoj Žižek, *The Fragile Absolute: Or, Why Is the Christian Legacy Worth Fighting For?* (London: Verso, 2000).

7. See, for example, "Radical Theology and Agamben," *An und für sich*, http://itself.wordpress.com/2008/07/07/radical-theology-and-agamben/. (The comments section is somewhat illuminating in this regard.)

8. See, for example, Chögyam Trungpa, "Cool Boredom" in *The Essential Chögyam Trungpa*, ed. Carolyn Gimian (Boston: Shambhala, 1999), 87–90.

9. See Timothy Morton, "Hegel on Buddhism," *Romantic Circles Praxis*, http://www.rc.umd.edu/praxis/buddhism/morton/morton.html, accessed November 29, 2012. Roger Pol-Droit, *The Cult of Nothingness: The Philosophers and the Buddha* (Chapel Hill: University of North Carolina Press, 2003).

10. Thomas Carl Wall, *Radical Passivity: Levinas, Blanchot, and Agamben* (Albany: State University of New York Press, 1999).

11. See Fredric Jameson, *Valences of the Dialectic* (New York: Verso, 2010), 372; and Cazdyn's introduction to his essay in this volume.

TO LIVE IN A GLASS HOUSE IS A REVOLUTIONARY VIRTUE PAR EXCELLENCE

MARXISM, BUDDHISM, AND THE
POLITICS OF NONALIGNMENT

Marcus Boon

1

In 1937, while in exile in Svendborg, Bertolt Brecht wrote a poem entitled "The Buddha's Parable of the Burning House." The poem describes the Buddha's disciples questioning him as to the nature of "nothingness" beyond "greed's wheel." The Buddha does not respond, but confides in his close disciples that answering such questions is like answering the questions of those whose house is burning down, as to what the weather outside is like and so on. "These people," says the Buddha, "need to burn to death before they stop asking questions. Truly, friends / Unless a man feels the ground so hot underfoot that he'd gladly / Exchange it for any other, sooner than stay, to him / I have nothing to say." The poem goes on to compare the Buddha's situation to those of the communists "putting forward / Various proposals of an earthly nature, and beseeching men to shake off / Their human tormentors," when asked similarly irrelevant questions by those faced with "the approaching bomber squadrons of Capital."[1]

The lines about communism that follow the Buddha's "I have nothing to say" were a later addition to the poem, as if the parable's Marxist subtext risked being appropriated back into a Buddhist narrative (likely derived from the third chapter of the *Lotus Sūtra*) unless the meanings were concretely specified and articulated.[2] Brecht's poem resonates with a parenthetical remark made by his colleague Walter Benjamin in his essay "On Surrealism," in which, elaborating the qualities of what he called "profane illumination," he has a flashback to his 1927 visit to Moscow:

> (In Moscow I lived in a hotel in which almost all the rooms were occupied by Tibetan lamas who had come to Moscow for a congress of Buddhist churches. I was struck by the number of doors in the corridors that were always left ajar. What had at first seemed accidental began to be disturbing. I found out that in these rooms lived members of a sect who had sworn never to occupy closed rooms. The shock I had then must be felt by the reader of *Nadja*.) To live in a glass house is a revolutionary virtue par excellence.[3]

So Buddhist practice, according to Benjamin, could be a revolutionary practice. As the recent book *Red Shambhala* describes it, there were in fact prominent Bolsheviks during the post-revolutionary period who pursued contacts with Buddhist organizations. This was sometimes no doubt because of realpolitik and the question of how to integrate central Asian areas such as Buryatia, Kalmykia, and Tuva with significant Buddhist populations into the USSR. But at other times it was because Buddhism was seen as offering tools that supported a revolutionary practice. The "congress of Buddhist churches" that Benjamin refers to was probably the First All-Russian Buddhist Congress, held in Moscow in January 1927, at a point where the situation of Buddhists within the Russian Communist state was still undecided.[4] As Anya Bernstein notes in her recent study of Buryatian Buddhism, there was a significant Buddhist reform movement in

Buryatia in the 1920s, many of whose goals resemble those of contemporary/secular engaged Buddhists today. This reform movement was brutally crushed in the 1930s, with the almost complete suppression of Buddhism in the public realm—in Buryatia and elsewhere in the USSR.[5] Even if the invitation to Buddhist monks to come to Moscow was made for propagandistic purposes, even if the invitation was accepted because the monks were also using Buddhism as a vehicle for secular ethnic/nationalist political purposes, Benjamin's observation of a truth about a practice of revolutionary virtue still stands. And the door to it still stands open. But for whom?

Common wisdom, however, would have it that Marxism, or more broadly critical theory, and Buddhism stand in opposition to each other: the world-negating spirituality of the Buddha as ideological obfuscation versus the concrete struggle over material conditions of the Marxist militant on the one hand; the deadly consequences of violently pursuing an inevitably distorted and distorting materialist ideology versus the embodied awareness of love and wisdom happening in the here and now of the Buddhist practitioner on the other, one the dialectical inversion of the other. And there is plenty of historical evidence that would support both of these dialectical positions in the narratives of the encounters of traditional, colonial, and postcolonial Buddhist cultures and communities with Marxism and/or communism throughout Asia in the twentieth century—and the decimation of Buddhist sanghas by communist regimes in Russia, China, and various Asian countries.[6] Furthermore, the study of Asian religions, and arguments for a "Buddhist society" in Europe and America in the twentieth century were often associated with right-wing and/or fascist thinkers, who valorized Buddhism and other Asian religions in the name of anti-modern, anti-democratic, and anti-communist politics of various kinds.[7] Conversely, contemporary writers associated with "engaged Buddhism" say surprisingly little about Marx, or for that matter the long and complicated histories of the engagement of Marxism and Buddhism within Asian societies.[8] Following the work of Naoki Sakai, one might well inquire into the historical and other conditions under which "Marxism" and "Buddhism" have been presented so often as entirely separate or opposed entities.[9]

The dialectical critique of Buddhism has recently been taken up by critics Slavoj Žižek and Peter Hallward. For Žižek, the emergence of Buddhism in the West is a form of fetishistic disavowal of the material conditions of late capitalism, notably taking the form of an orientalist valorization of feudalist Tibetan Buddhist society and/or a fantasized position of removal from the "stress" of real material conditions via meditation and the doctrine of "no-self."[10] For Hallward, the turn to Buddhism is one of the symptoms of a postcolonial celebration of pure difference that results in a state of depoliticized disengagement from the world.[11] Both Žižek and Hallward in part develop their arguments in response to the work of Alain Badiou and his argument for a philosophy and practice that maintains fidelity with the idea of communism. Reading Badiou's *Being and Event* has provoked a rethinking of the critical spaces in which I engage both Buddhism and critical theory, just as it has provoked Hallward and Žižek.

Žižek and Hallward's descriptions of historical Buddhism are often wildly inaccurate.[12] For example, in *The Puppet and the Dwarf*, Žižek appears to believe that "bodhisattva" is the name of a particular historical person rather than a generic descriptive type or category of being (22–23). Similarly, Hallward, at the end of his book on Badiou, describes "Sunyata" and "Satori" as specifically "Hīnayāna" (i.e., Theravādan Buddhist) terms, which he then attempts to contrast with what he believes to be a Mahāyāna Buddhist philosophy.[13] Perhaps these errors are the result of their arbitrary sources: Žižek's main reference for his knowledge of Buddhism in *The Puppet and the Dwarf* is *Orthodoxy*, a 1908 apologia for Christianity by G. K. Chesterton; and Hallward's in *Absolutely Postcolonial* is a relatively marginal

1951 book by Christmas Humphreys.[14] Beyond that, Žižek relies on Brian Victoria's *Zen at War*, an important study of Japanese Zen Buddhists' involvement in Japanese militarism in World War II—certainly enough to disabuse anyone gullible enough to believe that all applications of Buddhism are by definition infallible. But as Ernst Benz suggests in his 1963 study *Buddhism or Communism: Which Holds the Future of Asia?*, the Japanese story is quite specific, and the actual historical relations between Buddhism and communism, imperialism, fascism or, for that matter, postcolonial empire have been variable.[15] Still, despite his ignorance of historical Buddhism, many of the criticisms Žižek makes of contemporary Western Buddhism are in my opinion quite accurate, both in regard to existing Buddhist communities in the West, and more specifically my own practice. Similarly, I find Hallward's interest in putting Buddhism into relation with developments in contemporary theory and literature intriguing. In both cases, I find myself wondering why it is necessary to take this detour through a radically distorted Buddhism in order to get to the materialist philosophies to which these thinkers are committed.

Against Žižek's portrayal of the Dalai Lama as a kind of Disney figure cheerleading global capitalism, I note that the Dalai Lama has repeatedly articulated his support for Marxism, stating, for example, that "the failure of the regime in the former Soviet Union was, for me, not the failure of Marxism but the failure of totalitarianism. For this reason I still think of myself as half-Marxist, half-Buddhist."[16] Buddhism is an event in any society in which it emerges, whether in India, China, or more recently Europe and America. In this chapter I will argue that the challenge of a Buddhist universalism, in the form of the Mahāyāna Buddhist vow to bring about the enlightenment of all sentient beings, represents a trauma for any society that encounters it, including our own. Conversely, the encounter of existing Buddhist societies with communism has also been a trauma, and I believe that this is what the Dalai Lama recognizes: that an avowed Buddhist universalism in premodern Tibet supported a feudal system that manifestly failed to carry out its own claims to universal liberation.

A few years ago, I attended an event in Toronto to celebrate the publication of Tibetan Buddhist teacher Dzogchen Ponlop Rinpoche's *Rebel Buddha: On the Road to Freedom*. I was attracted to the notion of "rebel Buddha" but also wary, given that rebellion is one of the principal tropes of consumer capitalism these days. My wariness grew when we were shown a PowerPoint presentation featuring music by the Rolling Stones and images of Stephen Colbert, the *Jon Stewart Show*, and Rinpoche's Twitter account. Rinpoche argued that Buddhism means rebelling against the status quo, "taking down the belief system in our heads . . . not an external authority." He claimed that this would lead, among other things, to a well-behaved citizenry. The status quo then would be an internally generated projection of the form an existing society takes, rather than something externally imposed—or, for that matter, the specific way in which the relations of "internal" to "external" are mediated in a particular society. Later in the day, Rinpoche mused that it's unclear what an external system that could be imposed internally could actually be, except perhaps "language."

It became clear to me that Ponlop Rinpoche had no understanding of ideology, of the way in which the internal subjective world is structured and interpellated by particular social and political structures that are essenceless or empty, but nonetheless situationally effective. Whether one can say more generally that Buddhism has no theory of ideology is a problem that this essay seeks to address. Buddhist texts often speak of "habitual patterns," but habit is not merely an internally generated form of repetition. Rather, it is imposed through interpellation. In Althusser's classic definition, "ideology 'acts' or 'functions' in such a way that it 'recruits' subjects among the individuals (it recruits them all), or 'transforms' the individuals into subjects (it transforms them all) by that very precise operation which I have called *interpellation* or hailing, and which can be imagined along the lines of the most commonplace everyday police (or other) hailing: 'Hey, you there!'"[17] Indeed, even the dissemination of good habits—such as meditation practice, mind teachings such as recognition of the four noble truths, etc.—are external and social to some degree. There could be no "Buddhism" without such movements of interpellation, or without a teacher or Buddha who also said, "Hey, you there!" There are Buddhist teachings that could be considered teachings on ideological interpellation—for example, The Twelve Links of Dependent Origination in the Tibetan Mahāyāna tradition—yet the emphasis of those teachings is almost always on the internal nature of the problem.

Furthermore, one might ask to what degree Buddhism itself is an ideological formation whose particular forms have gone and will continue to be unexamined so long as one insists that Buddhist practice is internal, and therefore "beyond" the particular social, political and religious forms that exist in a particular Buddhist society or community. Debiprasad Chattopadhyaya makes the argument that "early Buddhism" in India (i.e., the Buddhism of the Pāli canon), operating under the influence of what he calls the "primitive Communism" of rural Indian life during the epoch of the Buddha, was both dialectical and if not materialist, certainly realist, built around a proposal for an egalitarian, casteless society, and *pratītyasamutpāda*, which he defines as "dependence on definite causes and conditions" and "universal flux." This early Buddhism proposed a critique of private or "personal" property—however, this critique goes no further than a withdrawal from the world, and, Chattopadhyaya argues, lacks the tools that were available to Marx and Engels, in terms of carrying out what is implied by *pratītyasamutpāda* in terms of the universal liberation of mankind. He continues that Mahāyāna and later forms of Buddhism ideologically obscure the radical, dialectical materialist aspect of the Buddha's teachings, in order to obtain the patronage of the royalty and wealthy

merchants. Setting aside the problematic rhetoric of original-
ity, earliness, and authenticity, so familiar in discourses on religion, Chattopadhyaya's argument uses the classic Marxist division between ideology (distorted descriptions of reality based
on class interests) and science (a "definite" materialist analysis).
For Chattopadhyaya, "original Buddhism" hovers somewhere
between ideology and science, since it lacks the tools to fully
develop itself as science and practice in a modern form. Still, we
might reverse Chattopadhyaya's argument and say that according to him, "original Buddhism" contains the elements of a productive stance on the problem of ideology.[18] I will return to this.

It's not hard to point to the weaknesses of historical Buddhist
societies that have resulted from the lack of open ideological critique: the now well-documented collaborations of the Japanese
Zen hierarchy with nationalist and militarist authorities in the
first half of the twentieth century; the feudal nature of Tibetan
society at the moment that Mao's Communist troops invaded in
1950; the problematic complicities between Buddhism and the
state in various Asian countries in the twentieth century. Even
recent studies of the politics of Buddhism struggle with this
point.[19] For example, in his admirable review of political Buddhism in Asia, Charles Keyes formulates the problem of political
Buddhism as the relation of Buddhism to the state.[20] Keyes demonstrates that this relation is historically quite variable, span-
ning the Buddha's own remarks on the topic as recorded in the
Pāli canon, to anticolonial opposition through theocracy. Yet
the essay nonetheless assumes that Buddhism qua Buddhism
is ultimately separate from the exercise of worldly power, even
when it appears to be fully incorporated into it, as in the case
of a theocracy. Implicit in Keyes's argument is the notion that
Buddhism is fundamentally anti-ideological, and can only be
appropriated into ideologies. As such, Buddhism by definition
cannot take a specific ideological stance, or bring into being its
own forms of political economy—or can do so only be betraying itself. But to what degree is such an absence of ideological

critique a necessary consequence of Buddhist thought, rather than a sign of an incomplete or unfinished analysis?

We should also ask to what degree critical theory, in its various contemporary Marxian iterations, has itself completely understood ideology. Much of Žižek and Alain Badiou's work can be understood as a critique of Althusserian renderings of ideology: in Žižek's case via the unresolved problem of the relationship between history (individual and collective) and the unconscious, via the equally unresolved problem of the historicity (or not) of the drives as mediators of the unconscious and (individual and collective) action; in Badiou's case, via the apparent split in Althusser between ideology and science, and the difficulty of generating philosophical criteria for distinguishing between the two.[21] I will argue that something like a Buddha flashes up within these problematics. Perhaps both Buddhism and Marxism are incomplete projects. If so, what do these incompletions share? And to what degree does the repeated presentation of Buddhism and Marxism as opposites obscure shared territories and possible solidarities?

2

I would like to begin to address some of these issues by looking at French philosopher Georges Bataille's interest in Buddhism and other Asian religions. Bataille is a key figure in the history of what we call theory. He was a direct interlocutor for the French existentialists, for psychoanalyst Jacques Lacan, for the Surrealists, and a powerful influence on Michel Foucault (who edited his collected works), Julia Kristeva, Jacques Derrida, and other members of the *Tel Quel* generation. Bataille's ideas are pervasive though often barely acknowledged in contemporary theory: his conception of sovereignty is one of the bases of Giorgio Agamben's work on bare life, Jean-Luc Nancy's rethinking of community and Achile Mbembe's concept of necropolitics[22]; both Judith Butler and Lee Edelman's work in queer theory have important links to Bataille via Kristeva's work on abjection and Lacan's structuration of excess[23]; the interest in "nothing" that is so important in the work of speculative realists like Ray Brassier, can be partly traced to Bataille through British philosopher Nick Land's monograph on Bataille and "virulent nihilism" in the 1990s.[24] Bataille's work on economy and exchange has also been crucial to anthropologists and philosophers such as Norman O. Brown, Michael Taussig, and Alphonso Lingis.[25]

Although Bataille's interest in religion is well known—and his interest in Christian mysticism has been examined in impressive detail by Amy Hollywood[26]—few have commented on the specific, intermittent, but quite substantial, discussion of Buddhism in his work.[27] Even a theory-savvy scholar like Bernstein, who refers to Bataille in her brilliant analysis of the *chöd* ritual among Buryat Buddhists, seems unaware that Bataille's concept of sovereignty likely came at least in part from his own readings about the *chöd* ritual.[28]

As evidence of Bataille's interest, we have a number of texts which mention yoga and a variety of meditation techniques— Buddhist, Hindu, Christian, and otherwise. We also have biographical information, mostly from one source, an essay written by Jean Bruno entitled "Georges Bataille's Techniques of Illumination" published in 1963 (the year after Bataille died) in *Critique*.[29] Bruno was a friend and colleague of Bataille's who worked at the Bibliothèque Nationale, and according to Surya, was probably the person who introduced Bataille to yoga. The word *yoga* (which means "union" in Sanskrit, the "yoking" of body to spirit, limited being to the divine) has been used in a variety of contexts by various Asian religions, notably Hindus and Buddhists. A yogi, to generalize, is one who seeks to bring about an inner transformation by using various techniques or methods that range from physical exercises (*āsana*), control of breath (*prāṇāyāma*), to prayer and meditation. In Buddhism, yoga is associated particularly (though not exclusively) with tantric practice.

Bataille's introduction to yoga came at a crucial moment of

his life, in the late 1930s, following the death of his lover and interlocutor, Colette Peignot, and the end of the Collège de Sociologie. It also followed the end of Acéphale, both the journal which Bataille edited and the secret society that he had convened, which fell apart when the group could not find a volunteer among its members for a proposed human sacrifice. Bataille had also been involved in the short-lived leftist Popular Front in the mid-1930s, and definitively and controversially gave up overtly political involvements around this time in favor of specifically religious practice and works, which were to be collected as *La somme athéologique* (*The Atheological Sum*). This multivolume work was to include the key Bataille texts *Guilty*, *On Nietzsche*, and *Inner Experience*, as well as the various writings included in the recently published collection *The Unfinished System of Nonknowledge*, notably the remarkable essay "Method of Meditation." It is in these works that Bataille developed the concept of *sovereignty* that is so important in his later work—the word, if not the idea itself, is not to be found in earlier texts such as "The Notion of Expenditure."

A yogi is one who practices, and it is in the context of practice that I will first situate Bataille's interest in Buddhism. The genealogy of the word *practice*, and its cognates in various European languages such as praxis, is a complex one. In Étienne Balibar et al.'s formulation, praxis

> refers, then, either to an Aristotelian version (*Nichomachean Ethics*) that opposes it to *poiêsis* and relates it to an ethics and politics of "prudence" (*phronesis*), or to a Marxist version ("Theses on Feuerbach") that identifies it with the effort to transform the existing world rooted in labor and class struggle (*umwälzende* or *revolutionäre Praxis*). Between these two poles there is a Kantian version of the practical element of action (*das Praktische*) and the "primacy of practical reason," which, by assigning to philosophy an infinite task of moralizing human nature (a task called "pragmatic" [*pragmatisch*]), consummates the break with naturalism and prefigures the dilemmas of collective historical action.[30]

Balibar et al. go on to assert a transhistorical "ambiguity of *praxis*"—evident in the English language in the complex, sometimes contradictory relations of "praxis" and "practice"—built around the tensions between individual and collective modes of practice, moral and technical framings of action, and idealist and materialist interpretations of agency.

Bataille's interest in practice is, however, further complicated by his introduction of notions of practice emerging from Asian religious traditions.[31] In fact, as we will see, it is decisive in his redefining of practice. I will try to remain specific about which Buddhist or Hindu tradition Bataille is discussing when he says "yoga" or "meditation," but given that Bataille often seeks to strip away all traces of tradition from those words, this is not always possible. Although Bataille devotes considerable energy to discussions of Christian mysticism, it is clear that when he talks about meditation, he is at the very least comparing Christian and non-Christian modalities. In a key passage from *Guilty*, after discussing his methods and experiences of meditation (without specifying what tradition they came from), he writes:

> In the first stage, the traditional teachings are irrefutable—they're wonderful. I got them from a friend, who got them from an Asian source. I'm not unaware of Christian practices, which are more authentically dramatic: they lack a first movement, without which we remain subordinated to speech.[32]

Thus Bataille differentiates between Christian and "Asian" religious systems by comparing their approaches to practice—and the difference he claims to find is in the way the that these practices negotiate the space between discourse and the non-discursive, or, to put in Bataillean terms, knowledge and non-knowledge. Insofar as Nietzsche's famous dictum that "God is dead" looms over Bataille's proposed "atheology"—the negation of Christianity's purported universalism opens up not only to an existential void, but to a space that is traversed by non-Christian religious doctrines and practices.

Setting aside for now Bataille's writings, there is little evidence that Bataille actually studied yoga with a teacher from any particular lineage (though there is a brief reference in *Guilty* to a meeting with a "Hindu monk").[33] Bataille had certainly read about Asian religions, including Buddhism and Hinduism, that involve yoga: we know that he read Eliade's *Yoga, essai sur les origines de la mystique indienne* in 1936, and that he possessed a heavily annotated copy of Vivekananda's *Raja Yoga ou conquête de la nature intérieur.*[34] From a review of a Louis Pauwels novel published in *Critique*, we know he was also familiar with Romain Rolland's two-volume biography of Sri Ramakrishna and Swami Vivekananda, *Essai sur la mystique et l'action de l'Inde vivante.*[35] Bataille's anthropological and sociological interests are also well known, and he was familiar with the work of Weber, Durkheim, and Mauss. As Alan Foljambe documents, Buddhism and Hinduism were also well known in the surrealist milieu in which Bataille moved: for example, Antonin Artaud had written letters to the Dalai Lama and "the Buddhist schools" which were published in *La révolutione surréaliste* in 1925.[36] Bataille, like Artaud, apparently planned a trip to Tibet in the early 1920s, but nothing came of it. He had read Alexandra David-Neel and Mircea Eliade on Tibetan Buddhism.[37]

Bataille apparently did more than read. Indeed what interested Bataille about yoga was that it could be a practice that produced particular kinds of experiences which went beyond knowledge to what he called "non-knowledge." Bataille argued that knowledge of yoga or other forms of mystical experience had to be regarded as an obstacle to the states of being or non-being which occurred within the experiences themselves. This remained the crucial paradox of yoga or mystical experience for Bataille—one which, as Sartre and others pointed out, added up to a philosophically incoherent system.[38] But this system, incoherent, unfinished or not, aimed at producing certain kinds of experience which could not be contained within the systems of philosophy (leading Bataille to say, contrasting himself to Heidegger, that he was not a philosopher but a madman or a saint).[39] If the word *yoga* has the traditional meaning of "union," it is linked then to the idea of communication that fascinated Bataille. For Bataille, communication meant a break or rupture of the boundaries of the subject that established a state of intimacy with the totality of the universe, and a "return to immanence" that he opposed to the transcendental impulse of most religions—as well as the totalizing systems of philosophy.

Apparently Bataille meditated. Working with Bruno in 1938, he meditated using techniques associated with the "southern" (i.e., Theravādan) Buddhist schools. This meant redirecting the mind away from the discursive activities of consciousness and unexamined but present emotional states to bodily functions such as breathing. Bruno associates this "stage" with the first meditations found in "The Practice of Joy before Death," first published in *Acéphale* in June 1939.

> "I abandon myself to peace, to the point of annihilation."
> "The noises of struggle are lost in death, as rivers are lost in the
> sea, as stars burst in the night.
> The strength of combat is fulfilled in the silence of all action.
> I enter into peace as I enter into a dark unknown.
> I fall in this dark unknown.
> I myself become this dark unknown."[40]

Thus: silence. Apparently Bataille reached states of joyful equanimity rather quickly, and grew dissatisfied with them by the beginning of 1939, when he began using "dramatization" or visualization techniques. Bataille gave a succinct account of these visualizations in *Guilty*. He wrote:

> I'm going to tell you how I arrived at an ecstasy of such intensity. On the wall of appearance I threw images of explosion and of being lacerated—ripped to pieces. First I had to summon up the greatest possible silence, and I got so as to be able to do this pretty much at will. In this boring silence, I evoked every possible way

there was of my being ripped to pieces. Obscene, ridiculous, and deadly thoughts came rushing out one after the other. I thought of a volcano's depths, war, and my own death. It wasn't possible any more to doubt that ecstasy dispenses with any idea of God.[41]

In the aforementioned "Practice of Joy Before Death," Bataille commented: "I remain in this annihilation and, from there, I picture nature as a play of forces expressed in multiplied and incessant agony."[42] To facilitate this, Bataille meditated on photographic images of torture, including those 1905 pictures of a Chinese torture victim which he was first shown by his psychoanalyst Adrien Borel, and which he later included in *The Tears of Eros*. Bruno notes that these meditations were difficult and were often followed the next day by feelings of depression. However, as the quote from *Guilty* above suggests, they also led to experiences of an atheological ecstasy (the term is both Bataille's and Bruno's, not mine), predicated on a rupture of the self, and an opening up to "communication" with that which is exterior to the self, whether figured as cosmos, the Real, or nothingness. In *Inner Experience*, Bataille writes: "If we didn't know how to dramatize, we wouldn't be able to leave ourselves. We would live isolated and turned in on ourselves. But a sort of rupture—in anguish—leaves us at the limit of tears: in such a case we lose ourselves, we forget ourselves and communicate with an elusive beyond."[43]

Bruno notes that Bataille's models for this kind of practice included the Ignatian exercises that he had done in his adolescence, as well as Zen meditation techniques (Bataille had read Suzuki's *Essays on Zen Buddhism*, first published in 1927, and discusses Zen in *On Nietzsche*). Bruno also points out that Bataille also knew of the Tibetan *chöd* meditation, in which the practitioner invites demons to devour his or her body as an ego-annihilating gift (but this meditation is predicated on the sense that the ego constructions that are devoured are false and that the demons are purifying the mind of the practitioner, ultimately leaving it stainless and in bliss).

Bruno argues (correctly, I think) that Bataille's meditation practice was closest to the tantric vision of the universe, where instead of a deceitful maya or illusory world of appearances behind which a transcendental real is to be found, the constant, immanent play of energy and exchange is emphasized. Tantra, itself an extremely complex and various ecology, plays a key role in Tibetan Vajrayāna Buddhism and in a variety of Hindu traditions. In its left-handed version, with which Bataille was apparently familiar, it can involve the ritual and transgressive use of alcohol, sexual intercourse, meat, dead bodies, and graveyards, as a means of arousing energy or shakti. In his unfinished book *La limite de l'utile*, an early and incomplete draft of *The Accursed Share*, Bataille ends his chapter on war by describing the activity of the Tibetan Buddhist tantric yogi who meditates in the graveyard. He takes this as an example of sovereign activity, a channeling of the energies of warfare against the self rather than the outside.[44] Bruno says that Bataille was planning a book on tantrism when he died, although no record of that has been found. Apparently, Bataille experimented at least once with sexual techniques similar to those of tantra, involving a stimulation of desire without ejaculation, and since the beginning of his interest in meditation he had explored various ways of making the *kundalini shakti* energy rise up his spine.[45]

But as Foljambe notes, Bataille was highly ambivalent about tantra, sometimes expressing fascination with it, at other times criticizing it (insofar as he understood it) for appropriating back into a world of means and ends, practices whose "purpose" should be to expose practitioners to non-knowledge, to universal principles of excess and loss, and to a universe finally beyond any principle or purpose. In an important note to *Inner Experience*, he writes:

> Tantric yoga uses sexual pleasure, not in order to ruin oneself in it, but to detach oneself before the end from the object, from the woman, whom they make use of (they avoid the last moment

of pleasure). In these practices, it is always a matter of an object having powerful prolongations within us—but an object which one disregards in one way or another, having only these prolongations in mind; it is always a matter of entering into possession of interiority, of acquiring the mastery of inner movements, detached from the objects of our life.[46]

Bataille, in fact, was against methods of any kind, preferring to improvise, or to rely on spontaneous mystical experiences (which he also wrote about in *Critique* in 1946). Bataille argued that too much reading or instruction actually disrupted any spiritual progress, and that the freedom to improvise was essential in any real development of "inner experience." In his 1947 text "Method of Meditation" he called for a yogic manual "stripped of moral and metaphysic beliefs," though his own notes at the end of this essay, on laughter, sacrifice, meditation, and other forms of the "sovereign operation," hardly constitute instructions.[47] Apparently, after his "successes" in 1939, Bataille abandoned the use of formal meditation practices, having reduced them to the production in himself of silence, and a mode of intensification, described by Bruno as "a revolt against the limits of the human" which would put him in a state of ecstasy.[48] In *Inner Experience* he observed that "I know little, at bottom about India . . . the few judgments which I abide by—more in antipathy than in receptivity—are linked to my ignorance. I have no hesitation about two points: the Hindus' books are, if not unwieldy, then uneven; these Hindus have friends in Europe whom I don't like."[49] Much of the interest in tantra during the interwar and postwar periods in Europe came from thinkers on the Right—Julius Evola and Mircea Eliade are only the most obvious examples—which no doubt accounts for much of Bataille's ambivalence. Furthermore, much of Bataille's terminology can itself be found in thinkers of the European Right. "Inner experience" was a phrase used by the German right-wing writer Ernst Jünger, whose work on "war as inner experience"

Bataille discussed in *La limite de l'utile* in the section preceding his discussion of the Tibetan yogi. As Gustavo Benavides shows, "the Sacred," "sovereignty," and the transcendence of economic considerations were all important tropes of key figures of the European intellectual Right including Jünger, Carl Schmitt, Tibetologist Giuseppe Tucci, Eliade, and others. When these ideas were presented in the name of a political elite, Benavides argues that "we can understand the theorists of the heroic death, of the *atto puro*, of the irrational experience, as ideologists and priests of sacrifice: as those who by glorifying deprivation purified the consumption of those in power."[50]

One should ask to what degree Benavides's comments can be applied to Bataille too. Bataille's interest in yoga can be seen as a continuation of the work of the Collège de Sociologie, a research group whose express concern was to mobilize religion and myth at the service of an antifascist politics. But it's not clear that this work was successful—especially since it was pursued, at least for a time, by a secret group, Acéphale, who however powerless they were, politically and practically, certainly bear many of the characteristics of the elites that Benavides describes. At the same time, it is possible to understand Bataille as proposing a reconfigured tantrism of the Left—a project that would become more familiar in the 1960s in the work of Beat writers like Allen Ginsberg.

Julia Kristeva frames her discussion of Bataille and the concept of *practice* in the following terms: "Marxism inherits from Hegel an ambiguity with respect to the 'active subject' within the concept of *practice*," she observes. "Classical Marxism does not bring out the 'active subject' of practice and slips toward a concept of practice that resembles a practice without a subject." In other words, a "praxis." Kristeva argues that it was only with the advent of Maoism that a concept of practice adequate to this active subject came into being, and uses Mao Tse-tung's 1937 essay "On Practice" as her main source—an essay written at the same historical moment of Bataille's turn toward practice.[51] It is Mao's emphasis on personal participation, and on immediate experience, in the struggle to transform reality that forms the basis of this new and active subject. But there are obvious differences between Mao's version of practice, in which knowledge is tested by the moment of experience and non-knowledge, only to be further consolidated, and Bataille's: indeed the inevitable inoperativity of any Bataillean practice that results from its reimmersion in the negative may be precisely what differentiates Bataille from the fascists—and from Mao.

Bataille turned to yoga and Buddhism in order to find ways of negotiating the confusing space in which knowledge turns to non-knowledge, "practice" becomes "real," and the subject that would guarantee experience in Western philosophy disappears in the very movement of "experience." How is practice different from experience? Practice, at least in a Buddhist and/or yogic sense, seeks to slowly rework the parameters by which experience is defined—but it does so by a process of engagement with and examination of experience. The discipline of practice consists of not taking the initial constituents of experience as a given, and seeks, by examination and other techniques, to transform these constituents—for the most part, the mental aggregates. "Method" in spiritual practice is not indicative of a dogma to be repeated in submission to one who proclaims it, but a set of operations to be initiated because the transformation or success that is sought after has reliably and repeatedly been produced by others who have used such methods in the past. In this sense, the aim of practice in Buddhism (and elsewhere) is often spoken of as a stable sense of recognition of a more fundamental state.[52] But there is an obvious paradox involved in instrumentalizing what is in a sense an ontological wager, and this is where spiritual practice departs from what Sloterdijk has recently called the "anthropotechnics" of practice.[53] Bataille was well aware of this paradox.

Anthropologically, the existence of "methods of meditation," and the evidence that at least some of these methods have some efficacy for some people, indicates the possibility of different approaches to the now familiar themes in contemporary critical theory of the nondiscursive Real and the limits of linguistic or discursive models of philosophy. At the same time, these "methods of meditation" such as yoga, cannot entirely separate themselves from the realm of the discursive, either. As Bataille writes in "Method of Meditation," "on the subject of yoga, the question is rigorously posed: if *resorting to means* defines the sphere of activity, how can we ruin this sphere, when from the onset we speak of *means*? Yoga is nothing if not this ruin."[54] Here Bataille identifies the paradox of practice, when considered as a method of accessing a nondiscursive Real: as soon as such access is instrumentalized as "method," it risks obscuring, or even negating the Real as such, turning it back into a kind of ideology.

I don't believe that Bataille was necessarily right on this point—in her recent book on yoga, *Between East and West*, Luce Irigaray writes of yoga as the cultivation of discernment in the development of consciousness, a slow turning away from that which harms or clouds it.[55] This positivistic account is in accord with texts like the *Yoga Sūtras*. There is no way to ruin an illusion—once it is recognized as such it is already "ruined," so long as one does not then continue to act as though the illusion were real. But at that point, a specifically political question emerges: if what is "ruined" by this practice is ideology, then what political configuration could ever be commensurate with such "ruin"? I will address Bataille's response to this question in the next section.

But there remains another paradox, which Bataille points to: that at the very moment of their success, disciplines of cultivation, as well as the discourses that accompany them, must disappear into the groundless plenitude or nothingness of being. Practice easily becomes a fetish object, a sign of a state of attainment that it may in fact obscure or destroy. "Means" not only bring the realm of discourse—and along with it yoga classes, meditation retreats, gurus, and so on—but also the commodification of yoga and Buddhism and their signs in retreats, acces-

sories, and lifestyles. Bataille recognized that we live in a culture obsessed by "use" and, perhaps in ways he could not have
imagined, by "the use value of the impossible"—meaning that
the most useless, sovereign aspects of our lives and being are
precisely those that are most rigorously commodified and pack-
aged as "useful" forms of withdrawal from a "stressful" system.
If this is true, then we are also particularly prone to "using" yoga
and other spiritual practices for particular kinds of profit and
structure. It was perhaps the most Bataillean of contemporary
Tibetan teachers, Chögyam Trungpa Rinpoché, who named this
appropriation of spiritual practice "spiritual materialism"—
and no coincidence that Trungpa's first key book addressed
to Western practitioners was entitled *Cutting through Spiritual
Materialism*.[56] He might as well have said "ruining the sphere
of activity."

Still, reading Irigaray alongside Bataille reveals the violence
in his desire for "self-annihilation," "rupture," and so on. Not
that this violence is unique to Bataille. Nor, for that matter, is
it clear that Irigaray can necessarily avoid violence in her yoga,
any more than Bataille does. Another way of articulating the
problem is, as Žižek does in his recent book on Hegel, through
the psychoanalytic concept of the drive:

> What Freud calls the "drive" is not, as it may appear, the Buddhist
> Wheel of Life, the craving that enslaves us to the world of illu-
> sions. The drive, on the contrary, goes on even when the subject
> has "traversed the fantasy" and broken out of its illusory crav-
> ing for the (lost) object of desire. And therein lies the difference
> between Buddhism and psychoanalysis, reduced to its formal
> minimum: for Buddhism, after Enlightenment . . . , the Wheel no
> longer turns, the subject de-subjectivizes itself and finds peace;
> for psychoanalysis, on the other hand, *the wheel continues to turn*,
> and this continued turning-of-the-wheel is the drive.[57]

Here Žižek appears to be repeating (in apparent ignorance)
what is basically the Mahāyāna Buddhist critique of Theravādan

Buddhism. One can agree with him that drive is indeed an important problem—but in the above passage, the Wheel of Life surely corresponds to the craving for the (lost) object of desire, not to drive itself. The Wheel of Life is thus only one possible configuration of the energy of the drive: other configurations are possible, and Buddhism examines, indeed catalogues them.

Yet if the issue is the persistence of drive, then, as Bataille and various Buddhist traditions were well aware, the issue can only be addressed in terms of practice. Still, the relation of drive to practice is a very subtle one, and opens up an important territory which allows us to rethink the problem of ideology, as I have set it out above. Practice is clearly collective, even if today it is often presented in terms of individual choice. As a collectively established or generated form, it could be bracketed as always the product of ideology "in the last instance." But Bataille's crucial question—"if resorting to means defines the sphere of activity, how can we ruin this sphere, when from the onset we speak of means?"—sees in yoga a very specific kind of practice, one that "is nothing if not this ruin." Bataille situates yogic practice on the side of useless expenditure, on the generative excess of the drive experienced as such rather than appropriated to some project, even those of enlightenment or revolution. Implicit in Bataille's question is the problem of how this practice can be collective and social—a form of what Nancy would later call *désoeuvrement* or "unworking"—without becoming "useful" and thus negating itself; or, conversely, if it remains merely an "inner experience," how such a practice can exert any influence at all on "the sphere of activity." This is the core of Bataille's interest in yoga and Buddhism, and, as I will now show, Bataille was at least partly aware of its political significance.

3

Bataille abandoned his meditation practice by the late 1940s. Perhaps he was dissuaded by Sartre, who wrote a scathingly astute critique of his work in 1943, accusing him of promoting a mysticism of negation.[58] Bataille and Bruno's claims to have mastered various yogic techniques should be viewed skeptically. Practice, at least in the Buddhist version, is not just something that happens for a brief period, after which one moves on. But Bataille's own theories of excess and general economy are themselves the product of, and if you like, profit from, his meditation practice. Meditation, a practice of sovereignty, of the "non-useful," was precisely used by Bataille as a secret source of the theory of sovereignty.[59] Which, ironically, was the critique Bataille made, somewhat erroneously, about mystical traditions: that they used an experience as a foundation for a doctrine.

Bataille devotes a chapter of arguably his most important book, the first volume of *The Accursed Share*, to "Lamaism" (i.e., Buddhism as practiced in premodern Tibet).[60] The book consists of a series of case studies of the ways in which different forms of human society are organized around the problem of the necessary expenditure of a surplus that is always in excess of what any society needs. In this sense it resembles Max Weber's works of religious sociology (including his books on Chinese and Indian religions), but where Weber focuses on a traditionally defined economy of resources produced and consumed by humans (this Bataille will call a "restricted economy," based on exchange and equivalence), Bataille expands the domain of the economic, using the work of Russian scientist Vernadsky on the circulation of energy in the biosphere, to include all possible expenditures and exchanges, human or nonhuman. This he calls "general economy."[61]

The book is arranged chronologically, and the chapter on Lamaism is placed next to a chapter on Islam, contrasting an "extreme" example of nonviolent expenditure to Islam's supposedly total commitment to militarization. Setting aside, once again, the questions of what Bataille really knew about Tibet (the chapter is built around a biography of the thirteenth Dalai Lama written by a British colonial official, Charles Bell, who lived in

Tibet and met the Dalai Lama in the early twentieth century), and the erroneous claim that premodern Tibet constituted an "unarmed society,"[62] the chapter remains a remarkable attempt to think of Buddhism and yoga in terms of a political economy that goes beyond Marx and Weber. And although Buddhism is bracketed within the book to part of the "historical data"— before industrialization, Russian Communism, and the Marshall Plan—Bataille also says explicitly that Lamaism presents the model of what he means by sovereignty, which he considers to be the only true solution to the problem of expenditure:

> If the different stakes are all played on the same board, then Lamaism is the opposite of the other systems: it alone avoids activity, which is always directed toward acquisition and growth. It ceases—true, it has no choice—to subject life to any other ends but life itself: Directly and immediately, life is its own end. In the rites of Tibet the military forms, evoking the age of the kings, are still embodied in the figures of the dances, but as obsolete forms whose loss of authority is the object of a ritual representation. In this way the lamas celebrate the victory won over a world whose violence is crudely unleashed toward the outside. Their triumph is its unleashing within. But it is no less violent for all that.[63]

The chronological, indeed Hegelian, structure of the book relegates this "solution" to the past. Yet there are places in the chapter where Bataille's sympathy for "Lamaism" as not merely an attempt at facilitating individual experiences of sovereignty, but as a collective decision concerning the orientation of an entire society around sovereignty, is apparent:

> Of course, while monasticism is a pure expenditure it is also a renunciation of expenditure; in a sense it is the perfect solution obtained only by completely turning one's back to the solution. But one should not underestimate the significance of this bold solution; recent history has accentuated its paradoxical value. It

gives a clear indication concerning the general conditions of economic equilibrium. It confronts human activity with its limits, and describes—beyond military or productive activity—a world that is unsubordinated by any necessity.[64]

The problem, as Bataille was no doubt aware, was that the "Lamaist" attempt at building an "inoperative community," in Nancy's term, ultimately relied on the productive labors of others.[65] The sovereign, at least in historical Tibetan society, was not simultaneously the generator of excess and its consumer. Bataille does not mention the fact that the Chinese Communists were invading Tibet at exactly the moment that he was writing about them. But his analysis is historical, and he presents "Lamaism" as a dialectical response to the other configurations of expenditure of excess surrounding Tibet: imperialism (European, Russian, Chinese, and Mongolian), militarism, and capitalism. He is obviously fascinated with the (Hegelian) situation of the thirteenth Dalai Lama who "had learned little beyond the captivating and peaceful lamaic meditation, which is structured by meticulous speculation and a deep mythology and metaphysics," but who is exposed to modern geopolitical realities such that he "became aware of the external play of forces, which could not be ignored or denied with impunity."[66] The thirteenth Dalai Lama attempts reforms, including the modernizing of the army, but provokes a monastic rebellion, described as a festival of protest and "fairy-like ceremonies" which sees reform as the undermining of a full societal commitment to the monastic project.[67]

One is left with the impression of a practice that Bataille has considerable sympathy with, but which cannot find a form of life that can respond to the forces around it, and which cannot reconcile or move beyond the contradictions of feudalism, in which the labors of the peasant population produce a surplus that is then spent by the monasteries. At times Bataille actually seems to be projecting himself onto the thirteenth Dalai Lama, since one could describe in similar terms Acéphale and the College of Sociology, Bataille's two failed attempts at producing a community, in the wake of his participation in the also failed Popular Front in France in the mid-1930s. In all of this, the substance of Buddhist practice has an indeterminate status:

> The piety of the monks is another matter: It is of secondary importance, but the system would be inconceivable without it. And there is no doubt that lamaic enlightenment morally realizes the essence of consumption, which is to open, to give, to lose, and which brushes calculations aside.[68]

The details matter here. Without a practice that actually produces enlightened beings, there is, as Bataille realizes, no point to the "Lamaist" system. At the same time, it is evident that despite Robert Thurman's claim that traditional Tibetan society was a machine for producing Buddhas, that even though the monastic system produced remarkable individuals, in fact, inequality and its correlate, suffering, were present in that society.[69] But is the core problem then that the practice itself was a failure in producing the goal it claimed to be directed toward—the liberation of all sentient beings? Or is it that that the practice was inadequately developed in relation to that goal—that it in fact required, and still requires, a passage through modernity in its various forms, in order to overcome the contradictions that mark and limit its traditional forms?

Here a gap opens up between the concepts of *practice* and *praxis*. Do these words, in a post-Marxian, post-Kantian context, have different meanings or not? In his recent book on practice, Sloterdijk uses the word *praxis* to denote state-run programs that enforce particular practices as universal or mandatory.[70] There is an implied contrast, then, between such programs and what Sloterdijk calls "the planet of the practicing," which is heterogeneous, multiplicit, etc. Twentieth-century communisms floundered precisely in their violent assertions of particular modes of praxis (collectivization, for example)—the Cultural Revolution can be looked at as a disastrous attempt to reopen the issue of "practice" in and against that of state-sponsored "praxis," and to somehow assert "practice" as "praxis." Yet if one entirely abandons the notion of praxis (i.e., universal programs), then one ends up with our current world in which individualized "practice" flourishes and where the only "praxis" is that of the free market.[71] While I basically agree with the distinction that Sloterdijk makes, it is worth reflecting on the apparent impossibility of speaking of a "Buddhist praxis" or a "Marxist practice"— and perhaps learning how to live in that impossible space.

Bataille continues on, laboriously working through the Reformation, capitalist accumulation, Soviet Communism, and the Marshall Plan. But at the very end of the book, he takes a strange, but very Hegelian turn, in which he reintroduces the concept of sovereignty, as a form of intimacy, a relating to an interiority or inner space which is the true location of that which most societies seek without, in sacrificial expenditures of things exterior to themselves.

> If *self-consciousness* is essentially the full possession of intimacy, we must return to the fact that all possession of intimacy leads to a deception. A sacrifice can only posit a sacred *thing*. The *sacred thing* externalizes intimacy: It makes visible on the outside that which is really within. . . . But a *point* must be uncovered where dry lucidity coincides with a sense of the sacred. This implies the reduction of the sacred world to the component most purely opposed to *things*, its reduction to pure intimacy. This comes down in fact, as in the experience of the mystics, to intellectual contemplation, "without shape or form," as against the seductive appearances of "visions," divinities and myths.[72]

Here, a number of key Bataillean non-concepts come together: "intimacy," "*l'informe*" (an ontological formlessness), and intimacy's correlate, "communication," out of which the possibility of a new non-identitarian kind of community will arise. Nevertheless, this remarkable quote is clearly a restatement of what Bataille has already noted in the chapter on "Lamaism" but which he conveniently forgets by consigning the source to history—even though the "Lamaist State" still existed in 1949. Bataille goes on to set out the problem of self-consciousness in terms that are remarkably similar to that of the later Lacan, or recent Žižek—that of the relationship of drive with an evanescent but always returning (thus empty) object:

> It is a question of arriving at the moment when consciousness will cease to be a consciousness of *something*; in other words, of becoming conscious of the decisive meaning of an instant in which increase (the acquisition of *something*) will resolve into expenditure; and this will be precisely *self-consciousness*, that is, a consciousness that henceforth has *nothing as its object*.[73]

Bataille could have gone a lot further, but he stops the book there, because he does not know where to go from there. Even though superficially a meditation that rejects visions for formlessness could be said to be Buddhist—there are indeed particular practices in various Buddhist schools that are called formless meditation—such a version conforms to the stereotypical nineteenth-century European view of Buddhism as a "religion of nothingness" examined by Roger-Pol Droit.[74] While it is arguable that certain Theravādan texts and practices go no further than the negation of form, Mahāyāna Buddhism is insistent on the undecidability and/or interdependence of form and formlessness. That core text of Mahāyāna Buddhist scripture, the *Heart Sūtra*, says:

> When this had been said, holy Avalokiteśvara, the bodhisattva, the great being, spoke to venerable Śāriputra and said, "Śāriputra, any noble sons or daughters who wish to practice the perfection of wisdom should see this way: they should see insightfully,

correctly, and repeatedly that even the five aggregates are empty of inherent nature. Form is empty, emptiness is form, Emptiness is not other than form, form is also not other than emptiness. Likewise, sensation, discrimination, conditioning, and awareness are empty. In this way, Śāriputra, all things are emptiness; they are without defining characteristics; they are not born, they do not cease, they are not defiled, they are not undefiled. They have no increase, they have no decrease.

Therefore, Śāriputra, in emptiness there is no form, no sensation, no discrimination, no conditioning, and no awareness. There is no eye, no ear, no nose, no tongue, no body, no mind. There is no form, no sound, no smell, no taste, no texture, no phenomenon. There is no eye-element and so on up to no mind-element and also up to no element of mental awareness. There is no ignorance and no elimination of ignorance and so on up to no aging and death and no elimination of aging and death. Likewise, there is no suffering, origin, cessation, or path; there is no wisdom, no attainment, and even no non-attainment."[75]

From this point of view there is no nothing, nor is there "a consciousness that henceforth has nothing as its object." A propos of Žižek's recent claims, there is also no "less than nothing." To quote the final and more nuanced line of *The Accursed Share*: "More open, the mind discerns, instead of an antiquated teleology, the truth that silence alone does not betray."[76] Yes: "If you meet a Buddha, kill the Buddha," as the Ch'an master Linji says.[77] Enlightenment as teleology actually blocks the possibility of full opening to the immanence of Buddha nature. In the Dzogchen teachings, "don't meditate!" is a key instruction—for meditation.[78] But again, here we return to the problem of practice. In another Tibetan Buddhist teaching, the Lojong, it is suggested that one practice free of all concepts of the three spheres (subject, object, and meditation practice that examines both). To practice thus is not to submit to aphasia, or "autistic jouissance," or for that matter, "nothing." We do not need to trans-

form practice into "praxis" in order that "knowledge" or awareness or even consciousness be included in practice. To realize,
to become enlightened, is to drop all labels, but not to eradicate
that which they refer to, including cognition or even language.
Here we observe the importance of the tripartite scheme in the
Buddhism of the Pāli canon, of *pariyatti* ("theory"), *patipatti*
("practice"), and *pativedha* ("direct realization"). Indeed, it is arguably "direct realization" rather than "practice" that presents
the real challenge here.

What remains unclear is the nature of the relationship
between the vast movements of history and the general intellect on the one hand, and the self-consciousness that Bataille
prescribes on the other. In another key text from this period,
the record of a two-evening lecture and discussion from 1948,
Bataille sets out for an audience, including historian of religions
Mircea Eliade, the themes which would later form his *Theory of
Religion*. Bataille discusses the difference between Buddhism and
Christianity when it comes to negation and transcendence. The
lecture restates the argument of "Method of Meditation": that
Buddhism is a rejection of all subjective action, and a turning of
a violence, usually directed outward at objects and the world,
back on the self. Bataille argues that, in so doing, Buddhism un-
derestimates action and the world, insofar as it thinks of it as
not meriting a response.[79] As a result, the complete immanence
that Bataille is interested in does not occur in Buddhism, since
"the position of subject as an object, which is not destroyed [un-
til after?]; which is maintained during the project of destroying itself, and also the position of things themselves in the rest
of the world is left intact."[80] Bataille goes on:

> What the Buddhist or Christian worlds miss, is the fact that the
> profane world is left, by the Buddhist and Christian worlds, free.
>   To this, revolutionary action, such as Marxism has defined it,
> is opposed, but it is also opposed to a possibility which I will now
> try to set out: . . .

What matters in the present world, is not creating the possibility of a mystical experience, or of opening new religious possibilities, there are perhaps none, but it's about igniting religious action in the profane world.

The profane world, must in its turn be destroyed as such, which is to say that everything in the capitalist world which is given as a thing which transcends and dominates man, must be reduced to the state of an immanent thing, by being subordinated to consumption by man.

This is profoundly opposed to all ascetic attitudes, such as are found in Buddhism as well as Christianity, to all Buddhist and Christian moral restrictions which are founded on transcendence. At a certain point, it is necessary to propose the consumption of the produced object outside of all utility, as the final end, because the final end of man is to destroy what he has made.[81]

I think the criticism Bataille makes of Buddhism is somewhat justified. The quote from the *Heart Sūtra* above does set out emptiness exclusively in terms of a critique of the subject, and as such leaves the position of things in the world "intact"— albeit knowing that because of impermanence, nothing actually remains "intact." The doctrine of the bodhisattva proposes the liberation of all sentient beings as a goal, but leaves it to the dissemination of Buddhist practice for this to happen. But this practice also includes doctrines, institutions, and communities, which certainly mark and order the worlds they are part of, even today.

Many Asian Buddhist traditions do have their own versions of sacrificial logic that cannot simply be opposed to the Native American practices of potlatch by which Bataille was so fascinated.[82] The political practice of self-immolation undertaken by Vietnamese monks in the Vietnam War, and more recently by Tibetan monks in China, are, as John Whalen-Bridge points out, crucial parts of the iconography of Buddhism today, reaffirming orientalist fantasies of Buddhism as a "religion of self-annihilation" but at the same time, emerging precisely in the Bataillean space of a confrontation between Cold War powers, a troubling sovereign act of nonalignment and auto-destruction.[83]

At the same time, I believe that Bataille's conception of practice is inadequate, and that the experience of consumption in itself is not a final end, but rather is quite easily integrated today into the order of global capitalism. So long as consumption has a private, "unavowable" quality, so long as it remains "experience," there can be no communication, or immanence—only repetition, and the reproduction of the relations of production via the consumption of "experiences." Strange, but true: there is no experience in the immanence that is the goal of Buddhist practice. The value of practice, at its most profound, is that it traverses experience, in the same sense that Lacan says the goal of psychoanalysis is to "traverse the fantasy." But not all forms of practice are equal in their ability to traverse experience.

I cannot see that it makes any difference whether we destroy the profane world in its materiality. Emptiness is empty because it is impermanent, because everything is impermanent. Violence can only mimic or repeat this impermanence, in an attempt to performatively control it on behalf of a self or subject that seeks to transcend impermanence through this enaction. It cannot. Thus "sovereignty," even in the act of self-immolation, becomes a mere simulation of itself. An image is emitted, a body is sacrificed—the political canceling itself out at the moment of its own articulation. I will take up this issue in a broader discussion of Buddhist contributions toward a political theory of the gift in the next section of this essay.

Bataille's striking formulation of the need to destroy the profane world by igniting a religious action has its origins in Durkheim's *Elementary Forms of Religious Life*, and Durkheim's claim that religion is defined not in reference to a supreme being, but to the way in which a particular community forms in relation to a particular division of the universe into the sacred and the profane. Buddhism plays a crucial role in Durkheim's argument, since he uses it to demonstrate that there are religious communities that are avowedly atheistic, but who nonetheless are formed around the positing of certain things as sacred (the four noble truths, etc.) in relation to others that are not (*saṃsāra*).[84] Bataille's criticism of Buddhism is that it observes the separation of the sacred and the profane, maintaining the sacred as a purified interiority in relation to the profane exteriority of the material world. But just as Durkheim's description of Buddhism is problematic, so is Bataille's. In fact, Buddhism offers some other ways of framing general economy—for example, the concept of *pratītyasamutpāda*/interdependence, which suggests that every thing that is, is simultaneously the product of its lack of inherent self-existence, and the product of a vast chain of dependent originations, such that it appears, contingently, in a particular way at a particular place and moment. Moreover, in proclaiming the equivalence of *saṃsāra* and *nirvāṇa*, Mahāyāna Buddhism already rigorously deconstructs the separation of sacred and profane that Bataille finds so problematic.

More challengingly, but more intriguingly too perhaps, one might consider the doctrine of karma as an alternative form of general economy.[85] Thanks to the "kitschification" of this term by North American countercultures in the 1960s, the philosophical and religious meanings of the word have been obscured. Buddhist teachers I've studied with have said that the topic of karma is "subtle." Karma is the universal law of cause and effect. In terms of general economy, and the ways in which Bataille frames Buddhist notions of sacred and profane in relation to inner/outer and subject/object, karma provides a way of understanding the interpenetration of notions of inner and outer. Karma is not simply a cosmic discourse of reward and punishment, such that a good act will be rewarded with karmic air miles that can be spent in the future, and a bad act will result in a karmic brick falling on your head at some point in the future. Karma is phenomenological. By which I mean that any entity's perception of a particular world/gestalt is itself the product of particular karmas. Thus the concept of the six realms in Buddhism: hell, hungry ghost, animal, human, jealous gods (*asuras*), and gods (*devas*), each of which is associated with a particular kind of gestalt. And one of the most important ways of framing practice from a Buddhist perspective is that practice produces a karmic shift such that there is also a phenomenological shift in a particular or collective subject's framing of the world. Thus, there is a cycling of provisional designations of inner and outer, subject and object, through a chain of multiple but provisional equivalences (i.e., "economies").

Perhaps the most powerful critique that has been made of Bataille's notion of sovereignty has been that of Giorgio Agamben in *Homo Sacer*. Agamben compares Bataillean sovereignty—built around an anthropology of the sacred and "the interiority of the subject, to which the experience of this life is always given in privileged or miraculous moments"—with political theorist Carl Schmitt's definition of the sovereign as the one who has the power to decide the state of exception (in which the law is suspended) and who has the right to kill. [86] Bare life, as Agamben defines it, is thus simultaneously the Bataillean exposure of individuals and collectives to non-knowledge a.k.a. bare life, and the process by which political power is exercised on individuals and collectives in reducing them to bare life, or nonhuman status.

Agamben specifically criticizes Bataille's ideas regarding sovereignty for failing to take into account what Foucault will formulate as modern biopolitical regimes and their attempts to reduce human society to the administrative regulation of bare life. In this sense, the practice of Bataillean non-knowledge, Buddhist or otherwise, would amount to a naive assent to being the material of a biopolitical regime. But as I have shown, the Bataillean politics of sovereignty are more complex than Agamben gives him credit for—Bataillean sovereignty implies a possibility of agency and assent that is not present in middle-period Foucauldian presentations of biopolitics and power—and which

Foucault himself revised in his late work on practices of friendship. The political meaning of "inner experience" in Buddhist communities has a history that Agamben is apparently unaware of. Nevertheless, the figure of the Buddhist, misrecognized or not and considered within a specific historical epoch, can be seen to come to stand for what Agamben calls the "Bataillean paradox of sovereignty": in other words, the Buddhist is both the one who voluntarily exposes him or herself to death, emptiness, bare life out of the desire to become enlightened for the sake of all sentient beings—and also the one who may be killed with impunity because he/she ostensibly assents to be "nothing," to be other than human. Thus we see a potential connection between nonalignment and nonviolence in the politics of sovereignty— and it is this connection that I will now turn to, in the context of the post-WWII moment.

4

What interests me about Bataille's conclusion is that, despite his marginality or obscurity at the time he wrote *The Accursed Share*, his concerns find a strong echo in other parts of the world at precisely that moment. The period 1945–80 is that of the Cold War, of decolonization, in India, China and elsewhere; of American hegemony and American counterculture; of disenchantment on the global Left with Stalinism and Russian Communism; and of communist revolutions in various Asian societies including China, North Korea, Cambodia, Vietnam, Afghanistan, and Mongolia. That Buddhism should feature as a prominent trope or idea during this period, in Bataille's work or elsewhere, is by no means obvious, yet in the period of decolonization, most of the Asian societies and nations in which Buddhism played a historic role had vigorous leftist movements and sometimes regimes. While in many cases Buddhism represented a powerful but residual force of tradition, often transfigured by and adapted to European colonial regimes, Buddhists were often important factors in the development of anticolonial forces. And, in the moment of decolonization, the Fanonian problematic of the way in which a society emerging from colonialism engaged with its precolonial traditions often took the form of a debate about Buddhist ethics in Asian societies.[87]

To list a few specific cases: In India, decolonization in 1948 more or less coincides with the restoration of Bodhgaya, the historical site of the Buddha's enlightenment, as a place of Buddhist worship, with an internationalist framing. Gandhi's colleague B. R. Ambedkar, born in the untouchable (Dalit) caste, converted to Buddhism in 1956, along with 500,000 of his supporters. The same year he wrote an important essay entitled "Buddha or Karl Marx" in which he compares the two:[88]

> It is clear that the means adopted by the Buddha were to convert man by changing his moral disposition to follow the path voluntarily.
>
> The means adopted by the Communists are equally clear, short and swift. They are (1) Violence and (2) Dictatorship of the Proletariat.
>
> . . . . It is now clear what are the similarities and differences between the Buddha and Karl Marx. The differences are about the means. The end is common to both.

Decolonization in Burma in 1948 lead to U Nu's attempts to synthesize Buddhism and socialism as the basis of the Burmese state, over a period which lasted until the military takeover of 1962.[89] Debates about how to integrate Buddhism into a modern socialist state also occurred in Sri Lanka, Cambodia, Laos, and South Korea.[90] They were also part of attempts at reform of Buddhist sanghas in Japan after the end of the Second World War.[91] Similarly, the Chinese Communist government had a quite complex response to Buddhism in the first decade of its existence, one that was by no means unilaterally hostile.[92] It is clear that "Buddhism" was used as a part of propaganda campaigns by both sides in the Cold War, as a vehicle for foreign policy, or the pursuit of partisan internationalist agendas, just as attempts at a rapprochement with Marxism in Buddhist texts of the period can also be read as attempts by Buddhist institutions to ingratiate themselves with the new powers. Accounts of the politics of Buddhism in Asian societies written during the Cold War tend to be partisan and the topic remains seriously under-researched to this day, so that the extent to which actual Buddhist socialisms flourished remains hard to measure.[93] The least one can say, however, is that the meaning of Buddhism was very actively negotiated during this period.

These debates within and around Asian societies find a dim echo within European intellectual circles. The prevalent form of Buddhism within the European and American philosophical imaginary in this period is Japanese Zen, as taken up by John Cage and the Beats in the late 1940s in the wake of the Japanese defeat in WWII and through the work of D. T. Suzuki.[94] Heidegger, who had participated in collegial discussions with members of the Japanese Kyoto School since the 1920s, wrote his "A Dialogue on Language, Between a Japanese and an Inquirer" in 1953.[95] Lacan, Barthes, Foucault, Fromm, and others all investigated and wrote about Japanese Zen in the 1950s and 1960s (though it is interesting to note that both Heidegger and Lacan studied Chinese language for varying periods after World War II).[96] Some indication of the situation of Buddhism within Western intellectual circles after World War II can be gleaned from Maurice Merleau-Ponty's "The Yogi and the Proletarian" in his 1947 book *Humanism and Terror*, ostensibly an attack on former Marxist fellow traveler Arthur Koestler's disavowal of Marx in his 1945 book *The Yogi and the Commissar*. The chapter, which is the final one in the book, connects yoga to a "decline in ideology and proletarian action" and a choice between a reactionary depoliticization (connected to the figure of the yogi) and "terror" (i.e., the dictatorship of the proletariat) as a necessary stage of revolutionary progress.[97] Merleau-Ponty endorses

Koestler's own dismissal of the yogi ("The Yogi is wrong to neglect hygiene and antiseptics. He allows violence to occur and does nothing").[98] But then Merleau-Ponty points out that in practice, Koestler's position is not so different from the yogi's: "One senses he is tempted, not by religion, which has a feeling for the problems of the world, but by religiosity and escapism."[99] Merleau-Ponty argues that this becomes a kind of pseudo-humanism, that is bankrolled by appropriative violence on a massive scale: "The British Empire did not send Yogi missions into Indonesia, any more than the French in Indochina, to teach 'change from within.'"[100] What is ironic is that decolonization in Asia was at times associated with the figure of the yogi (Gandhi is only the most obvious example), and Buddhism did appear in some Asian countries after World War II as a way of refusing the choices of the Cold War. However, most attempts at building a politics from a Buddhist base floundered because of military takeovers (as in Burma 1962), because of communist attempts to disassemble the feudal or colonial political-economic basis of existing Buddhist societies, and/or because of the fading away of the politics of "nonalignment" at the end of the Cold War, and the gradual integration of Asian nations and societies into the global capitalist economy. Furthermore, at least in Ambedkar's case, despite his claim that Buddhism is relevant to politics and economy, specific Buddhist arguments about the form of political economy did not materialize.

Economist E. F. Schumacher, best known today as the author of the 1970s bestseller *Small Is Beautiful: A Study of Economics as if People Mattered*, offers the most literal rendering of the problem in his essay "Buddhist Economics" (1966), which was inspired by his trip to U Nu's Burma in 1955. For the most part, what Schumacher offers is a restatement of the modernity versus tradition dialectic, with "Buddhist economics" firmly on the side of tradition, and the Gandhian loom: "Buddhist economics is the systematic study of how to attain given ends with the minimum means."[101] The connections Schumacher draws between

Buddhism, of whatever kind, and economics, of whatever kind, are fairly tenuous, not going much further than the assertion of "right livelihood" as one of the aspects of the Eightfold Path. The emphasis of the essay is on withdrawal from consumption, and a reorientation away from the production of a worthless excess. "Buddhist economics must be very different from the economics of modern materialism, since the Buddhist sees the essence of civilization not in a multiplication of wants but in the purification of human character," Schumacher argues.[102]

This position is articulated more specifically as a political philosophy in American Beat poet Gary Snyder's short essay "Buddhist Anarchism" (1961). The essay was written while Snyder was in the middle of a seven-year period studying Zen in Japan, a year before Snyder made a trip to India with Joanne Kyger and Allen Ginsberg that included a visit to Dharamsala, residence of the newly exiled Dalai Lama. The piece was later republished as "Buddhism and the Coming Revolution."[103]

Snyder begins by setting out a political critique of existing Buddhist societies in terms very similar to those made by Žižek and others: that a focus on individual enlightenment has meant a neglect of the actual social and political conditions existing in such societies. He then sets out the situation of Cold War geopolitics, rejecting both sides, and proposing Buddhist ethics and practice as a transnational alternative:

The joyous and voluntary poverty of Buddhism becomes a positive force. The traditional harmlessness and refusal to take life in any form has nation-shaking implications. The practice of meditation, for which one needs only "the ground beneath one's feet" wipes out mountains of junk being pumped into the mind by the mass media and supermarket universities. The belief in a serene and generous fulfillment of natural loving desires destroys ideologies which blind, maim and repress—and points the way to a kind of community which would amaze "moralists" and transform armies of men who are fighters because they cannot be lovers. . . .

The mercy of the West has been social revolution; the mercy of the East has been individual insight into the basic self/void. We need both. They are both contained in the traditional three aspects of the Dharma path: wisdom (prajña), meditation (dhyāna), and morality (sīla). Wisdom is intuitive knowledge of the mind of love and clarity that lies beneath one's ego-driven anxieties and aggressions. Meditation is going into the mind to see this for yourself—over and over again, until it becomes the mind you live in. Morality is bringing it back out in the way you live, through personal example and responsible action, ultimately toward the true community (sangha) of "all beings." This last aspect means, for me, supporting any cultural and economic revolution that moves clearly toward a free, international, classless world. It means using such means as civil disobedience, outspoken criticism, protest, pacifism, voluntary poverty and even gentle violence if it comes to a matter of restraining some impetuous redneck. It means affirming the widest possible spectrum of non-harmful individual behavior—defending the right of individuals to smoke hemp, eat peyote, be polygynous, polyandrous or homosexual. Worlds of behavior and custom long banned by the Judaeo-Capitalist-Christian-Marxist West. It means respecting intelligence and learning, but not as greed or means to personal power. Working on one's own responsibility, but willing to work with a group. "Forming the new society within the shell of the old"—the I.W.W. slogan of fifty years ago.

The traditional cultures are in any case doomed, and rather than cling to their good aspects hopelessly it should be remembered that whatever is or ever was in any other culture can be reconstructed from the unconscious, through meditation. In fact, it is my own view that the coming revolution will close the circle and link us in many ways with the most creative aspects of our archaic past. If we are lucky we may eventually arrive at a totally integrated world culture with matrilineal descent, free-form marriage, natural-credit communist economy, less industry, far less population and lots more national parks.[104]

In this text, Snyder condenses much of what will later be called "engaged Buddhism" into a brief, specific, radical statement. Snyder is attempting to suture a Buddhist meditation practice aimed at individual transformation with an anarchist political practice that is collective and social, nonaligned in its rejection of existing nation-states and political structures. In the second paragraph quoted above, Snyder builds the connections between Buddhist ethics, the practice of meditation, and social and political transformation. But to what degree is there a necessary correlation of these factors? I am charmed by his vision, as I also admire the real work done by engaged Buddhists, but one has to ask: Why has what Snyder proposed not come to pass? Although Snyder is careful and specific in proposing something other than a marketplace libertarianism, the suture between personal practice and collective action remains speculative—indeed, as Balibar points out, the tension between the two is genealogically embedded within the concept of practice. A Žižekian critique of Snyder's Buddhist anarchism might argue that he fails to take into account an irrevocable rupture or gap that is constitutive of human subjectivity. This is Žižek's point, when he brings up *Zen at War* and the ways in which Buddhist practice and doctrine can be used to rationalize slaughter. But again, when Žižek concludes that meditation is "just a tool," meaning a morally neutral artifact, he misunderstands practice in a way that Mao, who sees it as dialectical, does not. Formally, the question remains: how are the elements of Buddhist practice, Buddhist ethics, and political theory and practice to be developed in relation to each other?

In the light of the politics of nonalignment in India and elsewhere, one can historicize the formula with which Bataille ended *The Accursed Share*: choose between Buddhism, communism, capitalism or what a succession of post-Bataillean theorists will variably call "the unavowable community" (Blanchot), "the inoperable community" (Nancy), "the community that is not one" (Lingis), "the coming community" (Agamben), "communitas" (Esposito).[105] The trope or trace of Buddhism at the moment of decolonization and the emergence of post-WWII Cold War geopolitics (symbolized for Bataille by the Marshall Plan, with which he ends *The Accursed Share*) bifurcates into a series of "discursive" Buddhisms, residually precolonial or colonial, Theosophical or "Western" . . . and . . . something else, which does not or cannot find a place within the existing or emerging paradigms of general economy, but which could, despite Bataille's forgetfulness, still go by the name of "Buddhism." Nonetheless, such a politics of nonalignment always runs, or ran, the risk of being a convenient symbol for the "peace" of detente during the Cold War—in other words, a "peace" that is merely a strategic gambit used to gain a military advantage. Conversely, nonaligned states, including Buddhist ones, had to work out how to respond to an overwhelming geopolitical militarization, the menace of Bataille's "external world," and in many ways they were simply unable to do so.[106] Bataille's gambit, if I can call it that, was to confront the logic of the Cold War with its implied teleology, that of an all-consuming excess. This is also possible from a Buddhist perspective, but it remains an open question what the political form of an egalitarian consumption of excess that is not focused on external practices of sacrifice—or global consumer culture—would actually mean.

The work of Tibetan writer Gendun Chopel, who has been celebrated as "the first Tibetan modernist," opens up a different perspective on these issues. Chopel was born in Amdo in eastern Tibet in 1903. His father was a noted Nyingma practitioner, but he was educated at Gelugpa monasteries—first at Labrang in Amdo, and later at Drepung in Lhasa, at that time the largest monastery in the world. At Drepung he apparently caused problems during the traditional dialectical debates that are an important part of monastic pedagogy, by asking philosophically pertinent questions that couldn't be answered within the prevailing discourse of the monasteries. In 1934, he dropped out and began working with an Indian Sanskrit scholar, independence activist and member of the Indian Communist party, Rahul Sankrityayan, who was doing research on extant Sanskrit Buddhist texts on logic.[107] He then moved to India where he traveled and wrote for twelve years, and participated in the activities of the Tibetan exile community in Kalimpong, including a revolutionary group that was planning the overthrow of the Lamaist state in Tibet. After his return to Tibet in 1946, Chopel was arrested by the government of the Dalai Lama for alleged subversive activities, and he died in 1951, arguably from the effects of his imprisonment.[108] Today, many Tibetans, both in Tibet and in exile, regard Chopel's story and writings as a missed opportunity in the development of a different, autonomous, modern Tibet. In this sense, the valorization of Chopel resonates with the theme of nonalignment, as a missed "third way."

However, what interests me in Chopel's work is the specific way in which the problematic of nonalignment is framed within a Buddhist context. And it is precisely in Bataillean terms, of locating a religious struggle and practice within the forms of the modern profane world, that the pathos and power of Chopel's thought emerge. Several of Chopel's most important books articulate the problem of a religious practice that does not avoid or ignore modernity: his otherwise somewhat mundane pilgrimage guide for Tibetans traveling in India gleefully includes the prices of railway transportation in rupees, plus tips for traveling by taxi; his *Treatise on Passion*, an improvisation on the *Kāma Sūtra* that includes frequent assertions of the importance of trying and testing the various positions and techniques described, sets out a nonutopian politics of sexual pleasure and relationship; finally, his travel journal/historical essay on his time spent in India and Sri Lanka, *Grains of Gold*, demystifies India for Tibetans who know it only through scriptural texts.[109] In each case, Chopel poses the problem of ideology as it is found in the belief systems prevailing in Tibet in the early part of the twentieth century. He reveals the ideological dimensions of Buddhism and Tibet through research, historiography, and the examination of experience, but he does so from the position of a committed Buddhist practitioner.

Chopel's most important text, *Adornment for Nāgārjuna's Thought*, is written as a response to the Indian Mahāyāna philosopher Nāgārjuna, who set out the core philosophical analysis of Mahāyāna Buddhism for some of its most significant branches: Indian, Tibetan, Chinese and Japanese. The core of Nāgārjuna's argument concerns the relation between the relative and the absolute, a core which was recently reformulated by analytic philosopher Graham Priest and Buddhologist Jay Garfield as Nāgārjuna's paradox: that every proposition or designation of a relative reality can be deconstructed and revealed to be empty and/or dependently originated.[110] This proposition, reinterpreted in the canon of the reigning monastic hierarchy in Tibet, the Gelugpas, through Chandrakīrti and Tsongkhapa, also formed a core of the scholastic curriculum in preinvasion Tibet. Chopel's text asks: How do we get from an intellectual recognition of the possibility of the union of absolute and relative to a realization of it? If only a Buddha has absolute knowledge, how can beings who see only the relative even understand teachings? The question contains an implicit criticism of the monastic hierarchy as not being reliable sources of wisdom and realization.

It is of course an eminently theoretical question, too. Hegel's introduction of the problematic of history into philosophy, and the necessary dialectical working through of specific concrete historical situations through the struggle for recognition, seeks to address this point. Hegel's work was then given a radical reinterpretation by Marx, precisely on the question of practice, starting with the *Theses on Feuerbach*. The Buddhist and Marxist responses to the question intersect in Lhasa, 1950—almost exactly the moment that Gendun Chopel is puzzling about how those of us stranded in the mire of delusion can ever actually achieve realization.

The problem has a particular political history in Tibet that takes the form of a centuries-spanning debate concerning the relation of the "two truths," (i.e., relative or conventional truth and absolute truth), defined in brief, but not unproblematic terms as discursive and nondiscursive framings of the Real. [111] This debate had serious consequences, and contributed to the establishment of a hegemonic Gelugpa orthodoxy on the topic, as well as the banning of heterodox texts (such as Gorampa's) and sects (such as the Jonangpa) for significant periods of time. The Gelugpa position on the problem is established via the doctrine of "valid cognition," meaning that one should accept authorative statements concerning existing relative reality as being true, and arguably therefore also the commands of the reigning monastic hierarchy. And indeed, Chopel's tract was read at the time as an anti-Gelugpa diatribe enacting the "mistakes" of some of the other Buddhist schools, such as those of the Nyingmapa, whose response to the question might be quite different. While it is easy to stereotype the diversity of views and practices within the history of the Gelugpa, it is also worth emphasizing the importance in Tibetan history of those non-monastic practitioners whose political image might be the great mountain yogi saints such as Milarepa or Yeshe Tsogyal, and who are characterized by engaged autonomy. [112]

The two truths debate is a debate about ideology—or rather, the ideology of ideology. One of the radical aspects of Chopel's work is that he is pointing out that the Gelugpa doctrine of valid cognition is an ideology, and, having pointed it out repeatedly, he struggles with the broader problem of ideology and its relationship with truth. He writes:

> In general, for us common beings, there are many beliefs, things that we believe willingly, things we believe unwillingly, and things that we believe with no choice, but their basis is nothing other than merely our own belief in our own perceptions. What is meant by "belief" is the mind being required to engage in a particular object involuntarily through the force of habit. [113]

Of course it then depends what is meant by "habit"—but even if Chopel situates habit as something internal to mind and only implicitly suggests that it is the productive of a particular monastic training, the question of how beliefs structure particular societies has been raised. One can interpret much of Chopel's work as exposing ideological structures within premodern Tibetan Buddhist society: from his now famous critique of the traditional Tibetan doctrine that the earth is flat, to the more subtle philosophical ideologies underpinning the dominance of the Gelugpa in Tibet.[114] But there is also a more general articulation of the problem of ideology, as the cause of a distorted being in the world (i.e., *saṃsāra*).

The core of Chopel's argument, beyond his refutation of Gelugpa orthodoxy, is the relation between practice and what he calls "the inconceivable." It is only by practicing within the context of the inconceivable that Chopel believes the paradoxes of ideology and our own deep embedding within discursive structures can be even potentially overcome. What does Chopel mean by the "inconceivable"? It is not simply a utopia, or a beyond, or even something transcendent. Nor is it simply a linguistic concept or label, or even a formalism by which one could conceptually elaborate that which is not conceptual or conceivable. The inconceivable is there even if it is not present to the senses or mundane consciousness, and insofar as it is formally posited, it is only posited with reference to a practice or practices which engage with "it." In a key section of the text, Chopel elaborates on those practices that open one to the inconceivable: through the negations of the Prāsaṅgika Mādhyamaka system that Chopel discusses, which refute the consistency of all philosophical assertions or concepts (sections 73–84); and through meditation practices that reveal nonduality (section 87). In section 89, he notes:

> One should know that the union which nondualistically mixes as one such things as object and subject, desire and hatred, hot and cold, pure and polluted, is the body of great wisdom or the body of wisdom, the mixture of body and mind in one entity.[115]

It is striking in this passage that it is the body that it is the site of the inconceivable—not the body qua body, but the body as a point of practice, the site of non-knowledge. Chopel continues in a strikingly Bataillean manner, arguing that all of the practices of visualization in Tibetan Buddhism as well as the various tantric practices (involving sex, eating meat, alcohol etc.) "are only for the purpose of turning upside down this present valid knowledge . . . for the purpose of smashing to dust the conceptions of the ordinary, together with the reasoning of logicians."[116] He concludes:

> In brief, one should understand that taking the impure as pure and the improper as proper and so on is only set forth for the sake of reversing the conception of the ordinary. The state of the great unsurpassed joining of contradiction . . . seems to be something to be discovered.[117]

Which is to say that the point is to transgress (i.e., smash to dust), conceptual systems so that one is left with the inconceivable, with "nonlocatability" and "nonobjectification."[118] This would also be the only situation in which one could speak of "noncontradiction" (for more on Buddhism and the law of noncontradiction, see Timothy Morton's essay in this volume)—or openness.

This openness is accessible through eroticism (as it is for Bataille). Toward the end of his *Treatise on Passion* (1938), Chopel writes:

> Sometimes, seeing a goddess is revolting.
> Sometimes, seeing an old woman is arousing.
> Thinking, "This is it," something else comes along.
> How can the deceptions of the mind be counted?

> Having understood well and become weary,
> When the root of all conceptions is destroyed,

That is the great relaxation of bliss.
Another word for it is liberation.

To those who have not seen it, Lake Manasarovar is two
    miles wide.
When you arrive beside it, it is a puddle.
When the things of samsara have been bowed down to and
    experienced,
It is true that there is no wonderful essence at all.

Still, the race of men and women is the same size.
It is easy for them to find each other.
And if they desire each other, craving is a greater sin than
    copulation.
Thus, it is always right to rely on the enjoyment of sex.[119]

Practices of eroticism and intimacy open up the sphere of non-
knowledge, "self-arisen bliss" associated with orgasm and jouissance. Still, like Bataille, Chopel takes a very specific swerve in
the face of any universalization of a specific practice, since, with
the exception of "true divine dharma," "nothing in this life does
not make us sad."[120] It comes down again to a matter of practice. Since what appears, if it does, is the social, is sexual beings,
eroticism contingently matters. Insofar as it is the form drive
takes, eros should be honored, worked with. The last stanza of
the text concludes with a prayer that such a practice be possible:

May all humble people who live on the broad earth
Be delivered from the pit of merciless laws
And be able to indulge, with freedom,
In common enjoyments, so useful and right.[121]

It's a wonderfully modest universalism—a prayer for equality
based on a shared or common erotic pathos. It is not specifically
human since:

The blind ant runs for the sake of pleasure.
The legless worm crawls for the sake of pleasure.
In brief, all the world is racing with each other,
Running toward pleasure, one faster than the next.[122]

Human eroticism is then just one form—"common," but "useful and right"—of a pervasive drive oriented toward pleasure, or, in theoretical terms, jouissance. Not that jouissance qua jouissance is the ultimate point either.[123] It is an aspect of emptiness and, as such, paradoxically a condition rather than a goal.

Although the *Adornment of Nāgārjuna's Thought* is an intervention in a particular debate within a particular religious tradition, we can draw from it a formal proposition concerning the relation between practice, concepts, and the inconceivable. But I would also like to make a historical point about this particular problematic as it emerged in a number of places around the world at the end of World War II. Chopel, like Bataille, could not find a political form adequate to his vision of the inconceivable. Both of them are positing a specific relationship between practice and the inconceivable in response to Marxist conceptions of practice—which Chopel had been exposed to in India via Sankrityayan, among others. But even if Chopel's politics remain vague, it is evident that Chopel's scholarly text was nonetheless viewed as a political document, as the embodiment of the threat of a politicization of Buddhism.[124] Tibet was absorbed, by military occupation, treaty, and more, into Communist China in the 1950s. This happened in the name of modernization, in the name of equality, in the name of Chinese hegemony. The communist critique of the feudalism that underwrote premodern Tibetan Buddhist society was a piercing one, no matter how much it comes down to a matter of realpolitik or gunboat diplomacy. At the same time, communist regimes, in China and elsewhere, have also struggled with the problem of adequate political forms.[125] If today one can still see Chopel's name and photograph on billboards around the Barkhor in the center of the Tibetan part of Lhasa, it is surely because the questions that Chopel articulated remain relevant today. And remain unanswered.

The moment of Buddhist socialisms or anarchisms was historically specific to the Cold War. It ended with the Cultural Revolution in China and Tibet, and the advent of Maoist vanguardist politics in Asia and elsewhere that sought to definitively expose religion as an ideological fantasy.[126] Some of the contradictions of this moment can be found in American Catholic monk and writer Thomas Merton's talk "Marxism and Monastic Perspectives," which was given at a conference in Bangkok in December 1968, the day before Merton's tragic death in a hotel room there. Merton had a long-standing interesting in Asian religions, particularly Buddhism, and had written extensively about Japanese Zen. In 1968, he traveled around Asia, visiting Catholic monastic communities there, but also meeting members of the Tibetan exile community including the Dalai Lama, the Nyingma lama Chatral Rinpoche, and a young Chögyam Trungpa Rinpoche, one of the principal figures in the popularization of Tibetan Buddhism in America and Europe.

Merton was also very much engaged with the student Left in America, and his final talk attempts to set out a stance that responds to the student Left in Europe and America, the Cultural Revolution and its analogues as they unfold in Asia, Christian monastic traditions, and his recent encounters with Tibetan Buddhist monks. Merton drily begins by noting that "this lecture might have been entitled 'Marxist Theory and Monastic Theoria.'"[127] He then specifies that he is particularly interested in the work of Herbert Marcuse: "You could say this is a lecture on the monastic implications of Marcuse at the present moment" (327). The talk moves restlessly between the various elements outlined above. Merton sets out what he sees as the commonalities of Marxism and monasticism: that of a critical attitude toward the world, one that aims at the transformation of the world via a shift in political economy in the former, via a "total transformation of consciousness" that is individual but transmittable in the latter. Merton argues against the engaged Buddhist stance in which a fantasy of a totalized ethical practice would prevail, noting that "we will be relevant in the world of Marxism in proportion not as we are pseudo-Marxists or semi-Marxist monks, or something like that, but in proportion as we are simply monks—simply what we are" (328). He notes that both communism and monasticism are based on a principle of equality—but that he believes that only a monastery, and not a communist society can realize such equality. He then introduces Marcuse, and his double critique of existing communist and capitalist societies, through a reading of *One Dimensional Man*. Like many of the figures I've discussed in this section, Merton sets out a formal problem of nonalignment, of what a society that rejects the alienation of both capitalist and communist materialisms would look like. It is at this point that he introduces his recent meetings with various Tibetan monks, whose flight from the Chinese Communists he describes, while noting that the Dalai Lama recognizes the inequalities of premodern Tibet. He is surprised by a question that the Dalai Lama asks him about whether Christian monastic vows imply "a commitment to total inner transformation of one sort or another—a commitment to become a completely new man" (337). Thus the difference between Christian and Buddhist monasticism, for Merton, emerges in the historical forgetting of this commitment by contemporary Christian monastic groups—a commitment which Merton then wishes to reaffirm.

Merton goes on to recall something Trungpa tells him—a remark made to him by another lama at the moment of the Chinese invasion of Tibet, who tells him "from now on, everybody stands on his own feet" (338). Merton gives this a very specific interpretation: it is not a call to a kind of bourgeois individualism, but a recognition "that we can no longer rely on being supported by structures that may be destroyed at any moment by a political power or a political force" (338). It is at this point that Merton's talk tips over into a Bataillean politics of nonalignment. For Merton recognizes that the appropriation of societal excess into monasteries is no longer viable. But that leaves us then with a double problem. Firstly, what is a viable form that supports the total transformation of human beings, individually and collectively? Secondly, given the fundamental nature of excess over societal stability, what will happen to that excess—at least from the point of view of religious community—when it can no longer be channeled into the monasteries as locations of the sacred? Merton's answer to this question is subtle and surprising. He begins by considering a Zen *kōan*: "Where do you go from the top of a thirty-foot pole?" (338) A life in that situation seems inconceivable, as does a life without the monasteries, or without "structures." Merton describes the traditional icon of the Buddha, with a begging bowl in one hand, his other hand touching the earth. The hand on the earth attests to the immanence of enlightenment in the very "materiality" of the space in which we find ourselves. The begging bowl "represents the ultimate theological root of the belief not just in a right to beg, but in openness to the gifts of all beings as expression of the interdependence of all beings . . . when the monk begs from the layman and receives a gift from the layman, it is not as a selfish person getting something from somebody else. He is simply opening himself in this interdependence, this mutual interdependence, in which they all recognize that they are all immersed in illusion together, but that the illusion is also an empirical reality that has to be fully accepted, and that in this illusion, which is nevertheless empirically real, nirvana is present" (341–42).

Gift economy, interdependence, the inconceivable: these are all elements of a Bataillean general economy. They are also elements of a Buddhist description of the human condition. Yet the gift economy that Merton is describing also exists within a specific historical form of political economy—and the prevailing global political order after WWII, which includes both existing communist and capitalist nation-states, blocks or limits the

flourishing of an explicit Bataillean general economics, of a realized Buddhist community, of a politics of nonalignment. This
situation has recently been given a startlingly clear and concise
reformulation in Karatani Kōjin's *The Structure of World History*.[128] Like Bataille (who is mentioned only once in a footnote),
Karatani takes up Marx and Weber's descriptions of the historical development of global political economy.[129] He argues first of
all that the Marxist emphasis on modes of production needs to
be adjusted, and proposes to describe world history in terms of
the generation of different modes of exchange. He says there are
four of these: A—gift exchange; B- feudalism; C—commodity
exchange; D—something else. In category D, Karatani includes
religious movements, insofar as they refuse modes B and C and
propose a radicalized version of A in which gift exchange is no
longer simply gift-countergift (Mauss's argument), but gift giving without reserve (i.e., Bataille's notion of expenditure). He
also considers communist and anarchist movements of varying
kinds as belonging to D. He argues that, historically, category D
appears only as an unsustainable flash before being reabsorbed
back into B or C; that mode D has never yet fully and stably manifested itself, but that it haunts history, and insists itself on the
horizon of history as that which must be realized—for Karatani
in the form of a world republic built around associationism.

This model is extremely helpful in understanding the Buddhist politics of nonalignment in the postwar years. Although
U Nu's Burmese republic, organized around Buddhist principles,
did in fact last from 1948 to 1962, and left us dazzling texts such
as his *Towards a Socialist State* (1958), the difficulty, even impossibility of realizing those principles in the form of a stable society remains—not the least because of the potential for mis-
treatment of minorities under a hegemonic Buddhist state.
The same questions surround Snyder's Buddhist anarchism.
Of course much depends on whether one decides that "impossible" simply means impossible, and that the horizons of global
political reality as they are presented today within mainstream

political science and media are self-evident truths, or whether one decides that "impossible" is an ideological category that prevents us from conceiving and acting upon what has merely been hitherto inconceivable. Karatani himself ends his book rather abruptly, presenting the formal possibility of mode of exchange D without specifying what it is, or might be, beyond a few intriguing details. Yet Karatani—like Bataille—does formally present this possibility as one in which certain religious modes of thought contain in them a proposal concerning mode D and the global overcoming of nation/state/capital. And in this sense, the writers examined in this section offer ways to think of mode of exchange D from a Buddhist perspective. But how?

5

Chinese historian/philosopher Wang Hui has an astute reading of the apparent polarization of Marxism and Buddhism that took place in Western countercultures in the 1960s:

> From these two similar but quite opposite directions taken by Western youth in the 1960s, we can see that this move back to ancient philosophy via the mediation of the spirit of Tibet is, in fact, closely related to the political ideology of the Cold War period. We can say that those young people who looked toward China in seeking out the socialist ideal were following the Enlightenment tradition in moving toward Marxism, and those who believed that "the alliance of happiness and justice would no longer come about through the individual quest for wisdom but through the rebuilding of society as a whole. And before building a new society, the old one first had to be completely destroyed" found in the concept of "revolution" the possibility of combining theory and practice. On the other hand, the "liberal revolution" rejects the idea that the individual can find salvation by belonging to a collectivity, and believes that this idea will bring about political totalitarianism. Tibet thus provides a way of conceiving of modern society outside the Enlightenment tradition.[130]

Theoretical debates about Buddhism and Marxism today remain a product of this ideological split (not necessarily two ideologies but the split itself as ideology)—within Asia perhaps as much as in Europe and America. And, to say it again, it is precisely in the gap or space between these two ostensibly polarized visions that I situate Bataillean notions of community, and the problem of political Buddhism.

The 1960s and 1970s saw a number of extreme attempts to eradicate religion in communist-controlled Asian societies. In Cambodia, between 1975–79, the vast majority of Buddhist monasteries were shut down, and it is estimated that around 63 percent of monks were executed at the hands of the Khmer Rouge—the rest either disrobing or fleeing into exile.[131] In Tibet, both prior to and during the Cultural Revolution, the vast majority of monasteries were shut down, and the public practice of religion more or less disappeared.[132] In China, virtually all monasteries and temples were closed by September 1966, and remained so for the following decade, as part of the campaign to "Smash the Four Olds."[133]

These brief sentences and summaries obviously do not do justice to the events of those years, nor do they convey a sense of the geopolitical context in which they need to be understood—yet the absence of any acknowledgment of these events in the work of Žižek et al. seems much more problematic. Beyond the figure of the Buddhist as bare life to be subjected to biopolitical management of his/her religious beliefs, there rises Mbembe's necropolitics, which he defines as "contemporary forms of subjugation of life to the power of death."[134] In his essay on this topic, Mbembe argues that "the subject of Marxian modernity is, fundamentally, a subject who is intent on proving his or her sovereignty through the staging of a fight to the death. . . . Terror and killing become the means of realizing the already known telos of history."[135] Even if this is a sweeping generalization, it has relevance to the period we are discussing. This fight to the death staged the "ideological illusions" of religions against a scientific, materialist practice of critique, enacted through violent force. Insofar as religious belief systems claimed to guarantee protection from destruction for believers, those belief systems suffered an almost total defeat. But the evident resurgence of religious faith and practice both in former Soviet territories and in various Asian societies, after the exhaustion of communist attempts to eradicate all material signs of them, suggests that neither biopolitical nor necropolitical management of religion were in the end effective, or—insofar as effectiveness is a measure of truth—adequate in their understanding of religion.

Since the end of the 1970s, there has been a Buddhist revival in many Asian countries, which has run parallel with the expansion of market economies in those societies in the wake of the demise of socialist projects. Today, Buddhism exists primarily within variably secular regimes, who variously support, tolerate, repress, and market it as a simulacrum for tourists. Thus we encounter curious paradoxes: a Buryat lama who now funds the activities of his temple by working as an Amway distributor after reading the writings of an American former monk trained in the Gelugpa tradition[136]; Tibetan lamas in Sichuan and the Tibetan plateau whose flourishing monasteries are funded by wealthy Chinese sponsors.[137] Although the histories of "Asian Buddhism" and "Western Buddhism" are treated as separate, they are converging in ever more complex new forms in the emerging global economy and society. Bernstein, no doubt accurately, describes this phenomenon as a "post-socialist" one. But, to restate a well-known Žižekian thesis, it is precisely at this moment in which so many feel they are done with Marxism that it is worthwhile to think of Marxism and Buddhism together, and to remain open to the possibility that they hold other answers to the problem of consumption that Bataille saw at the core of the world-historical evolution of capitalism—and to which, he insisted, capitalism lacked an adequate response.

Bataille already saw (as Nietzsche did) that universally applied social justice was a necessary but not sufficient goal for human beings. Bataille's notion of sovereignty attempts to address this issue, and, as we have seen, this is a theme in Buddhism too, where liberation cannot simply be seen in terms of social justice. Although the various writers who have subsequently taken up Bataille on the theme of community do in a sense seek to address the problem of community beyond utility and/or distribution, there is a way in which Bataillean sovereignty has yet to be explored seriously—or refuted. Even those contemporary thinkers influenced by Nick Land's work—including Ray Brassier, or for that matter other "speculative realists" such as Meillassoux or Harman or Negarastani—have failed to address the issue of sovereignty—in other words, what being exposed to "nothingness" or an ontological gap means for a subject or subjects. Harman, for example, argues that any object-oriented ontology is beyond both theory and practice—but has said very little as to the consequences or decisions implied for the subject of such an ontology. Here Peter Sloterdijk's recent work is perhaps the most relevant, especially insofar as it takes up the theme of the Nietzschean superman, who is also a model for Bataillean sovereignty. Yet Sloterdijk oscillates between sports and experimental modernism as examples of "the planet of the practicing," and thus is unable to grasp the essentially religious nature of the problem of sovereignty. In this sense Žižek's call for a rethinking of the problem of political theology is more compelling, yet because it essentially sees religion as a matter of expediency, sovereignty does not come up in the way that it did for Bataille, or for Chopel. In other words, there is nothing at stake for Žižek in any transformative practice of subjectivity, which remains "in the last instance" the product of external conditions.

There has been a now well-known reevaluation of communism in contemporary theory over the last decade, including the two recent Idea of Communism conferences co-organized by Žižek. This reevaluation is associated with the work of Alain Badiou. For Badiou, whose communist sympathies are at this point well known, the Cultural Revolution was a necessary, radical, but ultimately failing attempt to move toward the achievement of a human society based on equality.[138] It forms a limit to our ability to think the political, a limit which we have retreated from over the last thirty years. I make no endorsement of Badiou's views on the Cultural Revolution. But it is impossible to think of Tibetan Buddhism today without thinking of it in the light of the Cultural Revolution and "the Communist idea," as it manifested in China, Mongolia, and the Southern Russian republics, some of which also practiced forms of Tibetan Buddhism prior to the advent of the Soviets.

It is evident that Buddhism has not disappeared in the way that communist ideologues thought that it would do, in Asia or elsewhere. Anyone who studies with a Buddhist teacher today, Tibetan or otherwise, is studying a Buddhism after communism—a Buddhism that bears with it the traces of the encounter with communism. Conversely, it must be said that anyone interested in the communist idea today is interested in an idea whose historical and philosophical trajectory is what it is because of, among other things, an encounter with Buddhism.

Badiou's philosophy is dense and requires a more detailed response than I can give it in this essay.[139] Still, there are striking similarities between Badiou's mature philosophical system and Mahāyāna Buddhist thought.[140] Consider Badiou's most decisive innovation: his development of a subtractive mathematical ontology in which infinite multiplicities develop out of/as the void, or zero, or empty set, rather than a transcendental One that would serve as their ground. This doctrine is strikingly similar to the Mahāyāna Buddhist notion of śūnyatā or emptiness—which was itself a response to the monism contained in the Upanishads. However, Badiou develops this ontology in a surprising way: he demonstrates the possibility of the production of truths via exposure to this void, and a reconfigured relation of knowledge to non-knowledge. As Bruno Bosteels astutely points out, it is this possibility of what Badiou calls truth procedures (formally associated with what he calls "forcing") that distinguishes him from other contemporary thinkers' renderings of the relation of thought to the void.[141] Badiou specifies four such truth procedures: love, art, science, politics. Badiou conceives of these truth procedures not only as a formal possibility, but as having a specific political meaning, one emergent out of his own commitment to Maoist politics in France. In this sense, and no doubt via his interest in Lacan, Badiou can be said to be responding to the Bataillean problematic that I've set out.

If both Buddhist philosophers and Badiou are agreed on a model of reality consisting of infinite multiplicities grounded in a groundless or essenceless void, the consequences of this model are, as I've said, radically different. One could accurately describe the history of Buddhist philosophy and practice in terms of truth procedures and their relation to the event of the Buddha's enlightenment (this would bring us back to the two truths debate discussed earlier). For Badiou, the infinite has no religious dimension because it is not transcendental and is merely the way in which the everyday appears as everyday. In a certain way, Buddhist thinkers would agree: Buddhism is not a theology and has no transcendental God, and as even the crudest stereotypes of Japanese Zen in the West indicate, enlightenment equals recognition of the coincidence of the infinite (and all possible orderings thereof), the zero and the everyday. But Buddhists ascribe this recognition the highest value. Badiou does not. Or does he? Badiou's void or emptiness is split into a mathematical void that is banal and meaningless and a traumatic event that sets in motion a truth procedure. This split marks off Badiou's "materialism" and he is dogmatic on this point, yet it also introduces a bifurcation into the zero. How can the zero be both traumatic and banal? I ask not because I think the coincidence of trauma and banality is impossible, but because I don't find an explanation in Badiou's work.

There is no way that one can remain a materialist in the strict sense of the word when one takes Badiou's position, because to insist on a materialist position is precisely to separate the event from the zero and thus reify it. This is why Mahāyāna Buddhism is not a materialist philosophy: because it refuses to reify emptiness. Furthermore, there is no particular reason why there should be only four domains of truth procedure, except that only four can be found that are strictly "materialist" and therefore acceptable. Yet limiting these domains to four introduces an obvious ethnocentrism into Badiou's work, a defensiveness against the radical implications of what he is actually proposing. Furthermore, it deforms that which in Badiou should be an argument in favor of practice, defined as the open negotiation of the truth of the event, into what I glossed above as "praxis"—in other words, a practice whose structure has already been predetermined and prescribed in such a way that it can take one of only four forms.

In his book on Saint Paul, Badiou locates the truth procedure of Christianity as one belonging to the domain of love.[142] One might conclude from this that religion is incompatible with philosophy, which stands outside of the various truth procedures but whose job it is to clarify them. But what is intriguing about Buddhism is that it is both philosophy and truth procedure—indeed, according to a very standard Tibetan formula, it is the union of wisdom/knowledge and compassion/love. What Buddhism points to is a different configuration of theory and practice that disturbs the separation of philosophy from truth procedures. Badiou sees this separation as an eternal truth, but it is merely one particular historical iteration—and perhaps not the final, or the most significant one at that. We might then wonder about the political consequences of a redistribution of the relation of philosophy to truth procedures—and whether it is precisely this potential for a disturbance of philosophy's positionality that makes the misrecognition of Buddhism so important for followers of Badiou.

6

Many of the questions formulated above have been articulated by a group of American thinkers associated with a project called speculative non-Buddhism, in the form of a series of lively and dense blogs that have appeared over the last five years, including *Speculative Non-Buddhism*, *The Faithful Buddhist*, *The Non-Buddhist*, and *Der Unbuddhist*; as well as a book, *Cruel Theory, Sublime Practice, toward a Revaluation of Buddhism*, written by Glenn Wallis, Tom Pepper and Matthias Steingass, which sets out many of their core arguments and critiques.[143] This work has proven controversial, at least in the hazy world of Internet blogs and comments sections, partly because of the sometimes belligerent tone of the writing, partly because of the challenge it poses to mainstream European and American Buddhist sanghas.

The arguments of Wallis et al. have two important elements. Firstly, they develop Žižek-inspired critiques of the integration of Buddhist techniques and communities into a consumer-friendly Buddhist ideology that is adapted to the world of global corporate capitalism. Unlike Žižek, who shows little evidence of any knowledge of existing Buddhist communities, these critiques are obviously insider jobs, often malicious, sometimes very funny and accurate, made with the intensity and bitterness often found in disenchanted former believers of whatever kind. One of the most recent posts on *Speculative Non-Buddhism* discusses a YouTube video made at a Google employees' conference in San Francisco, in which a corporate mindfulness workshop is suddenly interrupted by antipoverty activists accusing Google of decimating local communities through the influx of wealth and the resulting gentrification of San Francisco neighborhoods.[144] The mindfulness trainer responds to this protest by advising the attendees on how to dissociate themselves mentally from the protest that is going on. This example of a Buddhist practice being ideologically appropriated is critiqued using a theoretical vocabulary that includes Marx, Althusser, Badiou, Žižek, and others. The value of this critique consists in its attempt to stage a philosophically rigorous conversation from within Buddhist communities about the uses and misuses of existing Buddhist theories and practices in a global capitalist economy—and to engage the resistance that such a critique generates, while still remaining part of the community.

The second element consists in the development of a formal theoretical model that can be used to think about and practice Buddhism: that of speculative non-Buddhism. The framework for non-Buddhism is derived from speculative philosopher François Laruelle's work, and specifically his critique of philosophy as a whole, as being characterized by a certain decisionism regarding the Real. Non-philosophy, Laruelle's proposed alternative, consists of the possibility of generating valid axioms and practices based on a generic refusal of this decisionism.[145] Laruelle himself writes of "non-Marxism" and other "non-"s. Wallis adapts Laruelle's thought to generate a speculative "non-Buddhism," characterized by a refusal of what he sees as a ubiquitous Buddhist decisionism within existing Buddhist communities, which he refers to as "X-Buddhist," meaning "any community that commits itself to the decisionism of doctrinal belief in Buddhism." This decisionism amounts to "Buddhism as ideology," or, more colloquially, an irrational obedience to the authority of tradition. The refusal of this decisionism, within a Buddhist context, is an attempt (among other things) to fully engage the problem of ideology as it relates to Buddhist theories and practices. Indeed, the major problem with Wallis et al. is that their recognition of the problem that Buddhism has negotiating ideology is overdetermined and lacking in subtlety and, I would say, compassion.

Wallis et al.'s work illuminates Bataille and his notions of sovereignty and non-knowledge, which I have shown to be emergent from his thinking through of Buddhism and yoga. In a sense, what Bataille did with Buddhist meditation practices and philosophy was precisely to strip them of their configuration within an existing tradition, and then to use them to displace philosophical and political theory, exposing the limited economy of knowledge to the general economy of non-knowledge. Bataille's major contribution in terms of philosophy was to assert the vitality and capaciousness of the "non" or "NOTHING," and to assert the possibility and value of a life exposed to this nothing.

A liberal critique of Wallis et al.'s non-Buddhism would begin by asserting that the supposed separation of X- and non-Buddhisms is hardly absolute, and that historically what has in fact been non-Buddhism consists of all the doctrinal disputes, heretical figures, and texts which constitute the reality of the flourishing of the multiplicity of schools that Wallis et al. define as X-Buddhist. Within the history of Tibetan Buddhism, for example, figures like Dolpopa and Gorampa were heretical in relation to hegemonic Gelugpa philosophies, and were effectively banned for hundreds of years, only to later be reintegrated or at least tolerated. But they still saw themselves as Buddhists. Furthermore, the figure of the yogi—Milarepa, for example—is defined by a certain autonomy relative to existing religious institutions.

Again, returning to the theme of this essay, one might ask whether Gendun Chopel is a non-Buddhist or an X-Buddhist. If, as Donald Lopez suggests, Chopel's most significant contribution was to raise the issue of enlightenment in a context where it had been more or less bracketed, it becomes clear that the separation of non-Buddhism and X-buddhism made by Wallis et al. isn't totally coherent.[146] Non-Buddhism must presuppose the possibility of enlightenment as the minimal criteria for its own existence: without it, one might as well argue that an installation manual for an air conditioner or a trip to the dentist are "non-Buddhist" (there might well be "Zen" arguments along these lines that are significant, but let's set them aside for now). Furthermore, "the possibility of enlightenment" has a specific meaning: it implies practice, and it is noteworthy that Wallis continues to lead or participate in a meditation group ("or something like it," as his website says).[147] Therefore non-Buddhism and X-Buddhism actually share something crucial. "Non-Buddhism" reopens the possibility that fields that are not explicitly Buddhist might be highly relevant to the universal realization of enlightenment. It endorses the necessity of theory interrupting theory in a historically contingent but necessary way, of practice interrupting theory, and of theory interrupting practice.

What Wallis et al. do signal, in terms of the concerns of this essay, is the emerging relationship between Buddhism and the emerging paradigm of cognitive capitalism—which can be thought of as an extension of "the informatization of production" or the development of "affective labor."[148] The validation of neuroscientists such as Thomas Metzinger, who argue that Buddhist models of self/no-self correlate with the discoveries of contemporary neuroscience, represent a temptation for Buddhists, precisely because the truth claims that are being made with such correlations have a particular ideological value in the cognitive capitalist marketplace. [149]

The core question remains: What is the relationship between Buddhism and politics? As much as I value the actually existing work of engaged Buddhists, I am actually inclined toward a more difficult, less appealing answer to the question. I am haunted by both Bataille and Chopel's insistence that in the end it comes down to the mind—and I am also struck by the way in which neurocognitive capitalism is tending toward a similar conclusion. Obviously, there are ways in which certain versions of Buddhism can become a kind of (a)theological Prozac, serving to enable global capitalism through a certain ideology of distancing, purity, etc. But to what degree does Buddhism support the development of other modes of collective interiority that are necessary? If Karatani is right, and what beckons on the horizon of the world of contemporary formations of capital is an as-yet inconceivable form of gift economy, one of the crucial questions that emerges is, What kinds of collective modes of subjectivity can actually sustain or articulate a gift economy? Going beyond the general insight that many religions propose ethics of hospitality, egalitarianism, love and compassion, is there a specific reconfiguration of this problem that Buddhism proposes—or can respond to? One of the principal figures of contemporary theorizations of community is that of depropriation (Esposito) or dispossession (Butler and Athanasiou).[150] If what human beings share is finitude, exposure to death, a being without property/properties, desire—in Buddhist terms, the first noble truth, that of suffering—then what are the qualities that can sustain, indeed deepen our familiarity with and solidarity in that exposure? Buddhist meditations on interdependence aim at precisely this point—interdependence is a figure of the Common, and conversely, a theoretical understanding of the nature of the Common deepens a meditative understanding of interdependence, loosening up deeply held ideological formations of subject and object as private property. It is in this regard that I've previously examined the politics of the copy in terms of Buddhist (and non-Buddhist) philosophy.[151]

If there is something like a Buddhist trace that runs through critical theory all the way to Žižek's current disavowals, it is the Buddhist insistence on an extra-discursive dimension to reality, one that is accessible through practices of various kinds. It seems like such a minor point, almost nothing at all. So easy to misrecognize. And yet for all three thinkers, something crucial is at stake in what Bataille calls "non-knowledge," Chopel "the inconceivable," and Badiou "the event." If Hallward, Žižek, and other Marxian thinkers take the effort to critique a Buddhist position on these matters, it is because something is at stake for them, too. What Bataille, Chopel, and Badiou share is an interest in the politics of that which is sometimes labeled as nothing. Is it less than nothing, an infinity "grounded" in nothing, simply nothing, or, to paraphrase Levinas, other than nothing? Bataille believes that ontologically there is nothing. Nonetheless, he believes that abandoning oneself completely to that nothing can be lucky. In other words, that some kind of *jouissance*, pleasure, knowledge, ecstatic nonknowledge, revealed by chance or whatever the source of "luck" is, will be consequent. So, despite his differences with Bataille, does Badiou. If the event is capable of sustaining a truth procedure, it is because in some way, the zero or nothing which Being is sutured to is still capable of giving truth—ecstatic or not.

Chopel orders a strikingly similar problematic in a different way. The negation of all appearances, all conceptual formulations about Being, opens up the possibility of "the inconceivable," a.k.a. the nonconceptual, a.k.a. emptiness. Beyond concepts does not mean "nothing." It means empty. Empty means "empty of inherent existence." Empty of self/empty of other. This is the significance of the two truths. What Chopel establishes is in fact a Buddhist theory of ideology, where all assertions of conventional truths are ideologies which stand as imaginary or false in relation to an ultimate truth that is beyond concepts. The coexistence of the two truths is a breach of the law of noncontradiction, and ideology is the result of the attempt to force a resolution or resolve the contradiction between the two levels of truth prematurely. Prematurely because, as Chopel says, the point of practice is to attain a state of enlightenment which would be the resolution of "the great contradiction." The question nevertheless remains: Can there be any political significance to this inconceivable that is other than nothing, or will it always amount to an abdication of the political, even the social—or, conversely, a reified ideological form, as one finds with Snyder? For Badiou, the answer is to "force" the contradiction and thus "resolve" it. For Bataille, there are at least two possibilities: one, to abandon oneself to the aleatory force of the drive, beyond knowledge, thus affirming excess; two, to commit oneself to what has been called "radical passivity" (a position that Blanchot, Nancy, Agamben, et al. elaborate). With Chopel, the answer is less clear—although, not coincidentally, Chopel also paid the highest price for not censoring the political implications of his argument, with its specific critique of the ruling Tibetan orthodoxy. But it would be a mistake to limit Chopel's politics to a particular position within a theological debate between hegemonic and non-hegemonic Buddhist sects in mid-twentieth-century Tibet, just as it is a mistake to believe that Chopel was simply arguing for modernity against theocratic feudalism. Read as part of a continuing politics of nonalignment that is still present with us today, even after the end of the Cold War, Chopel's work articulates a desire for a different future.

I would like to return to Agamben's critique of Bataillean sovereignty as ignoring the modern biopolitical appropriation of "bare life" into an administrative regime—not to mention Mbembe's recent revision of Agamben and Foucault with his concept of "necropolitics"—in other words, the instrumental use of the right to kill and of death and dying, not only as a state of exception claimed by the sovereign, but as an integral part of the day to day functioning of states and other political entities. How does one think the contemporary politics of Buddhism outside of biopolitics or necropolitics? To quote my friend Charles Stein: "But the challenging and really difficult 'violence' is that enlightenment is not pro-life. Not pro-death either. As Yeats had written on his tombstone: 'Cast a cold Eye/ On Life, on Death./ Horseman pass by!'"[152] Stein puts the word "violence" in quotes to show the way that the Buddhist worldview can be experienced as a kind of violence by those who believe that biopolitics and/or necropolitics constitute the field of the political in toto today. Practicing Buddhists need to take the question seriously and ask what the relationship is between states of nonconceptual "bare life" achieved in states of meditation, and the kinds of social and political structures that are generated, ostensibly around such practices. But equally theorists such as Žižek need to examine their own fear of bare life, and their avoidance of consensual practices that examine and realize states of non-knowledge.

So: have we learned anything that allows us to think further than Žižek's conclusion to *Less Than Nothing*: that it's *Gelassenheit* (more or less radical passivity) vs. class struggle, with Buddhism relegated to the former position, usually as an enabler of liberal capitalist ideology? In researching this essay and reading the descriptions of the brutalities inflicted on Buddhists, among many others, during the period of the dictatorship of the proletariat and the consolidation of various communist states, I return to Freud's caustic remarks concerning Russian Communism in *Civilization and Its Discontents*.[153] Freud asks who the Communists will unleash their aggressive instincts on if and when the Russian bourgeoisie has been vanquished and an egalitarian society formed. The issue is not fundamentally that of class struggle, it is that of human inclination—or, if you like, drive. In this sense, we have hardly even begun to ask the right questions concerning the relationship of a Buddhist politics to sexuality and sexual difference[154]—indeed, these questions haunt this essay, from Bataille to Chopel to Snyder—as evidently they haunt those critical theorists who have been most attuned to the practice of Asian religions: Barthes, Foucault, hooks, Irigaray, Kristeva, Sedgwick, Ronell. They also haunt Buddhist communities, whether through the problem of monasticism as a radical attempt to neutralize issues of sexuality and gender, or that of tantra as a "secret" negotiation of sexuality in the cause of enlightenment.

The question—historical, materialist, otherwise—is, What will cause human beings to act differently? Thus it is a question of practice—as Bataille, Chopel, Snyder, and Badiou variably recognize. But what kind of practice? Chopel says, "In the end it comes down to what you do with your mind." Or what we do collectively with our minds. The struggle then cannot be merely a private or personal one. Emerging work on collective phenomenologies is instructive: what we need is a collective phenomenology of an ontological contradiction, the contradiction of what is.[155] I argue that Buddhist practices constitute, or could constitute important elements of such a phenomenology. Such practices open up onto the inconceivable, or to use a word recently explored by Lauren Berlant and Lee Edelman, "the unbearable."

As my Buddhist teachers say, the measure of the success of the practice is the capacity for kindness, compassion. Perhaps this is what Benjamin meant when he said that "to live in a glass house is a revolutionary virtue par excellence." The practice of those monks in the Moscow hotel in 1928 is both interior and social.

But basically what I'm saying is *meditate*. Do it. Right now.

Beyond that, the answers to the questions raised in this essay are not simply theoretical—or practical—or a combination of the two. There is an important research question involved: namely, what kinds of Buddhist socialism, Marxism, or anarchism were generated in the twentieth century, in Asian or non-Asian societies? It is a difficult research question because the most interesting answers may come not from institutional archives, but from the details of very fragile historical lives, individual and collective, as they struggled to articulate themselves in the middle of fierce material conditions.

NOTES

The author gratefully acknowledges the support of a Canadian SSHRC Standard Research Grant, and a York University Faculty of the Arts Fellowship, for work on this project. For teaching me about Buddhism, many thanks to Khenpo Tsultrim Gyamtso Rinpoche, Gelek Rimpoche, and Khenpo Sonam Tobgyal. For advice and comments on this essay, many thanks to John Whalen Bridge, Jr., Donald S. Lopez Jr., Stuart Kendall, Charles Stein, Ian Harris, Elena Basile, Gabriel Levine, and Christie Pearson.

1. Bertolt Brecht and John Willett, *Poems* (London: Methuen, 1976), 290–92.

2. *The Lotus Sūtra*, trans. Burton Watson (New York: Columbia University Press, 1993), 56–79.

3. Walter Benjamin, "On Surrealism," in *Selected Writings*, vol. 2

(Cambridge, MA: Belknap Press of Harvard University Press, 2003), 209.

4. Benjamin mentions the Buddhist monks in the entry for January 25, 1927, in *Moscow Diary* (Cambridge, MA: Harvard University Press, 1986), 104. See also Andrei Znamenski, *Red Shambhala: Magic, Prophecy, and Geopolitics in the Heart of Asia* (Wheaton, IL: Quest/Theosophical Publishing House, 2011); Alexandre Andreyev, *Soviet Russia and Tibet: The Debacle of Secret Diplomacy 1918–1930* (Leiden: Brill, 2003).

5. Anya Bernstein, *Religious Bodies Politic: Rituals of Sovereignty in Buryat Buddhism* (Chicago: University of Chicago Press, 2013), chap. 1, loc. 1043–1079.

6. See Ian Harris, "Buddhism and Politics in Asia: The Textual and Historical Roots" in *Buddhism and Politics in Twentieth-Century Asia* (London: Pinter, 1999), 1–26.

7. Horst Junginger, ed., *The Study of Religion under the Impact of Fascism* (Leiden: Brill, 2007). Gustavo Benavides, "Giuseppe Tucci, or Buddhology in the Age of Fascism," in *Curators of the Buddha: The Study of Buddhism Under Colonialism*, ed. Donald Lopez Jr. (Chicago: University of Chicago Press, 1995), 161–95.

8. For example, the recent collection edited by Melvin McLeod, *Mindful Politics: A Buddhist Guide to Making the World a Better Place* (Boston: Wisdom, 2006) does not mention Marx, and contains almost no mention of any historical material, suggesting that Buddhist politics is an almost entirely a prospective thought. Christopher Queen and Sallie King's seminal edited volume *Engaged Buddhism: Buddhist Liberation Movements in Asia* (Albany: State University of New York Press, 1996) only contains one chapter (Santikaro Bhikkhu's essay on Thai monk Buddhadasa Bhikku's "dhammic socialism"—see 165–75) that engages Marxism; Queen's subsequent collection, *Engaged Buddhism in the West* (Boston, MA: Wisdom, 2000) does not mention Marx at all; neither does the third volume edited by Queen, Charles S. Prebish, and Damien Keown, *Action Dharma: New Studies in Engaged Buddhism* (London: RoutledgeCurzon, 2003). *Buddhism and Politics in Twentieth-*

Century Asia, which is not specifically about "engaged Buddhism" does have relevant essays by Harris on Cambodia, and Stuart-Fox on Laos, in particular. Trevor Ling's pamphlet *Karl Marx and Asian Religion* (Bangalore University, 1978) has a helpful discussion of the territory.

9. Naoki Sakai and Jon Solomon, "Introduction: Addressing the Multitude of Foreigners, Echoing Foucault," in *Traces*, vol. 4: *Translation, Biopolitics, Colonial Difference* (Hong Kong University Press, 2006), 1–35.

10. Chronologically, Žižek's remarks on Buddhism can be found in the following works: "From Western Marxism to Western Buddhism," *Cabinet*, Spring 2001 (http://www.cabinetmagazine .org/issues/2/western.php, accessed 05/14/13); Slavoj Žižek, *The Puppet and the Dwarf: The Perverse Core of Christianity* (Cambridge, MA: MIT Press, 2003), 13–33; "Revenge of Global Finance," *In These Times*, May 2005 (http://inthesetimes.com/article/2122/, accessed 05/04/13); the chapter "Lacan against Buddhism" in Žižek's *Less than Nothing: Hegel and the Shadow of Dialectical Materialism* (London: Verso, 2012), 127–35; and Slavoj Žižek, *Living in the End Times* (London: Verso, 2010), 286–89. There is also a series of three lectures given at the European Graduate School in 2012, "The Buddhist Ethic and the Spirit of Global Capitalism," "The Irony of Buddhism," and "Lacanian Theology and Buddhism," which can be accessed on YouTube.

11. Peter Hallward, *Absolutely Postcolonial: Writing between the Singular and the Specific* (Manchester, UK: Manchester University Press, 2001), 10–11, 284–90.

12. For a series of informed responses to a Žižek piece on Tibet in the *London Review of Books*, see the letters column for the June 5, 2008, issue, archived at http://www.lrb.co.uk/v30/n11/letters (accessed June 30, 2014).

13. Peter Hallward, *Badiou: A Subject to Truth* (Minneapolis: University of Minnesota Press, 2003), 318.

14. Žižek, *Puppet and the Dwarf*, 13; Hallward, *Absolutely Postcolonial*, 10.

15. Ernst Benz, *Buddhism or Communism: Which Holds the Future of Asia?* (Garden City, NY: Doubleday, 1965).

16. Dalai Lama, *Beyond Dogma: Discourses and Dialogues* (Berkeley: North Atlantic Books, 1996).

17. Louis Althusser, *Lenin and Philosophy, and Other Essays* (London: New Left Books, 1971).

18. Debiprasad Chattopadhyaya, *What Is Living and Dead in Indian Philosophy* (New Delhi: People's Publishing House, 1976), 518–43. See also his essay "Some Problems in Early Buddhism," in *Buddhism: A Marxist Approach* (Delhi: People's Publishing House, 1970). See also Gustavo Benavides, "Economy," in *Critical Terms for the Study of Buddhism*, ed. Lopez Jr., 77–102, for a discussion of some of the same material.

19. Brian Daizen Victoria, *Zen at War* (Lanham, MD: Rowman & Littlefield, 2006); Melvyn C. Goldstein, *A History of Modern Tibet, 1913–1951: The Demise of the Lamaist State* (Berkeley: University of California Press, 1989); Tsering Shakya, *The Dragon in the Land of Snows: A History of Modern Tibet since 1947* (New York: Columbia University Press, 1999).

20. Charles Keyes, "Buddhists Confront the State," in *Buddhism, Modernity, and the State in Asia: Forms of Engagement*, ed. Pattana Kitiarsa and John Whalen-Bridge (New York: Palgrave Macmillan, 2013), 17–40.

21. Slavoj Žižek, "The Spectre of Ideology," in *Mapping Ideology*, ed. Žižek (London: Verso, 1994); Alain Badiou, *The Concept of Model: An Introduction to the Materialist Epistemology of Mathematics*, trans. Zachary Luke Fraser and Tzuchien Tho (Melbourne: re.press, 2007).

22. Giorgio Agamben, *Homo Sacer: Sovereign Power and Bare Life*, trans. Daniel Heller-Roazen (Stanford, CA: Stanford University Press, 1998); Jean-Luc Nancy, *The Inoperative Community* (Minneapolis: University of Minnesota Press, 1991); Achile Mbembe, "Necropolitics," *Public Culture* 15 (2003): 11–40.

23. Judith Butler, *Gender Trouble: Feminism and the Subversion of Identity* (New York: Routledge, 1990); Lee Edelman, *No Future:*

Queer Theory and the Death Drive (Durham, NC: Duke University Press, 2004).

24. Ray Brassier, *Nihil Unbound: Enlightenment and Extinction* (Basingstoke, UK: Palgrave Macmillan, 2007); Nick Land, *The Thirst for Annihilation: Georges Bataille and Virulent Nihilism* (London: Routledge, 1992).

25. Norman O. Brown, *Apocalypse and/or Metamorphosis* (Berkeley: University of California Press, 1991); Michael Taussig, *Defacement: Public Secrecy and the Labor of the Negative* (Stanford, CA: Stanford University Press, 1999); Alphonso Lingis, *Violence and Splendor* (Evanston, IL: Northwestern University Press, 2011).

26. Amy Hollywood, *Sensible Ecstasy: Mysticism, Sexual Difference and the Demands of History* (Chicago: University of Chicago Press, 2002).

27. An important exception is Alan Foljambe, *An Intimate Destruction: Tantric Buddhism, Desire and the Body in Surrealism and Georges Bataille* (PhD Dissertation, University of Manchester, 2008). See also comments by Donald Lopez Jr., in *Prisoners of Shangri-La: Tibetan Buddhism and the West* (Chicago: University of Chicago Press, 1998), 8, 211–12.

28. See Bernstein, *Religious Bodies Politic*, loc. 3037.

29. Jean Bruno, "Les Techniques d'illumination chez Georges Bataille," *Critique* 195–96 (1963): 706–20.

30. Étienne Ballibar, Barbara Cassin, and Sandra Laugier, "Praxis," in *Dictionary of Untranslatables: A Philosophical Lexicon*, ed. Barbara Cassin, trans. Steven Rendall et al. (Princeton, NJ: Princeton University Press, 2014), ePub, loc. 2874.

31. On the concept of practice in Buddhism, see Carl Bielefeldt, "Practice," in *Critical Terms for the Study of Buddhism*, ed. Lopez Jr., 229–44. In Pāli, *pariyatti* is scriptural mastery, *patipatti*, the putting into practice of the teachings and *pativedha* direct realization of truth—but we might also consider the importance of Pāli/Sanskrit words such as *bhāvanā* ("meditation") and *sādhanā* ("technique"), as well as their translations and modifications in other Asian languages.

32. Georges Bataille, *Guilty*, trans. Bruce Boone (Venice, CA: Lapis, 1988), 37.

33. Bataille, *Guilty*, 44.

34. Michel Surya, *Georges Bataille: An Intellectual Biography*, trans. Krzysztof Fijalkowski and Michael Richardson (New York: Verso, 2002), 553.

35. Georges Bataille, "Expérience mystique et littérature," in *Oeuvres complètes* XI (Paris: Gallimard, 1988), 83–86.

36. Antonin Artaud, "Address to the Dalai Lama" and "Letter to the Buddhist Schools," in *Antonin Artaud: Selected Writings* (New York: Farrar, Straus and Giroux, 1976).

37. Foljambe, op. cit., offers the most thorough documentation of the Surrealists' and Bataille's interests in Asian religions. See also Andrew Hussey, *The Inner Scar: The Mysticism of Georges Bataille* (Atlanta: Rodopi, 2000).

38. See Sartre's comments in "Discussion on Sin," in Georges Bataille's *The Unfinished System of Nonknowledge*, trans. Michelle Kendall and Stuart Kendall (Minneapolis: University of Minnesota Press, 2001), 52; and Jean-Paul Sartre, "A New Mystic"/"Un Nouveau Mystique" originally published in *Cahiers du Sud* in 1943 and then in *Situations I* (Paris: Gallimard, 1947), 133–74.

39. Bataille, *Unfinished System of Nonknowledge*, 285.

40. Georges Bataille, *Visions of Excess: Selected Writings, 1927–1939*, trans. Allan Stoekl, with Carl R. Lovitts and Donald M. Leslie, Jr. (Minneapolis: University of Minnesota Press, 1985), 237.

41. Bataille, *Guilty*, 32–33.

42. Bataille, *Visions of Excess*, 237.

43. Georges Bataille, *Inner Experience*, trans. Leslie Anne Boldt (Albany: State University of New York Press, 1988), 22.

44. Bataille, *Oeuvres complètes* 7 (Paris: Gallimard, 1976), 258.

45. Bruno, "Les Techniques d'illumination chez Georges Bataille," 718.

46. Bataille, *Inner Experience*, 183. See also *Guilty*, 20, for Bataille's comments on Eliade's book on yoga.

47. Bataille, "Method of Meditation," in *Unfinished System of Non-Knowledge*, 77–99.

48. Bruno, "Les Techniques d'illumination chez Georges Bataille," 713.

49. Bataille, *Inner Experience*, 17.

50. Gustavo Benavides, "Irrational Experiences, Heroic Deeds and the Extraction of Surplus" in Junginger, ed., *Study of Religion under the Impact of Fascism*, 272.

51. Julia Kristeva, "Bataille, Experience and Practice," in *On Bataille: Critical Essays*, ed. and trans. Leslie Anne Boldt–Irons (Albany: State University of New York Press, 1995), 258–60. Mao Tse–Tung's essay "On Practice" can be found in Mao Zedong, and Slavoj Žižek, *On Practice and Contradiction* (London: Verso, 2007), 52–66.

52. See, for example, the references to stability in the Tibetan Lojong teachings.

53. Peter Sloterdijk, *You Must Change Your Life* (Oxford: Polity, 2013).

54. Bataille, "Method of Meditation," 78, italics in original.

55. Luce Irigaray, *Between East and West: From Singularity to Community*, trans. Stephen Pluháček (New York: Columbia University Press, 2002), 9.

56. Chögyam Trungpa, *Cutting through Spiritual Materialism* (Boston: Shambhala, 1987).

57. Žižek, *Less Than Nothing*, 131, italics in original.

58. Jean-Paul Sartre, "Un Nouveau Mystique."

59. Many of Bataille's finest commentators, including Kristeva and Klossowski, use the word "meditation" casually, and without any real examination of what the word might mean.

60. Georges Bataille, *The Accursed Share: An Essay on General Economy* (New York: Zone, 1988).

61. For a broader review of Bataille's sources re. general economy see Stuart Kendall, "Toward General Economy," *Scapegoat 5* (2013), "Excess," 27–32.

62. See Donald Lopez Jr., *Prisoners of Shangri-La*, 8–9.

63. Bataille, *Accursed Share*, 109–10.

64. Ibid., 110.

65. Nancy, *Inoperative Community*.

66. Bataille, *Accursed Share*, 101.

67. Ibid., 104.

68. Ibid., 109.

69. Robert Thurman, *Inner Revolution: Life, Liberty, and the Pursuit of Real Happiness* (New York: Riverhead, 1998).

70. Sloterdijk, *You Must Change Your Life*, 445.

71. On the history of the concept of praxis within Marxism see John Roberts, *Philosophizing the Everyday: Revolutionary Praxis and the Fate of Cultural Theory* (London: Pluto, 2006).

72. Bataille, *Accursed Share*, 189, italics in original.

73. Ibid., 190, italics in original.

74. Roger Pol-Droit, *The Cult of Nothingness: The Philosophers and the Buddha* (Chapel Hill: University of North Carolina Press, 2003).

75. *The Heart Sūtra* at http://www.lamrim.com/hhdl/heartsutra .html, accessed 05/07/13.

76. Bataille, *Accursed Share*, 190.

77. Burton Watson, trans., *The Zen Teachings of Master Lin-Chi: A Translation of the Lin-chi lu*, (New York: Columbia University Press, 1999).

78. Tulku Urgyen Rinpoche, *Blazing Splendor: The Memoirs of the Dzogchen Yogi Tulku Urgyen Rinpoche, as Told to Erik Pema Kunsang & Marcia Binder Schmidt* (Kathmandu, Nepal: Rangjung Yeshe, 2005).

79. Bataille, *Oeuvres complètes*, 7:431.

80. Ibid., 7:433.

81. Ibid., 7:437.

82. On Buddhist articulations of sacrifice and the gift, see Bernstein, *Religious Bodies Politic*, chap. 5 and Reiko Ohnuma's essay "Gift" in Donald Lopez Jr., ed., *Critical Terms for the Study of Buddhism*, 103–23.

83. John Whalen-Bridge, "Angry Monk Syndrome on the World Stage: Tibet, Engaged Buddhism, and the Weapons of the Weak," in Whalen-Bridge and Kitiarsa, eds., *Buddhism, Modernity, and the State*, 163–208.

84. Emile Durkheim, *The Elementary Forms of Religious Life*, trans. Joseph Ward Swain (New York: Free Press, 1965), 45–52.

85. The topic of course is not limited to Buddhist presentations of karma. See Gananath Obeyesekere, *Imagining Karma: Ethical Transformation in Amerindian, Buddhist, and Greek Rebirth* (Berkeley: University of California Press, 2002).

86. Agamben, *Homo Sacer*, 112.

87. Frantz Fanon, *The Wretched of the Earth* (New York: Grove, 1965).

88. B. R. Ambedkar, "Buddha or Karl Marx," in *Modern Buddhism: Readings for the Unenlightened*, ed. Donald S. Lopez (London: Penguin, 2002), 92–97; Johannes Beltz and Surendra Jondhale, eds., *Reconstructing the World: B.R. Ambedkar and Buddhism in India* (New Delhi: Oxford University Press, 2004).

89. Benz, *Buddhism or Communism*, 45–55, 79–85; Tilman Frasch, "The Relic and the Rule of Righteousness: Reflections on U Nu's *Dhammavijaya*," in *Buddhism, Modernity, and the State*, eds. Whalen-Bridge and Kitiarsa, 115–38.

90. On Laos, see Patrice Ladwig, "Schools, Ritual Economies and the Expanding State: The Changing Role of Lao Buddhist Monks as 'Traditional Intellectuals,'" in *Buddhism, Modernity, and the State*, eds. Whalen-Bridge and Kitiarsa; on Sri Lanka, see Mahinda Deegalle, "'Foremost Among Religions': Theravada Buddhism's Affairs with the Modern Sri Lankan State," in *Buddhism, Modernity, and the State*, eds. Whalen-Bridge and Kitiarsa, 41–62; on Cambodia, see Ian Harris, "Cambodia's Experiment in Buddhist Socialism: Sihanouk and the Wider Southeast Asian Context," in *Buddhist Socialisms in Asia*, ed. Patrice Ladwig (New York: Routledge, forthcoming). See also the material in Benz, *Buddhism or Communism*.

91. See the Soka Gakkai's interest in "human socialism," in Daniel Metraux, "The Soka Gakkai: Buddhism and the Creation of a Harmonious and Peaceful Society," in *Engaged Buddhism*, ed. Queen and King, 385.

92. Holmes Welch, *Buddhism under Mao* (Cambridge, MA: Harvard University Press, 1972); Benz, *Buddhism or Communism*, 138–69.

93. Patrice Ladwig's edited volume, *Buddhist Socialisms in Asia*, cited above, is awaited eagerly.

94. Shoji Yamada, *Shots in the Dark: Japan, Zen, and the West* (Chicago: University of Chicago Press, 2009); Rick Fields, *How the Swans Came to the Lake: A Narrative History of Buddhism in America* (Boston: Shambhala, 1992).

95. Martin Heidegger, *On the Way to Language* (New York: Harper & Row, 1971), 1–54. See also Reinhard May, *Heidegger's Hidden Sources: East Asian Influences on His Work* (London: Routledge, 1996).

96. Jacques Lacan, *Seminar X: Anxiety*, unpublished ms., 202–10; "Michel Foucault and Zen: A Stay in a Zen Temple," in *Religion and Culture: Michel Foucault*, ed. Jeremy Carrette (New York: Routledge, 1999), 110–15; Jay Prosser, "Buddha Barthes: What Barthes Saw in Photography (That He Didn't in Literature),"*Literature and Theology* 18, no. 2 (June 2004), 211–22; Erich Fromm and Daisetz Teitaro Suzuki, *Zen Buddhism and Psychoanalysis* (New York: Harper & Row, 1960).

97. Maurice Merleau-Ponty, *Humanism and Terror: an Essay on the Communist Problem* (Boston: Beacon, 1969), 149.

98. Ibid., 162–63.

99. Ibid., 163

100. Ibid., 176.

101. E. F. Schumacher, "Buddhist Economics," in *Small is Beautiful: A Study of Economics as if People Mattered* (New York: Vintage, 1993), 42.

102. Schumacher, "Buddhist Economics," 40.

103. "Buddhist Anarchism" was first published in *Journal for the Protection of All Beings* 1 (City Lights, 1961). The revised version was published as "Buddhism and the Coming Revolution" in *Earth House Hold* (New York: New Directions, 1969), 90–93.

104. Gary Snyder, "Buddhism and the Coming Revolution," in *Earth House Hold: Technical Notes and Queries to Fellow Dharma Revolutionaries* (New York: New Directions, 1969), 92–93.

105. Maurice Blanchot, *The Unavowable Community* (Barrytown, NY: Station Hill, 1988); Nancy, *Inoperative Community*; Alphonso Lingis, *The Community of Those Who Have Nothing in Common*

(Bloomington: Indiana University Press, 1994); Giorgio Agamben, *The Coming Community* (Minneapolis: University of Minnesota Press, 1993); Roberto Esposito, *Communitas: The Origin and Destiny of Community* (Stanford, CA: Stanford University Press, 2010).

106. *The Non-Aligned Movement and the Cold War: Delhi-Bandung-Belgrade*, ed. Natasa Miskovic, Harald Fischer-Tiné, and Nada Boskovska (New York, Routledge, 2014).

107. Indeed, Sankrityayan's essays, such as "Buddhist Dialectics" (reprinted in *Buddhism: A Marxist Approach*) show that he was attempting to think Marxism and Buddhism simultaneously—and surely he must have discussed such matters with Chopel on their travels together.

108. For Chopel's biography, see Donald Lopez Jr.'s introduction to *The Madman's Middle Way: Reflections on Reality of the Tibetan Monk Gendun Chopel* (Chicago: University of Chicago Press, 2006), 1–46; Heather Stoddard, *Le Mendiant De L'Amdo* (Paris: Société d'ethnographie, 1985;); Luc Schaedler, *Angry Monk: Reflections on Tibet: Literary, Historical, and Oral Sources for a Documentary Film* (doctoral diss., University of Zurich, Faculty of Arts, 2007).

109. Gendun Chopel, "Treatise on Passion," in *Tibetan Arts of Love*, ed. Jeffrey Hopkins and Dorje Yudon Yuthok (Ithaca, NY: Snow Lion, 1992); Amdo Gendun Chopel, *The Guide to India: A Tibetan Account*, ed. Toni Huber (Dharamsala, India: LTWA, 2000).

110. Jay Garfield and Graham Priest, "Nāgārjuna and the Limits of Thought," *Philosophy East and West* 53, no. 1 (2003): 1–21.

111. See Georges Dreyfus and Sara McClintock, eds., *The Svātantrika-Prāsaṅgika Distinction: What Difference does a Difference Make?* (Ilford, UK: Wisdom, 2003); *Moonshadows: Conventional Truth in Buddhist Philosophy*, ed. The Cowherds (Oxford: Oxford University Press, 2010); Sonam Thakchoe, *The Two Truths Debate: Tsongkhapa and Gorampa on the Middle Way* (Boston: Wisdom, 2007).

112. *The Hundred Thousand Songs of Milarepa*, trans. Garma C. C. Chang (Boston: Shambhala, 1999). *Sky Dancer: The Secret Life and Songs of Lady Yeshe Tsogyal*, trans. Keith Dowman (Ithaca, NY: Snow Lion, 1996).

113. Chopel, *Madman's Middle Way*, 60.

114. Donald Lopez Jr., *Buddhism and Science: A Guide for the Perplexed* (Chicago: University of Chicago Press, 2010).

115. Chopel, *Madman's Middle Way*, 68.

116. Ibid., 69.

117. Ibid., 69.

118. Ibid., 70.

119. Gendun Chopel, *Treatise on Passion*, trans. Donald Lopez Jr., forthcoming. For an alternative translation see Chopel, *Tibetan Arts of Love*, 271.

120. *Treatise on Passion*, n.p.; see also Chopel, *Tibetan Arts of Love*, 271.

121. *Treatise on Passion*, n.p.; see also Chopel, *Tibetan Arts of Love*, 275.

122. *Treatise on Passion*, n.p.; see also Chopel, *Tibetan Arts of Love*, 268.

123. Indeed, the question of how to translate the Tibetan word *bde ba* in the original, which can mean both "pleasure" and "bliss" (Donald Lopez Jr., personal communication) according to context ("pleasure" for "ordinary" enjoyment, "bliss" for tantric rituals), is an intriguing one, and suggests that there is a significant politics of translation to be explored in the ways in which pleasure is designated as ordinary and extraordinary (consider *plaisir* and *jouissance* in the French psychoanalytic context too).

124. See Donald Lopez Jr.'s comments in Chopel, *Madman's Middle Way*, 230–44.

125. See Wang Hui, *The End of the Revolution: China and the Limits of Modernity* (London: Verso, 2009).

126. Again, this remains a highly under-researched topic. See Ian Harris' *Buddhism in a Dark Age: Cambodian Monks Under Pol Pot* (Honolulu: University of Hawai'i Press, 2013).

127. Thomas Merton, "Marxism and Monastic Perspectives," in *The Asian Journal of Thomas Merton*, ed. Naomi Burton, Patrick Hart and James Laughlin (New York: New Directions, 1973), 326. All further page references are in parentheses.

128. Karatani Kōjin, *The Structure of World History: From Modes of Production to Modes of Exchange*, trans. Michael K. Bourdaghs (Durham, NC: Duke University Press, 2014).

129. Ibid., 312.

130. Wang Hui, *The Politics of Imagining Asia* (Cambridge, MA: Harvard University Press, 2011), 152. Hui quotes from Jean-François Revel, in *The Monk and the Philosopher: A Father and Son Discuss the Meaning of Life* (New York: Schocken, 1999), 21.

131. Harris, *Buddhism in a Dark Age*, chap. 6.

132. Shakya, *The Dragon in the Land of the Snows*, chap. 12.

133. Welch, *Buddhism under Mao*, 340–51; Vincent Goossaert and David Palmer, *The Religious Question in Modern China* (Chicago: University of Chicago Press, 2011), 164–65.

134. Mbembe, "Necropolitics," 39.

135. Ibid., 20.

136. Bernstein, *Religious Bodies Politic*, chap. 6.

137. Dan Smyer Yü, *The Spread of Tibetan Buddhism in China: Charisma, Money, Enlightenment* (London: Routledge, 2012).

138. See the special issue of *Positions* on Badiou and the Cultural Revolution: vol. 13, no. 3 (2005).

139. See Marcus Boon, "Buddhism after Badiou," lecture presented at Middlesex University, 2009.

140. Badiou's key works are: *Theory of the Subject*, trans. Bruno Bosteels (London: Continuum, 2009); *Being and Event*, trans. Oliver Feltham (London: Continuum, 2005); *Logics of Worlds: Being and Event, 2.* trans. Alberto Toscano (London: Continuum, 2009).

141. Bruno Bosteels, *Badiou and Politics* (Durham, NC: Duke University Press, 2011).

142. Alain Badiou, *Saint Paul: The Foundation of Universalism*, trans. Ray Brassier (Stanford, CA: Stanford University Press, 2003).

143. Glenn Wallis, Tom Pepper, and Matthias Steingass, *Cruel Theory/Sublime Practice: Toward a Revaluation of Buddhism* (Roskilde, Denmark: EyeCorner Press, 2013).

144. Glenn Wallis, "Mineful Response and the Rise of Corporatist Spirituality," http://speculativenonbuddhism.com/2014/02/17

/mineful-response-and-the-rise-of-corporatist-spirituality/, accessed 07/14/14.

145. A good introduction to Laruelle's thought is François Laruelle, "What Can Non-Philosophy Do?," trans. Ray Brassier, *Angelaki* 8, no. 2 (2003): 169–89.

146. Donald Lopez, interview in Schaedler, 239.

147. http://www.glennwallis.com/meditation-group/, accessed 07/14/14.

148. Arne de Boever and Warren Neidich, eds., *The Psychopathologies of Cognitive Capitalism* (Berlin: Archive Books, 2013); Michael Hardt and Antonio Negri, *Empire* (Cambridge, MA: Harvard University Press, 2000), 280–303; Hardt and Negri, *Multitude* (New York: Penguin, 2004), 108ff.

149. Thomas Metzinger, *The Ego Tunnel: The Science of the Mind and the Myth of the Self* (New York: Basic Books, 2009).

150. Esposito, *Communitas*; Judith Butler and Athena Athanasiou, *Dispossession: The Performative in the Political* (Cambridge: Polity, 2013).

151. Marcus Boon, *In Praise of Copying* (Cambridge, MA: Harvard University Press, 2010).

152. Charles Stein, personal communication, June 2014.

153. Sigmund Freud, *Civilization and Its Discontents* (New York: Norton, 1962).

154. Bernard Faure, *The Red Thread: Buddhist Approaches to Sexuality* (Princeton, NJ: Princeton University Press, 1998).

155. Eric Chelstrom, *Social Phenomenology: Husserl, Intersubjectivity, and Collective Intentionality* (Lanham, MD: Lexington, 2012).

ENLIGHTENMENT, REVOLUTION, CURE

THE PROBLEM OF PRAXIS AND THE
RADICAL NOTHINGNESS OF THE FUTURE

Eric Cazdyn

THE PROBLEM OF PRAXIS

Let's begin with the following claim: *enlightenment* in Buddhism is analogous to *revolution* in Marxism, which is analogous to *cure* in psychoanalysis. With this analogy established, we are tempted to move in one of two directions. The first is to criticize the oftentimes sloppy and reactionary mobilization of these three terms. Enlightenment, for example, is criticized as the original and mystical Buddha nature that enables all manner of poetic obfuscation, sappy metaphysics, and excuses for not critically engaging in the world. Revolution is criticized as the wishful thinking that blinds naive dreamers to the political realities of the here-and-now. And cure is criticized as the key ideological fantasy of which psychoanalytic patients must be disabused. The other direction stresses the more radical dimension of enlightenment, revolution, and cure. Without enlightenment charging Buddhism, it becomes gratuitous spiritual practice or limited liberal-humanist critique. Without revolution charging Marxism, it becomes idealist political philosophy or quick-fix social-democratic reform. Without cure charging psychoanalysis, it becomes toothless psychotherapy or orthodox psychoanalytic technique. In this more radical direction, enlightenment, revolution, and cure are not simply moments that can be reached or that always already exist, but are better understood as *symptoms of a particular mode of praxis.*

Praxis is today generally understood as putting theory into practice, or, even more reductively, as simply a code word for action, or for practice as such.[1] Even though praxis is often understood this way—consistently undertheorized and misidentified throughout the varied histories of Buddhism, Marxism, and psychoanalysis (sometimes by the masters themselves)—this is very different from how praxis actually functions in these three discourses. Our first task, therefore, is to retheorize praxis from the ground up, which will require disregarding complacent and confusing mobilizations of the term *praxis* in favor of understanding praxis as a problem, *as the problem of the relation between theory and practice.*

It should not be forgotten that there are different traditions of this term, and that Aristotle put praxis in relation to both *poesis* and *theoria.* But to argue that praxis names the problem of the relation between theory and practice is to argue that when theory hits its limit, only ground-changing practice can make it through the brick wall of history; likewise, when practice hits its limit, only theoretical rigor can open up the situation. Most importantly, we must accept that there is no actual answer to the theory-practice problem—not even the clever recognition that theory is a practice, just as practice is a theoretical event.[2] There are only more or less effective failures at resolving the problem. Praxis names the desire to unite theory and practice, however impossible such a project is fated to be. Praxis drives—and is driven by—this incommensurability. Praxis is the ceaseless movement among thinking, meditating, understanding, experimenting, acting, attaining, losing, and changing—none of which exist autonomously, but all of which are always supplemented by the others, and always inextricably tied to the logic of the historical moment during which they are at work. This tension—the irreducible gaps that structure these categories—is as inescapable in the temple for the Buddhist as it is on the street for the Marxist, as it is in the clinic for the psychoanalyst.

But to say that praxis is a central problem of Buddhism, Marxism, and psychoanalysis is to say that Buddhism, Marxism, and psychoanalysis themselves are problematics. This is a point that Fredric Jameson persuasively makes in response to those who criticize Marxism as old-fashioned, or as a failed nineteenth-century philosophy and social theory. Jameson writes that as a problematic, Marxism "can be identified not by specific positions (whether of a political, economic, or philosophical type), but rather by the allegiance to a specific complex of problems, whose formulations are always in movement and in historic rearrangement and restructuration, along with their object of study (capitalism itself)."[3] As Jameson goes on to argue, "what is productive in the Marxian problematic is its capacity to generate new problems."[4]

To take our contemporary moment, for example, the current system, dominated by finance capital and neoliberal strategies of dispossession, is constituted by ideologies that are no longer underwritten by the Cold War political justifications of freedom and democracy. The demand to either starve or work one's fingers to the bone so as to protect liberty against foreign enemies falls on deaf ears. Rather, today's post post–Cold War ideologies of sacrifice openly justify the economic logic of sustainability and growth. You die because the logic of capitalist profit and expansion requires a withholding of your lifesaving medications. The most vulnerable, in other words, are told the truth: that the global capitalist system cannot afford to save their lives . . . at least if it wants to manage its own contradictions. This ideological shift, from idealistic political reasoning to practical economic reasoning, is effected by—and effects—the relation between labor and capital, and thus the current possibilities and limitations of human freedom. It is revolution itself (both the condition of and the desire for it) that becomes the new problem generated by such a situation. Not that revolution hasn't always been at the bottom of a Marxist critique—it has, of course; but a retheorization of revolution in relation to the current dispensation of global capitalism is now required, and this process in itself generates new possibilities of thought and action.

As for what comes after revolution, if we knew in advance what that was then it would not be revolutionary. Which is another way of saying that revolution is not a destination to be reached—like the last pages of a developmental narrative—but rather the spark that keeps thought and action fresh, and which reminds us that a radically different way of thinking and acting is possible only within a radically different historical formation . . . and that a radically different historical formation is always possible!

Revolutionary desire has come to mean a certain kind of transcendent or wishful thinking about impossibilities. But to accept this meaning is to misunderstand the significance of the concept of revolution both for Marxism and for understanding praxis. If revolutionary desire engages the impossible, it does so with the ultimate aim of shifting the realm of possibility. Since what is historically possible is shaped by—and shapes—that which is historically impossible, and the engagement with the impossible becomes at once an engagement with the possible. By crashing into the impossible—not the liberal impossible of, say, trying to produce social equality within capitalism, but the radical impossible of imagining and struggling for a noncapitalist future within the limiting space of capitalism—Marxism mobilizes revolution as a sort of reality check, a reality check against so much cynical reason and gratuitous theory and politics.

In this same way we can view psychoanalysis less as an early twentieth-century theory of mind or psychology, and more as an allegiance to a reformulation of the problem of the unconscious in relation to the current logic of global capitalism. The unconscious flashes a radically different future (the unconscious actually comes from this future), and today points forward rather than backward. In this way, cure is not directed back at uncovering past traumas (however much this practice might be therapeutically effective); rather, it is reformulated so as to flash future traumas, most significantly the trauma of redefining the very category and possibilities of the future itself. This termination of the present-future in lieu of a radically different future (what might be called a future-future) necessarily includes a killing off of the subject, or at least a cure for the subject's desire to manage the present-future. What is most productive in the psychoanalytic problematic today is its capacity to generate this new problem of cure—cure after we have given up on cure . . . cure after we have given up on the liberal-humanist subject that desires this cure.

The reversal of fortunes over the past thirty years of psychoanalysis, from the preeminent "talking cure" (whether as a cure of psychological symptoms or a cure of the desire for cure itself) to the embarrassing uncle that the field of psychiatry would rather keep hidden, is related to the decentering of cure today, and to the tremendous growth of cognitive behavior therapy and psychotropic medications. Many are familiar with Freud's quip about cure in his 1895 *Studies in Hysteria* written with Joseph Breuer: "Transforming hysterical misery into common unhappiness."[5] But it is the next line that is often forgotten: "With a mental life that has been restored to health, you will be better armed against that unhappiness."[6] Indeed, common unhappiness is not the end, for this would be merely a *management* of symptoms, instead of a more radical transformation, leading toward the following play on the classic Marxist thesis: "The psychoanalysts have only interpreted the subject, the point is to change it." Common unhappiness, therefore, should not be considered the good-enough cure. Rather, common unhappiness is a means to an end, a means to a more productive struggle with unhappiness, and even, possibly and however momentarily, to happiness itself. For Lacan, the desire for a cure was limited but crucial nonetheless: "All the same, cure always seems to be a happy side-effect . . . but the aim of analysis is not cure."[7] What needs to be teased out here is a psychoanalytical theory of cure that exceeds the cure of neurotic or psychotic symptoms to reach the wider philosophical and political stakes of the underlying category. Without cure charging desire, charging the desire of the patient and of the analyst, charging the desire of psychoanalysis itself, we have left the realm of psychoanalysis. Perhaps this is another way to distinguish between psychoanalysis and psychotherapy: analysis is no longer possible without some mobilization of cure (even as a negative category that, although unachievable in any complete way, still functions to preserve the possibility of substantive change); therapy, in contrast, can manage quite successfully without it.

Likewise, we can view Buddhism less as an ancient Eastern religion or spiritual practice, and more as a commitment to the problem of enlightenment, and to the problem of how the very act of desiring enlightenment keeps us trapped in cultures built upon stoking and reproducing this very desire. The key question is how to retain the desirability of enlightenment without desiring it—this is a restructuring of the problem of enlightenment for the current moment. In this case, enlightenment represents an unthinkable, undreamable, unknowable state that can only be thought, dreamed, and known from a state of non-enlightenment, or delusion. Like revolution for Marxism and cure for psychoanalysis, this paradox of enlightenment has defined Buddhism since its beginning. Here we might want to recall the distinction between "craving" (*trsna*) (understood as harmful, insofar that it emerges from an attachment to permanence) and "motivation" (*bodhicitta*) (understood as nourishing, insofar that it emerges from compassion or a nonattachment-based desire for enlightenment).[8] Still, as a problem, enlightenment functions differently today within the current space of global capitalism and requires refocused attention—if only to counter the way that enlightenment is appropriated in a reactionary mode by the mainstream culture, so that, for example, it has been eviscerated of its radical charge, and has become just another commodity marketed and sold to shore up radical desire. Simultaneously, enlightenment has been ridiculed and criticized to such a degree so that all that remains is nothing but the desire to cling to the feeble mantras of living "one day at a time" or being "in the present," so as to protect against the radical threats of an unknown future.

Over the past twenty years, one of the most interesting and explosive debates within Buddhism, spearheaded by Hakamaya Noriaki and Matsumoto Shirō, two renegade Buddhist scholars from Japan, has concerned enlightenment. In the name of what they call "Critical Buddhism," Hakamaya and Matsumoto argue that almost all of Japanese Buddhism is effectively non-Buddhist. They claim that a certain type of *hongaku shisō*—an ethos that wrongly views the inherent enlightenment of all things, the identity of *saṃsāra* and *nirvāṇa*, the nativist mobilization of *wa* (or harmony), the transcendence of all dualities (including good and evil), and the nondifferentiation of native Japanese gods and the Buddhas—is pervasive throughout Japanese history and is responsible for all of its black marks, from Japanese fascism during WWII to gender inequality, environmental destruction, and the extensive antipathy toward critical thinking in today's Japan.[9] Nothing is safe from Critical Buddhism's critique, and it extends not only to those Western Buddhists who resort to Buddhism as a way of meditating away their class contradictions, but also to just about every Japanese Buddhist, from D. T. Suzuki to the Shinto-infused Buddhism of the Japanese emperors, to the great Japanese Buddhist Dōgen himself (who, nonetheless, remains the touchstone for the Critical Buddhist's radical revisions of contemporary thought and practice). This represents a quite breathtaking development, especially for those of us connected to Japanese studies, who have always respected the Kyoto School philosophers while finding it hard to take some of their work seriously, knowing all too well the coordination of their Buddhism with the brutal Japanese imperialist project. But when the Dōgen scholar Hee-Jin Kim criticizes Hakamaya and Matsumoto's relentless denunciation of enlightenment for "throwing out the baby with the bathwater," he is on to something, and we can follow our argument about revolution and cure to develop this charge.[10]

By stressing the causality of historical time and the material realities of the present, and by downplaying enlightenment, the Critical Buddhists wish to engage more directly with the current political situation of globalized capitalism. More power to them. They also wish to expose the history of discrimination within their own Buddhist tradition of the Sōtō school, from the unjust treatment of the *burakumin* (outcast community) to the defrocking of monks on bogus treason charges.[11] This overt politicization and relentless critical spirit, coming from inside one of the most conservative institutions, has been a relief and inspiration to many longtime activists (Buddhist and non-Buddhist) who have been struggling on the margins of Japanese society. Moreover, the critique cuts particularly deep into the orientalizing dimension of so much Western Buddhism—at least the variety that uses watered-down Buddhist principles to justify its depoliticization and its reproduction of unjust social systems (corporate executives in the morning and meditating monks at night). Slavoj Žižek's critique of this sad loop, namely that a Buddhist ethics often turns into late capitalist ideology par excellence, is dead-on.[12] But the Critical Buddhists have been suggesting this for decades.

In the process of generating this phenomenal intervention, with all of its philological rigor and trenchant political critique of Japanese culture, the Critical Buddhists overextend their critique of enlightenment from one that fetishizes a moment of enlightenment (at the beginning or at the end) to one that limits praxis to single issues in a liberal mode—in effect they end up advocating for piecemeal political reforms at the expense of any larger revolutionary project. In the Japanese situation, this practical reform of the actually existing social situation is admirable and required (especially since there is such little political resistance to the machinery of Japanese power). But it is precisely this everyday reformism that coordinates with neoliberal ideologies too smoothly, naturalizing capitalism and squeeze-drying the imagination required to propose, dream, and struggle for alternative systems. To retain the radical dimensions of revolution, cure, and enlightenment is at once to retain the revolutionary spirit of Marxism, psychoanalysis, and Buddhism.

This mention of revolution brings us to the question of why the relationship among Buddhism, Marxism, and psychoanalysis should be pursued in the first place. One answer: don't do it. You'll just end up playing the fool, reducing all three discourses, and decontextualizing so many concepts and principles. The other answer: why not, especially when we recognize that Buddhism, Marxism, and psychoanalysis, at least in terms of the contemporary moment, share the historical context of global capitalism and, therefore, are struggling with similar limits. This is also an attempt to open up the three fields to those who feel alienated or excluded from them—experiences that are often quite legitimate, and which require serious attention on the part of those who still invest in these fields. Often, these negative feelings are simply our fantasy projections of what we think the three discourses stand for (reductive critique, opportunistic violence, smug moralization, idealism masquerading as materialism, ineffectual and gratuitous practice, failure), rather than a response to the genuinely capacious and indispensable analyses and modes of being that they are capable of producing. This is especially true at our contemporary moment. Once again, this is also an effort to understand Buddhism, Marxism, and psychoanalysis as problematics—as modes of engagement that prioritize the inextricable relation between their distinct forms of thought and action (and non-thought and non-action) on the one hand and the historical situation in which they are situated and generate new problems on the other hand.

We can now add another key problem to our list connecting

Buddhism, Marxism, and psychoanalysis, namely that of desire itself, and by extension the question of how the desire for enlightenment, revolution, and cure must return and be enlivened while the subject of this spiritual, political, and psychological desire must die—a desire without desire. It is only when such a desire without desire is realized that the radical core of Buddhism, Marxism, and psychoanalysis can be mobilized. I will argue that this core opens to a non-moralizing critique and to a radical future, both for individual subjects and for social collectives.

If there is a fidelity that the more intent adherents of Buddhism, Marxism, and psychoanalysis share, it is to the problematics themselves—of which the problems of enlightenment, revolution, and cure have moved toward the center, a center that is, and has always been, occupied by the fundamental problem of praxis. This implacable, irresolvable problem of praxis not only pressurizes the very coming-into-being of these three discourses and not only grounds the contradictions that kick-start each discourse, but also returns throughout their respective histories to breathe new life into them.

In psychoanalysis, for example, the problem of praxis challenged Freud from the outset. How can he theorize psychoanalysis without being properly psychoanalyzed himself? How, in other words, can Freud be anything but a fraud, since he inevitably broke the first rule of psychoanalysis, that all analysts must undergo an analysis of their own? But how can Freud be psychoanalyzed when there are no psychoanalysts? It was not only through the *Interpretation of Dreams* and his friendship with Wilhelm Fleiss that he tried to self-analyze himself, but it was also in the way he conducted his analyses with patients. What Freud realized early on was that when an analyst engages a patient, he or she *is* theorizing—and the particular, long-term relationship between analyst and patient (in which their very relationship itself becomes the practical material to be analyzed, or in this case theorized) is an ideal place to engage this principle of praxis.

The clinic is the place to theorize, just as much as it is the place to practice. In the same way, the psychoanalytic essay, case study, or seminar is a site of practice, just as much as it is a site of theory. Melanie Klein had no formal philosophical training, yet theorized her field-shifting object relations paradigm solely based on her work with children. D. W. Winnicot's psychoanalytic essays are deceptively simple, using language and problems, such as holding, play, and the true and false selves, in a way that did not adapt the clinic to the leading philosophical concepts of the day, but they created concepts right out of the stuff of the clinic itself. Who better than Jacques Lacan, moreover, to reestablish this point by way of his style—the way, for example, that the very form of his spoken seminars would actually produce the concepts themselves (as opposed to the seminars simply delivering the concepts).[13] Lacan was not the theorist in the seminar room and the practitioner in the clinic, but both, in both places.

For Marx, too, the problem of praxis revealed itself from the beginning. How could his own class position as a bourgeois intellectual not compromise his thinking? Why would Marx's own blind spots not undermine his theories, just as they did for the philosophers of German Idealism? Marx was able to produce Marxism precisely by placing the blind spot itself in the center of his critique—in this case as the absent presence called capitalism. For example, Marx does not make too many advances past the classical political economists; his labor theory of value, along with so many other key concepts, is already established by the time he starts to write. It is the way he puts the concepts in relation to each other, and in relation to this new totality (or logic) he calls capitalism, that things come into being. Like the unconscious for Freud, capitalism is the absent presence, the blind spot that informs all of its component parts just as these parts compose it. In this sense, the opposition between interpretation and change in the "11th Thesis on Feuerbach" is not a simple attack on philosophy in favor of action, but rather an attack on any action (be it philosophical or otherwise) that reproduces the *status quo*, that reproduces the blind spot called capitalism.

As for Buddhism, the problem of praxis is also there from the beginning: we see it in how Siddhārtha Gautama's very act of seeking, if not desiring, enlightenment seems to betray Buddhism's first principle: that one's seekings and desirings limit one's access to the truth of nothingness. Indeed, this problem returns for Dōgen, who is famous for instructing his disciples to "just sit!," "just meditate!," "just do zazen!" (*shikan taza*), despite Dōgen himself being best known as one of the most prolific and conceptually refined Buddhist thinkers and writers. As for the present turn toward a more socially conscious and politicized Buddhism, there is still the problem of violence and the spilling of blood that necessarily accompanies substantial social change. It is precisely this dirty reality of violence that seems to call into question the Dalai Lama's famous statement that he is half-Buddhist and half-Marxist, let alone many of the more liberal and even social-democratic solutions that are sustained by the inescapable contradiction of capitalist logic, such as the already-mentioned Critical Buddhist movement in Japan.[14] In fact, it is the Dalai Lama himself who proposes this very problem: knowing full well that the capitalist system is a system structured in inequality and violence, he is unable to countenance the full implications of revolution that might bring about the kind of Marxist-inspired world so desired. The Dalai Lama, it should go without saying, understands that today's market socialism in China is not a model for the type of Marxism he has in mind.

The Dalai Lama's impossibility of being half-Buddhist and half-Marxist within today's global capitalist system marks the return of the problem of praxis for the current moment.[15] If we accept this new working definition of praxis—that which registers the problem of the relation between theory and action— then we are compelled to ask how the problem itself might change from one historical moment to the next. And to complicate matters even further, we must remember that the problem of praxis might change that which constitutes the very category of change itself so radically that it, the change, might look like no change at all, from the place of the new historical moment.

My first claim, therefore, is that the origins of Buddhism, Marxism, and psychoanalysis are located where the problems of praxis are first produced and theorized as the crucible of each discourse. My second claim is that the recentering of the problem of praxis throughout the histories of Buddhism, Marxism, and psychoanalysis is always accompanied by a return (sometimes reactionary, sometimes radical) to the original production of praxis in each discourse, and always driven by the dominant contradiction shaping the historical moment during which the return is conducted. By tracking these shifts, we will arrive at my third claim, namely that at our contemporary moment, some of the most radical interventions into Buddhism, Marxism, and psychoanalysis are staged as reengagements with the problem of praxis, and that these are occurring off the cushion, off the factory floor, and off the couch . . . while remaining ineluctably based on the fundamental logics of the three practices in question, and inextricably tied to the categories of enlightenment, revolution, and cure.

To support these three claims and the legitimacy of the departing analogy, let's proceed by interweaving three narratives of praxis within the histories of Buddhism, Marxism, and psychoanalysis. I will begin with the Zen Buddhism of Dōgen in the early to mid-thirteenth century, and his monumental text on practice, *Shōbōgenzō*, before moving to Marx and a formal analysis of *The Communist Manifesto* and *Capital*, and finally to Freud and the writing of his tour de force, *The Interpretation of Dreams*. Braided into these three inquiries will be the various returns to the "origin moment" throughout the subsequent histories of each problematic.

This will set the stage for a shift in direction, toward the praxis of the great Japanese architect Isozaki Arata, who has incorporated into his diverse work over the past fifty years the concept of *ma* (a kind of negative time-space), which flashes a new way into the problems of enlightenment, revolution, and cure. Isozaki's *ma* will also serve as a way to mobilize the category of *nothing* that links our three problematics, as well as the three inquiries that organize this book, for *ma* turns out to be a materialist nothing (or the nothing of materiality), spectacularly activated by Isozaki in one of his more recent projects ("Ark Nova") in response to the 2011 Japanese disasters (earthquake, tsunami, nuclear meltdown). "Ark Nova" is a portable art-community space that can hold up to five hundred people before being deflated and transported to a future disaster, a disaster that has yet to occur but that is built right inside of our present. "Ark Nova" is an architecture of the future. Not a model for a future architecture, but an architectural figure for a radically different future, one that is at once different from our present, different from our wildest speculations on the future, and different from our very concept of the future itself.

Isozaki's work and its instantiation of *ma* will also provide us with the opportunity to invoke the category of "critical theory," which, however capaciously defined, and however tenuously connected to work ranging from the Frankfurt School to post-structuralism and beyond, will allow us to tease out a non-moralizing dimension of Buddhism, Marxism, and psychoanalysis, in order, ultimately, to return to my central claim that we can locate some of the more impressive interventions into Buddhism, Marxism, and psychoanalysis outside of their privileged spaces of practice (temple, street, clinic) and theory (publication, university, seminar). Even though Isozaki does not sustain a direct inquiry into our three problematics, his work surely constitutes one of the more impressive interventions into them.

This argument about Isozaki contains a final claim that will ground my thoughts here: that an engagement with a problem of a specific field can occur from any place and with any material, not only from within the disciplinary trajectory of the specific problem itself. Just as philosophizing oftentimes exceeds the domain perceived as philosophy proper, so might a radical political, psychological, or spiritual act look nothing like politics, psychology, or spirituality as we know it. This is another way of defining critical theory: for what distinguishes it from, say, Marxist philosophy, or Lacanian psychoanalysis, or Zen Buddhism is the recognition that one can—and often does—engage these disciplines from outside their generally understood theories and practices.

Critical theory, perhaps uniquely, opens up to, pursues, and even creates these unlikely connections and material mismatches. In the end, the rigorous engagement with a problem remains, while the disciplinary containment is overcome. Previously, I have named this role of critical theory a non-disciplined rigor, a fresh way of attending to the specificity of a problem and carefully mobilizing canonical scholarship, while effectively challenging the institutionalization of the field itself.[16] Critical theory is not just philosophy light, or cheap interdisciplinarity, but an alternative to the professionalization of knowledge, especially as it is congealed in the contemporary university.

Perhaps it is for this reason that Buddhism, Marxism, and psychoanalysis have never occupied a comfortable position in academia—for to radically pursue them challenges the university's rock-bottom assumption that the truth will set you free. No, the truth will not set you free. We can go as far as arguing that this is the ultimate lesson of Buddhism, psychoanalysis, and Marxism (and that this is another reason why they can be productively thought together)—in all three discourses, only praxis will set you free. Or, at least, the engagement with the problem of praxis can provide the room to recognize the contradictions and paradoxes, not to mention the magnificent and productive inescapability, of the desire to be free in the first place. But, and again, this is a specific form of praxis . . . one that puts the very implacable problem of the relation between theory and practice (thought and action) and its connection to radical change at the center of its project—and that thereby risks destroying its own foundation at every turn.

DŌGEN, ENLIGHTENMENT, AND BUDDHIST PRAXIS

Legend has it that it was Dōgen's profound doubt regarding enlightenment and practice that generated the Sōtō school of Zen Buddhism in the thirteenth century, which has become a hallmark for the subsequent history of Zen up until the present. Dōgen famously asked why anyone should submit to the rigors of daily meditation practice if they already possessed Buddha nature? In other words, if one is already endowed with original enlightenment (*hongaku*, the key principle representing the core of Buddhist teachings, and central to the Tendai school of Zen under which Dōgen was trained as a young monk), then why act with the intent of acquiring this very endowment?[17] It is often argued that it was this paradox that inspired Dōgen to travel to Sung China in search of an answer, and that generated an entire tradition of Japanese Buddhist thought and practice upon his return.[18] Dōgen resolved this contradiction by breaking open a whole new form of teaching, and by expressing the very problem itself, stressing what he called the "oneness of practice and enlightenment" (*shushō-ittō*) that calls the dualism itself into question. But to call the dualism into question, for Dōgen, does not lead necessarily to a monism or to an absolute critique of dualism as such. Rather, it is the negotiation of the dualism that marks Dōgen's genius—he simultaneously held and disintegrated it, and shifted his position on the limits and possibilities of particular dualisms in coordination with the shifting power relations of medieval Japan. It is this negotiation of the problem of dualisms (which, for Dōgen, is ultimately the negotiation of the Buddhist way) that marks the key moments of revisionism throughout the history of Zen Buddhism in Japan.

Charting the beginnings of Zen Buddhism in Japan is fraught with controversy, anachronism, and ideological interests.[19] With this in mind, let's begin with the following narrative. After Eisai (1131–1215), who brought the Rinzai Zen teachings to Japan following his first trip to China, Dōgen, along, with Shinran and Nichiren, was instrumental in establishing what is known as Kamakura New Buddhism during the Kamakura period (1185–1333).[20] As a young monk under the direction of Eisai, Dōgen cultivated his doubt about reigning Buddhist ideologies of enlightenment and practice. It is at this point that Dōgen is believed to have traveled to central China, where he studied with Ju-ching at the temple of Mount T'ien'-t'ung. Sitting meditation dominated Dōgen's practice, and he immediately took to the strict discipline of monastic life. Ju-ching would practice *zazen* (sitting meditation) for up to twenty hours a day, and represented a model that inspired Dōgen. One night after sitting for hours, Dōgen heard Ju-ching castigating fellow monks for falling asleep. Ju-ching is reported to have said, "In Zen, body and mind drop off" [this has also been famously translated as "the casting off of body and mind"]. Ju-ching followed this up with the question, "Why do you sleep?"[21] It is at this moment that Dōgen reportedly experienced enlightenment, and he would go on to stress the significance of casting off body and mind (*shinjin datsuraku*) throughout his subsequent writings and teachings. Before returning to Japan in 1227, Ju-ching presented Dōgen with a document verifying his enlightenment, and with the title of succession that subsequently represented the starting point of the Sōtō school of Zen in Japan.

When Dōgen returned to Kennin-ji temple in Kyoto, destruction, corruption, and violence was pervasive throughout Japan. This historical moment of medieval Japan is punctuated by a transfer of power from the powerful aristocratic families (*kuge*) of the imperial court to the samurai class (*bushi*), now in control of judicial and civil matters, and ruled by military families (*daimyō*) and warlords (*shōgun*). The dominant schools of Buddhism were necessarily implicated and complicit with the power dynamics of the day, but the young Dōgen, thanks to his time spent away in China, was able to keep his relative independence. After his return, it did not take long for him to gain a reputation as an important monk, and he gathered followers as well as critics. He soon moved to the town of Fukakusa outside of Kyoto, where he took up his work at the relatively small temple of Kōshō-ji. Dōgen's followers at the time, called the Daruma-shu, could be considered the first "zen" group in Japan, but were seen as heretics, banned by the Tendai order.[22] For the next decade, Dōgen practiced *zazen* at Kōshō-ji, taught his disciples, and began composing his masterpiece, the *Shōbōgenzō*.[23]

The *Shōbōgenzō* (its title can be translated as *The Treasury of the True Dharma Eye* or, more literally, *True Dharma Eye Treasury*) is a profoundly important text, and the foundation for all Buddhist practices and studies inspired by Dōgen. The problem is that the *Shōbōgenzō* is not one text, there is no agreement on what version of the *Shōbōgenzō* is most authentic, and there are as many different readings of the *Shōbōgenzō* as there are differences among Dōgen's various Buddhist followers. It is precisely this discursive struggle over the text itself, a struggle that returns from one historical period to the next, that shapes the various critical appropriations of Dōgen and his work, as well as the significance of these returns.

We will see the same kinds of struggle over the work of Freud and Marx, although they are perhaps less focused on single texts, and more on the stereotypes of the early Marx (philosophy) and late Marx (economy), or the early Freud (the topographical model) and the late Freud (the structural model). It should come as no surprise that an interested appropriation of origins would legitimate subsequent thinkers and movements. My own strategy here is to read each return as symptomatic of the historical moment during which it emerges, and to argue that the various perspectives on the original texts hold within it the theory of praxis espoused by subsequent thinkers and movements. With this in mind, let's look more closely at the *Shōbōgenzō*, and focus on how the production of the text itself is Dōgen's resolution to the problem of theory and practice.

The *Shōbōgenzō* is organized around sections called fascicles, each one foregrounding a central doctrinal issue, such as Buddha nature, Transmission, and Being-Time.[24] Dōgen composed the fascicles as commentaries, as lessons for his disciples, and as an opportunity to engage the most pressing debates of the day. Written between 1231 and 1253 (the year of Dōgen's death), there are ninety-five fascicles collected in the original Japanese collective works (*Dōgen Zenji Zenshū*). The dominant version of the *Shōbōgenzō* consists of seventy-five fascicles, which represent what sometimes is referred to as the old *Shōbōgenzō*, composed mostly in the middle part of Dōgen's life. There is also a newer version, discovered in the early twentieth century, made up of twelve fascicles and composed by Dōgen at the end of his life. The older version is understood to be more abstract and philosophical in nature, while the newer version is oriented toward practice, and commonly understood as simpler, with the purpose of teaching lay monks how to properly meditate. It is also notable that the *Shōbōgenzō* is written in Japanese, embedding passages in Chinese within the Japanese syllabary (*kana*), rather than being composed in classical Chinese, which, up until Dōgen's writing, had been the language of choice for most Japanese Buddhist texts.[25]

Dōgen's attention to language, and his decision to write in Japanese is significant for a number of reasons. Most importantly, he was one of the few monks to have traveled outside of Japan, for training with a teacher (Ju-ching) who was not particularly renowned, which gave him the confidence to write in a different language upon his return to Japan. Additionally, Dōgen's fluency in Chinese has been called into question. A poor command of the language could have accounted for his decision to write in Japanese, not to mention for some of his more radical appropriations of terms and concepts. Language itself, moreover, necessarily invokes the problems of mediation, signification, and representation—three problems, at once political and aesthetic, to which Dōgen, despite being wrongly understood as a quietist, shut-up-and-meditate taskmaster, was fully committed. It is precisely Dōgen's formal strategies as employed in his writing that flash the impossible unity of enlightenment and practice. His writings were always geared toward teaching his students, with many of them being direct transcriptions of dharma talks. For instance, let's look at how Dōgen articulates the relation between enlightenment and practice in the fascicle called the *Bendōwa* ("Discourse on the Practice of the Way"). This was one of the first fascicles he wrote, in 1231, but it was lost until the late seventeenth century, when it was adopted as the first fascicle in the ninety-five volume edition of the *Shōbōgenzō*.

Here, Dōgen writes,

> The view that practice and enlightenment are not one is a non-Buddhist view. In the Buddha-dharma they are one. Inasmuch as practice is based on enlightenment, the practice of a beginner is entirely that of original enlightenment. Therefore, in giving the instruction for practice, a Zen teacher should advise his or her disciples not to seek enlightenment apart from practice, for practice itself is original enlightenment. Because it is already enlightenment of practice, there is no end to enlightenment; because it is already practice of enlightenment, there is no beginning to practice.[26]

This passage suggests a radical critique of the dualism of practice and enlightenment, and an elevation of *hongaku* thought. This is precisely how the Dōgen scholar Abe Masao reads it. Abe writes, "[As] Dōgen realized through his experience of the casting off of body-mind, practice and attainment are not two but one and constitute a dynamic whole."[27] Abe goes on to argue that Dōgen's realization of the oneness of practice and attainment "includes a dynamism mediated by negation—it is a dynamic, nondualistic identity between practice and attainment that is mediated by the realization of impermanence-Buddha-nature."[28] Hakamaya has a similar reading of this section, but, unlike Abe, downplays the importance of the *Bendōwa* and other early fascicles as confusing, and as Dōgen's misguided elevation of enlightenment thought.[29] This is why Hakamaya and others who identify with the Critical Buddhist movement look to the later version of the *Shōbōgenzō*, which features only twelve fascicles and which is less abstract and less open to misinterpretation, while being much more critical of the opportunistic appropriations of Buddhism occurring at the time both by political and by spiritual leaders.

But Dōgen's passage also suggests a radical critique of the nondualism of practice and enlightenment. This is how Hee-Jin Kim chooses to read it. As Kim writes,

> Practice and enlightenment are neither the two complementary (and opposite) sides of the same reality, nor in a relationship of the periphery and the center. Neither are they related in terms of the surface and the core. To put it another way, the unity is not the nullification of differences between the two, nor is it a transformation of one into the other, or a fusion of one with the other. Practice and enlightenment are different, yet not two. Dialectical nonduality does not deny the *differences* between the two.[30]

Kim argues that Dōgen recognized there could be no outside to dualistic thought. This is because nonduality itself can only exist in relation to what it is not, namely duality, producing the fundamental dualism of nondualism and dualism. What is at stake here is the role of intellectual rigor in Dōgen's Buddhism, and whether the category of enlightenment makes room for philosophical speculation and historically situated criticism.

The emphasis on dualism or nondualism can only be evaluated in relation to what is occurring at the historical moment during which the argument is being made. For Dōgen, his work is necessarily implicated within the large-scale historical transformation from imperial to military rule. But with any historical transformation, there is never a radical break after which the past is absolutely past. At the same time, there is never a radical continuity through which the past is absolutely present. Rather, the historiographical problem of change, and of what constitutes this change (both for individuals and for the larger social structure), is specific to each moment. How to negotiate this historiographical paradox is always the fundamental aesthetic, psychological, and political question, and it is for this reason that I wish to read Dōgen's negotiation of the dualism of practice and enlightenment as a coded way of negotiating this dualism of historical continuity and discontinuity. Medieval Buddhist scholars, for instance, pay great attention to how Dōgen's trip to Kamakura, invited by the powerful military leader Hōjō Tokiyori in 1247, reflects his changed views on karma and the cause and effect of human behavior. Upon his return to his disciples, Dōgen made clear that he merely explained to Hōjō that "those who do good rise while those who do evil fall."[31]

What we see in the later work of Dōgen (as represented in the twelve-fascicle text of the Shōbōgenzō) is a more straightforward critique of a nondualistic view of original enlightenment, and of his more focused attention to causality and karmic retribution as it applies not only to his students, but also to the political leaders and Buddhist teachers of the day. Causality and karmic retribution include an ethics and an attention to worldly matters, whereas the principle of original enlightenment refers to a fundamental enlightenment that transcends the world and is a denial of cause and effect. For Hakamaya, this stress on enlightenment is a delusion. He writes, "This simplistic and one-dimensional notion of original enlightenment asserts that truth lies in a monistic, underlying enlightenment, which turns out to be the dominant force behind the perpetuation of social discrimination."[32] Hakamaya continues, "Without the slightest hint of discomfort one sits there and simply announces that the true is the provisional and the provisional is the true, that discrimination is none other than equality and equality none other than discrimination."[33]

Whether the principle of original enlightenment persists

through all of Dōgen's thought and writing, or whether an emphasis on karmic retribution can be located from the beginning, is beyond the scope of my argument.[34] For our purposes we can summarize the issue as follows: the karmic principle is prioritized for those scholars more concerned with the political and moral implications of Buddhism, while original enlightenment is prioritized for those who de-emphasize political and particular historical matters in favor of spiritual implications.[35] Significantly, it is precisely this reductive, and ultimately false, division between enlightenment and practice that is insinuated into the various returns to Dōgen's work.

By holding the tension of the duality of enlightenment and practice, and thus of duality and nonduality itself, Dōgen, however indirectly and unconsciously, produced a philosophy of history—one that proposed a double critique of the Heian past with its elitist social structure and of the medieval present with its militarist ethos. Quite remarkably, Dōgen holds this double critique in such a way that it does not cancel itself out into an ahistorical retreat, but, rather, creates a form of engagement that refuses to submit to the more tempting ideological conceits of his day. It is precisely this philosophy of history that gets reworked for different political reasons when we move to the first modern return to Dōgen at the beginning of the Meiji period.

Leading up to the Meiji Restoration in 1868, there was a growing anti-Buddhist resentment. Driven by the emergence of a national learning movement (*kokugaku*) that fed on a growing Confucianism and on native Shinto rituals and beliefs, and under so much pressure from corruption practiced by the various Buddhist sects (especially connected to those temples located in the rural areas associated with long-standing nepotism), Buddhism would have to be made over or be relegated to the dustbin of history. One way that the Sōtō School was able to perform this makeover was by returning to the work of Dōgen, specifically by translating his main teachings in the *Shōbōgenzō* into an easily accessible publication called the *Shushōgi*. The *Shushōgi* extracted sections of the *Shōbōgenzō* into five chapters, and was geared to a lay readership that perfectly coordinated with the Meiji ideology of nation building, and of civic responsibility in the name of a newly empowered emperor, who for centuries previously was relegated to an effete figurehead.

At first glance, the *Shushōgi* looks to focus on the political implications of karma, as the questions of birth and death, retribution, repentance, and moral behavior are what organize the text. In this way, the text could be read as a critique of the nondualistic principle of original enlightenment. But as Hakamaya argues in his essay "Thoughts on the Ideological Background of Social Discrimination," there is a crucial difference between the ways in which the significance of karma is presented first in Dōgen's *Shōbōgenzō,* and then in the subsequently published *Shushōgi.*[36] For Hakamaya, the Meiji return to Dōgen functioned to naturalize the socially constructed differences among people as well as specific forms of discrimination by interpreting karma as that principle which advocates for the *acceptance* of disparities based on past actions. What was once the royal road to equality and to acting on behalf of others had now been put in service of justifying pernicious differences, if not enacting policies to exacerbate them. Despite the focus on karmic retribution gestured to in the text's content, the *Shushōgi,* for Hakamaya, effectively performed the same ideological work as did earlier calls for the absolute nature of original enlightenment. In the context of the late nineteenth century, this ideology stoked the fetishization of the Japanese historical tradition at precisely the moment when a full-scale project of Westernization was taking place.

Watsuji Tetsurō is instrumental in facilitating this return to Japanese tradition, and to Dōgen in particular, during the interwar years. Before he had reached the age of twenty-five, Watsuji had already studied and written sustained works on Nietzsche, Kierkegaard, and Schopenhauer, and had taken a serious interest in Byron and other Romantic poets. But it was his early relationship with the great prose writer Natsume Sōseki, his reading of Nitobe Inazō's famous book on samurai ethics, *Bushidō: The Soul of Japan* (1900), and attendance of Okakura Kakuzo's lectures on Asian art that inspired Watsuji to dedicate most of his later work to the problems of modernity, and to the question of how a return to premodern Japanese thought could contribute to a universal ethics.

After studying with Heidegger for just over a year in the late 1920s, Watsuji returned to Japan and immediately began translating Dōgen's *Shōbōgenzō* while, at the same time, attempting to resituate his Western philosophical training into the Japanese context. For example, Watsuji wrote his masterwork *Fūdo* (*Climate and Culture*) as an attempt to supplement Heidegger's radical historicity in *Being and Time* with an emphasis on the specific details of Japanese climate and geography, thus producing his own radical spaciality, a sort of "Being and Space." Heidegger stressed that the subject is totally fashioned by the temporal logic of a given moment, and that the a priori conditions of this historical structure are flashed by dwelling in the singularity of these ordinary experiences and in the "equipment" of everyday life. Watsuji held on to these beliefs, but added a focus on geographical particularity. In the Japanese context, this meant combining unpredictable weather systems, which generate great vulnerability, with the clockwork-like regularity of the Japanese seasons and the confidence that such predictability instills. It is through these dualities between natural predictability and unpredictability as well as Japanese particularity and global universality that we can question the significance of Watsuji's engagement with Dōgen and the problem of praxis.

Dōgen's work existed in relative obscurity until Watsuji turned to him immediately before his studies abroad, and again immediately following his return from Berlin. By drawing a premodern Japanese thinker like Dōgen into the larger history of philosophy, Watsuji achieved two goals: first, to critique the orthodox and opportunistic dimension of so much Japanese Buddhism that had relied on vulgar interpretations of classic texts and the underappreciation of Dōgen's subtlety; and second, to critique the defilement of so much modern Japanese culture that Watsuji understood to be less tied to the logic of capitalist modernity, and more to certain unscrupulous attitudes that could be avoided by fetishizing the unique persistence of the aristocratic Japanese past, with, once again, special attention granted to Dōgen's thought.[37]

Watsuji began his early work on Dōgen with two questions directed toward himself. First, how could someone who is not professionally tied to Buddhist practice and thought, and who has not yet achieved enlightenment, say anything of substance about Dōgen?; and, second, "what would be the point of trying to make this great religious master's personality and his manifestation of the truth serve [Japan's] cultural and historical understanding?"[38] It is precisely because Watsuji was a layman, and not implicated within the corrupt Buddhist sects of his day, that he believed he was able to produce critical insights regarding Dōgen's thought. This resonates with the way Watsuji is usually understood as a key spokesperson for the insidious project of *nihonjinron*, or the discourse of Japanese uniqueness: that it is precisely a thinker like Watsuji (and by extension a nation like Japan)—being uniquely outside of Western intellectual, religious, and political trends while being uniquely inside of them insofar that he rigorously studied and was inescapable affected by them—who opens up the possibility to think and act *more* radically than those very thinkers and nations central to, but enclosed by, the most pressing debates occupying the modern world.[39]

Watsuji held out for a critical engagement with the world by holding on to the dialectic of absolute enlightenment and particularized practice, which led him back to Dōgen and to the persisting traditions of premodern Japan. But Watsuji overemphasizes the particularity of the present without accounting for the very structure, the very historicity, of the particularity itself—not the deep structure of Japanese culture and identity that Watsuji viewed as the persistence of aristocratic values as rendered in Dōgen's elegant solution to the oneness of enlightenment and practice, but the inescapably socializing logic of the particular historical formation of Japanese modernity, namely capitalism itself.

Watsuji was arguing for this idea of history at a geopolitical moment of colonialism that was itself driven by the global crisis of industrial capitalism. Japan's economy had been overstimulated during the war years (1914–18), as its heavy industries provided manufactured goods to its neighbors in lieu of the Western colonial countries' temporary departure from these Asian markets because of more immediate military concerns. After the war, however, the Western powers returned to their Asian markets, and Japan's boom in export surpluses plummeted, leading to severe recession. This reversal, exacerbated by the Great Kantō Earthquake of 1923 and acute depression in the agricultural industry, was responsible for over ten years of recession in the Japanese economy. By this point, the geopolitical logic was clear: either Japan would be colonized by a handful of Western powers (like the rest of Asia), or it would have to consolidate its own colonial project under the emperor and the desire of an East Asian co-Prosperity Sphere. It seemed almost impossible to imagine how to exceed this dualism of colonizer-colonized without submitting to one or the other. Only those Japanese thinkers who were able to hold a critique of the structuring logic of capitalism together with an unwavering critique of Japanese nationalism and nation building (such as Tosaka Jun and Miki Kiyoshi), or writers and filmmakers (such as Nakano Shigeharu and Kamei Fumio) held open the space of this difficult dualism, usually at great sacrifice.[40] Watsuji called his own attempt to resolve this colonize-colonized dualism a "double life," and fantasized an old Japan in the name of Dōgen, Buddhist thought, and the persisting aristocratic ways, in which the old would persist and serve as a bastion from the dominant logic of contemporary society. Watsuji, therefore, effectively promoted capitalism and its colonial logic, as he believed that their destructive effects could be avoided by the exceptionality of Japan. Harry Harootunian brilliantly sees through this precarious logic and argues that for Watsuji, "capitalism inevitably led to imperialist domination, driven by interest, yet Japan, already committed to a capitalist mode of production, had escaped the temptation of interest because its transformation had been driven by the necessity to survive and the desire to maintain the integrity of the national community."[41]

Along similar lines, Naoki Sakai smartly criticizes Watsuji's ethics, which, for Sakai, effectively ends up trusting the corporation and the state more than other people.[42] Rather than opening up to the contingency of strangers, Watsuji's humanism returns to the "authenticity" of individuals who are understood to always occupy stable subject positions. This authenticity is not original enlightenment, but an ethnocentric self that could easily lead to the most "violent jingoistic sentiment."[43] Without celebrating the mysticism of original enlightenment, Watsuji stressed the persisting dualistic nature of enlightenment and practice, with enlightenment signifying Japanese nativism and practice signifying the entangled, defiled, but indispensible work of criticism and historical awareness. Ultimately, this led to a politically suspect elevation of Japan and Japanese culture, a project that D. T. Suzuki, the single most important spokesperson of Zen throughout the Western world, shared, but which he achieved from the other direction, namely an overemphasis of Zen Buddhism as direct, ahistorical "pure experience" as well as of the nondualistic irrationality of Zen that coordinated perfectly with orientalist desires the world over (including the self-orientalism peculiar to Japan itself).[44]

Suzuki is not usually associated with Dōgen, as he was trained in the Rinzai tradition and rarely writes about Dōgen, let alone the *Shōbōgenzō*. But in his numerous books on Zen Buddhism, Suzuki invariably returns to the same argument about nondualism that functions as a concentrated and transparent attack on

Dōgen. In some of his earliest essays, Suzuki writes: "If you have been in the habit of thinking logically according to the rules of dualism, rid yourself of it and you may come around somewhat to the viewpoint of Zen."[45] And: "Hush the dualism of subject and object, forget both, transcend the intellect, sever yourself from the understanding, and directly penetrate deep into the identity of the Buddha-mind; outside of this there are no realities."[46]

Like Watsuji, Suzuki was born during the Meiji period, and was university-educated. And like Watsuji, Suzuki connected the radicalness of Buddhism with the rich specificity of Japanese culture, such as *ikebana* and poetry. But it was to the samurai ethic to which Suzuki most readily turned in order to argue for Japan's uniqueness. Suzuki writes, "Zen discipline is simple, direct, self-reliant, self-denying, and this ascetic tendency goes well with the fighting spirit."[47] What we see here is a return to the problem of praxis in which the dualism of enlightenment and practice is totally evacuated, with sudden enlightenment (*kenshō*) now celebrated as a destination that can only be achieved by an absolute authenticity undefiled by history or any worldly mediation—the historical context of the problem of praxis no longer matters.[48]

Simple, direct, self-reliant, unmediated, and ahistorical are code words for the category of "pure experience" that Suzuki appropriates from his close friend Nishida Kitarō, who developed the idea in his first book, *An Inquiry into the Good*, published in 1911. Nishida, the first and most influential philosopher of modern Japan, and the father of what later became known as Kyoto School thought, integrated the work of German idealism (Hegel, Husserl, and Heidegger, in particular) with Buddhist philosophy, Japanese aesthetics, and Zen practice. The absolute limit of Western philosophical thinking could only be overcome by a lifestyle of spiritual practice enacted by the philosopher himself, which led Nishida to Buddhist practice and to flirting with the inescapable horizon of nondiscursivity. Nishida's *An Inquiry into the Good* develops the idea of "pure experience" as "the state

of experience just as it is without the least addition of deliber-
ate discrimination."[49] Nishida begins his first book by writing,
"When one directly experiences one's own state of consciousness, there is not yet a subject or an object, and knowing and its
object are completely unified."[50] Here, Nishida is working with
the psychological research of Wilhelm Wundt and, in particular, with William James's "A World of Pure Experience" ("the
relations that connect experiences must themselves be experienced relations, and any kind of relation experienced must be
accounted as 'real' as anything else in the system.")[51]

Whereas Suzuki became more committed to an anti-
philosophical and ahistorical Buddhism, Nishida moved away
from Buddhist practice and toward a more historicized understanding of experience, exploring through his later work more
what William Haver has recently called an "ontology of production."[52] The role that Nishida has played in Japanese thought and
its political effects, and the way that subsequent scholars and
critics (both inside and outside of Japan) have mapped Nishida's
work, function as a lightening rod in any appraisal of the Kyoto
School thinkers, if not Japanese modernity itself. In general,
those committed to a project of comparative philosophy, or to
a more Japan-centric form of Japanese studies, tend to be more
sympathetic and celebratory of Nishida. In contrast, those who
identify with a project of critical Japanese studies, and who are
committed to a global analysis of Japan's modernity (such as
the powerful work of the aforementioned Harootunian, as well
as the sharp critique of Japanese studies in the brilliant cross-
cultural analyses of Masao Miyoshi), tend to be more dismis-
sive.[53] There is also the critique of Nishida and the Kyoto School
by Hakamaya and other Critical Buddhists, who see the work
as nothing more than "a mishmash of 'original enlightenment'
and German Idealism," as well as a reprehensible precursor to
and influence on so much "postmodern" Japanese thought that
they charge with caring little for rational criticism. But then
there is a scholar like Karatani Kōjin (a philosopher of Marx and
Kant and speculative thought in general), who criticizes Nishida

for the way he mobilized his leading ideas of "contradictory self-identity" and the "place of nothingness," themselves reworkings of Kant's "transcendental apperception" and Heidegger's "ontological difference," to signify the emperor system and rationalize the argument that Japan had to unify the various Asian countries that make up the Greater East Asia co-Prosperity Sphere.[54]

We will return to the differences of Hakamaya and Karatani in the context of the present situation and the function of enlightenment today; for now, however, it must be stated that it is impossible to ignore the role Nishida played in support of the emperor and the Japanese colonial project. Still, the more important point is to what effect the work can be mobilized today. With this in mind, Haver has recently effected a shift in this debate of Nishida's work, not by taking sides or trying to defend Nishida's fascist apologetics, but by focusing on Nishida's later essays, and making some unlikely connections between Nishida and Marx—opening up a new way of thinking about Nishida's view of praxis for our contemporary moment.

Whereas Watsuji's Buddhism pointed back to the classical past, and Suzuki's pointed out of history to a mystical authenticity, Nishida's Buddhism pointed to the future, a radically different future in which the presently configured subject becomes something totally other. Nishida writes, "The past is the past because it utterly negates the future; the future is the future because it utterly negates the past."[55] This radical future, for Nishida, is based on a reworking of the Aristotelian delineation of *praxis*, *poiesis*, and *theoria*. For Aristotle, *theoria* is the contemplation of that which is eternal and transhistorical, *praxis* refers to human activity that is contingent on historical circumstances, and *poiesis* refers specifically to production, to the purposeful making of something distinct from its human producer.[56] Nishida, rather, collapses these three terms and comes closer to an understanding of praxis as a conjuncture of contemplation, agency, and production, in which all three are active, mutually constitutive, and historically contingent.

Nishida writes, "The world of historical actuality is the world of the movement from the made to the making, the world of form-making activity."[57] To think and to see, for Nishida, is to act. But he does not argue that this leads to a nondualism in the way that Watsuji and Suzuki understand Dōgen's oneness of enlightenment and practice. Instead, Nishida writes, "to say that dialectically to see is to act is neither to say that acting and seeing become one nor that acting disappears. To speak of the form-making activity of the movement from the made to the making is to say that the thing, as the self-identity of what is absolutely opposed, is made and that, being self-contradictory, what is made is continually being destroyed, and that what is being destroyed itself becomes a condition, which is to say that a new thing comes into being."[58] For Haver, this new thing, which includes a radically new subject, is not based on any teleological destination determined in advance, which is to argue that Nishida's renegotiation of the *praxis-poiesis-theoria* conjuncture becomes "not a means to an end but an end in itself," and is therefore oriented "not toward what should be (the Good) but toward what we want, a more profoundly disturbing question than that of the Good."[59]

This is disturbing precisely because we can no longer deduce a praxis from the concept of the Good (a morality), but we must seriously consider what we want, how, in Haver's words, "to constitute the 'we' that is said to want," and how to orient ourselves within this desire.[60] This renegotiation of praxis and the questions of morality and desire will take us directly to Marx's and Freud's problem of praxis, and to the question of how a radical Marxist and psychoanalytic ethics is categorically different from the kind of moral and ethical projects to which so much political and psychological work submits.

But before making this move, we must first return to the Critical Buddhists in Japan, to see with what kind of understanding of praxis they affiliate, and what kind of ethics this implies. The whole project of Critical Buddhism turns on an argument about "criticism" that Hakamaya and Matsumoto offer in opposition to topicalism and topical Buddhism, which they disdain as "uncritical pseudo-Buddhism." When Hakamaya emphatically states that "only that which is critical is Buddhism," he is directly referring to the polarity of "critical philosophy" and "topical philosophy," as first framed by Giambattista Vico in the early eighteenth century. Vico writes, "For just as the invention of arguments is by nature prior to the judgment of their validity, so topical philosophy (Lat. *Doctrina*) should be given precedence over critical."[61] Hakamaya takes this to mean that Vico stressed the importance of rhetoric, invention, oratory, and imagination over rational scientific process, logical disinterest, and the deductive criticism of Descartes. Hakamaya then argues that it is precisely in Japan that Vico's "anti-philosophy" has been farcically taken up ("a tedious parroting of the latest Western fashions by Japanese intellectuals who are anxious to fuse our ancient, indigenous 'topical' worldview with this latest foreign import"[62]), and that it has poisoned so much intellectual work (from the Kyoto School to contemporary Japanese theorists of structuralism and post-structuralism), political policy (fascism, social discrimination, irresponsible environmental practices), and, of course, Buddhism (anything that is touched by *hongaku shisō*, such as *tathata* [suchness], *samatha* [tranquility], and other mystical ahistorical half-principles).

Hakamaya is emphatic about not essentializing the difference between Eastern and Western thought, but wants instead to view difference in terms of whether one commits to *topica* or *critica*. There is no doubt that topical criticism has been mobilized by the Japanese state for the purpose of committing atrocious violence, and that it is not difficult to associate thinkers like Watsuji, Suzuki, and Nishida with such a dispensation. But Hakamaya simply trades one essentialism in for another: in this case, he clings to the essentialism of topicalism itself. Topicalism cannot simply be thrown at the doorstep of Vico or Lao-tzu, or any number of other figures that Hakamaya accuses; likewise, criticalism is more subtle than a simple nod to Descartes or the work of the Critical Buddhists themselves. Topicalism and criticalism, rather, must be affirmed or denied based on the specific historical function they are performing, and must be rehistoricized within the contexts of every transformed situation. Criticism itself is conditioned by the topos, just as topos is shaped by the state of criticism.

Like the terms of any dualism, most notably the one between practice and enlightenment that Dōgen so subtly negotiated, critical philosophy and topical philosophy are always at risk of freezing up and losing any claim on the world. Karatani is most sharp about this when engaging the Cartesian ego, which for him looks nothing like Hakamaya's Descartes, who stands in for rational criticism and in whose name Hakamaya rails against all abstraction. But Karatani also criticizes the likes of Nakamura Yūjirō (post-structuralist critic of Descartes and Hakamaya's main target) and other Nishida apologists who essentialize topicalism and end up de-historicizing the dualism from the other direction—and Karatani, as we will see in the next section, does this without giving up on the radical dimension of enlightenment in the name of a more parallaxical engagement with dualisms of all sorts, which now starts to look more and more like the Marxist category of revolution.[63]

This mention of revolution, and the political more generally, should remind us that Hakamaya and Matsumoto are right about so much, but that the basis of their critique is naive and moralizing. Their critique of enlightenment is dead-on, and yet it starts to weaken the moment we extend the category of enlightenment not to its political effects (which has indeed been fascist), but to the effects of its analogous political category, that of revolution. Only by placing these two categories in relation to each other, each one affirming the other, we can see what is indispensable to each and why to give up on Buddhist enlightenment is tantamount to giving up on revolutionary politics. And these two categories will also require their triplet, cure, which at one and the same time invokes the psychoanalytic dimension of subjectivity, producing even more creative tensions among the three problematics. In this case, praxis is once again at the center of things, and it is time to see how a Marxist negotiation of praxis can open up the problematic of Buddhism even further.

MARX, REVOLUTION, AND PRAXIS

Marx and Engels's *The Communist Manifesto* (1848) is generally considered to be the exemplary text of praxis. It contains an overt desire to unite theory and practice and has, matched by only a few other select works, inspired immense transformations over the course of modern human history. In his *Poetry of the Revolution*, a remarkable book on the manifesto form, Martin Puchner reminds us that *The Communist Manifesto* shared a generic history with earlier manifestos, in particular the act of bringing something into the open and making it known.[64] But Marx and Engels also performed a crucial break with the genre, as their manifesto was the first that did not declare the will of the sovereign, but rather attempted to usurp "the authority it does not yet possess."[65] It was, as Puchner argues, a poetry of a future revolution, since as a literary form it cannot be more than a "call, a cry or a demand, an impatience with the fact that no matter how impassioned and effective, the manifesto will always remain a split second removed from the actual revolution itself."[66]

There is a certain impatience to *The Communist Manifesto*: "But let us have done with the bourgeoisie's objection to communism."[67] There is also intolerance: "In a word, you charge us with intending to put an end to your property. Precisely so; that is just what we intend."[68] And anger: "The bourgeoisie has stripped of its halo every occupation hitherto honored and looked up to with reverent awe. It has converted the physician, the lawyer, the priest, the poet, the researcher, into its paid wage-labourers."[69]

Then there is *Capital* (1868), the more patient, methodical, and rigorous text, the one that does not cry about anything, but lays out the more objective logic of how capitalism reproduces itself. Beginning from the beginning (vol. 1, chap. 1, on the "simple commodity") and ending at the end (with the system as a whole, in vol. 3, or the more refined theories on surplus value in what would have been vol. 4). But what if we turned this around, and read the *Manifesto* as a critique and *Capital* as a manifesto? What if *Capital* was the great praxis text of the Marxist canon? Or what if, in a grand dialectical reversal, like the one that generated the text, in the first place, out of Hegel's own system, *Capital* today has turned into the great praxis text of our generation—so that what functioned as a sober and scientific critique in the nineteenth century has now become the revolutionary call par excellence? What if, at our moment of a saturated media sphere in which polemics of all kinds are neutralized by commercialized news organizations and corporatized universities, the slow and thoughtful critique of *Capital*, which seemed to err on the side of "being too theoretical" and "too methodical," has become the text of radical action, all the while still holding to its theoretical rigor? What if, finally, it is the *Manifesto* that has turned into a piece of intellectual history, which has become a footnote in political theory, or simply a text that today hits the wrong affective note, while *Capital* now squares the circle and has become the great non-moralizing manifesto of change?

As a manifesto, *Capital* is a call to action—a call to read the text. One cannot just know what *Capital* is about; if one were to simply focus on all of the concepts, all of the equations, all of the different renditions of the base-superstructure schema, then one would be no closer to the Marxist project than so many anti-Marxist critics. Likewise, if we were to simply know how capitalism works, in all of its political-economic and ideological detail, we would be no closer to changing the system itself. One must actually read *Capital*, the same way that one must read a novel, rather than just know its plot development.

The text produces a skill set, one that is expressly directed toward teaching its readers how not to moralize—that is, how not to account for injustice based on the good or evil intentions of the individual actors involved. The whole project of *Capital* is formalized so as to teach us how the production of surplus value is what generates wealth, crisis, and the unequal division of social relations necessary to the reproduction of the capitalist system. And to teach us that this surplus value is produced when the system functions according to a set of fundamental principles, that it works most effectively when the contract is obeyed, the factories are clean and safe, and the workers are treated fairly. It is more often the case that it is the various acts of corrupt transgression by the national business leaders and overt physical violence by the state police that threaten capitalism.

Capital painstakingly reveals, therefore, how the economic system itself operates not through corruption or a relentless regime of repressive acts, but by the rational logic of commodity production and consumption. *Capital* also highlights how capitalism produces a key ideology, which is not a false consciousness hiding the various machinations of the system and controlling the masses by cultivating and maintaining their stupidity, but by producing a rather clever working class that can criticize and even understand the complexities of capitalism. The crucial ideology of capitalism is not one that keeps the truth from the masses, but one that produces a situation in which the masses produce their own truth that functions to shape their desire in such a way that, although critical and angry, it contains little revolutionary expectation.

This ideological effect turns on a dominant understanding and experience of time (built right into the laboring process itself) that prevents productive speculation on a future alternative to the capitalist mode of production. Like it was for Dōgen, for Marx, too, the problem of praxis is inextricably tied to the problem of history, of how to negotiate the continuities and discontinuities of historical transformation. And like the way I read Dōgen's negotiation of the dualism of practice and enlightenment as a coded way of negotiating the dualism of the Heian past and medieval present, I will read Marx suggesting that his production of the problem of praxis is inextricably tied to his engagement with the problems of time, history, and revolutionary change.

In the first volume of *Capital*, there are two key points at which Marx refers to the relation between praxis and time. The first has to do with Marx's invocation of Aristotle, in the section on the value form halfway through chapter 1; the other has to do with Marx's critique of mainstream arguments regarding the length of the working day, and regarding how surplus value is produced in relation to this duration. Let's first turn to Aristotle, who Marx respected as the first thinker to analyze the value form of goods.

In chapter 1, volume 1, of *Capital*, Marx has just finished making the crucial point that goods come into the world in the form of use values or material objects, but that they are only commodities "because they are at the same time objects of utility and bearers of value."[70] It is this primary dualism, built into the commodity itself, that structures Marx's other dualisms, from that of the two great classes of the proletariat and the bourgeoisie, to that of theory and practice, to that of how a nondualistic singularity is itself related to what it is not—namely, a stalled, historically specific dualistic logic. But just as with Dōgen, Marx's handling of the various dualisms in his work must itself be handled with care, for at the heart of Marx's work is a trenchant critique of the positing of any kind of ahistoricized dualism. The category of revolution would have no purchase if the various dualisms themselves were not contingent on the given historical logic.

At any rate, Marx here distinguishes what is peculiar about the equivalent form of value in the commodity, namely that its value arises not in relation to other goods, but by being an object that is recognized as value, as a congealed amount of labor. And then, this concrete labor takes the form of its opposite, abstract human labor.[71] This is followed by what Marx calls the commodity's third peculiar form, when abstract labor takes the form of its opposite, social labor—in capitalism, as opposed to earlier historical formations, the three peculiarities of the commodity are working as one; they, at once, exist in the commodity as the concrete, abstract, and social form of labor. It is here that Aristotle enters the text.

In the *Nicomachean Ethics*, Aristotle notes the first two peculiarities of the value form of the commodity, concrete and abstract labor. Aristotle gives an example in which five beds equal one house in value, and states that this is indistinguishable from how five beds equal a certain amount of money. Aristotle writes, "There can be no exchange without equality and no equality without commensurability."[72] But this is where Aristotle's analysis ends. In the *Ethics*, Aristotle stresses, "It is, however, in reality impossible that such unlike things can be commensurable."[73] The reason why Aristotle cannot go further is because he cannot think what is equal in both the bed and the house. He cannot think the category of equal human labor itself.

Marx writes, "Aristotle himself was unable to extract this fact, that, in the form of commodity-values, all labor is expressed as equal human labour and therefore as labour of equal quality, by inspection from the form of value, because Greek society was founded on the labor of slaves, hence had as it natural basis the inequality of men and of their labour-power."[74] The value form of the commodity could not be deciphered until the concept of human equality had "already acquired the permanence of a fixed popular opinion."[75] And Marx finishes with this: "Aristotle's genius is displayed precisely by this discovery of a relation of equality in the value-expression of commodities. Only the historical limitation inherent in the society in which he lived prevented him from finding out what 'in reality' this relation of equality consisted of."[76]

It is impossible to think outside of one's historical moment. One can only think and act inside it so as to change it, and thus change what counts as the impossible. The young Hegelians, and Feuerbach in particular, did not go far enough with their materialism (and from here we get the famous Eleventh Thesis). But as noted earlier, Marx was not criticizing all thought and interpretation, only thought and interpretation that did not progressively change the world. For Marx, therefore, no matter how radical thinking is, if it effectively reproduces the status quo, it is ultimately reactionary. The proof of thought is in change. But, and this is where the historical component becomes crucial, thought and interpretation are limited (indeed, structured) by the socio-historical moment. As evidenced by the conclusions Aristotle drew in his thinking about labor and value, we only set tasks that we can solve.[77] To think differently, we must first change the world. And to change the world, we must first think differently. This is the ground zero of the problem of praxis—a zero that always takes a different historical form. And different moments require different attempts to square this zero; as for *Capital's* attempt, it is intended to teach a form of critique that can flash the logic of the whole system rather than the good or bad acts of individual capitalists and workers.

When one does not recognize the historical limits of one's own thought, a moralizing tendency invariably creeps in. This takes us to the second great moment of praxis and time in *Capital*, volume 1, when Marx takes to task the renowned Oxford professor of economics, Nassau W. Senior, regarding the length of the working day. Senior argued that to shorten the working day as proposed in the Factory Act of 1833, by even one hour, would destroy any net profit and thus compromise the whole capitalist system. This is because, for Senior, the entire net profit is derived from the last hour, which specifically meant that children must continue to work an eleven-and-a-half-hour, if not a fourteen- or sixteen-hour, working day.[78] Marx shows that the last hour is not special at all, but that surplus value is extracted during every hour and that it is not the extra time that is the key, but time as such, as it functions abstractly within the laboring process.

Many commentators focus on Marx's sarcastic and ad hominem response to Senior, including his criticism of Senior's style (comparing him, at once, to both a sentimental novelist and a nasty prizefighter). It might seem like this is Marx the moralizer—histrionic, bitter, acerbic—but Marx in fact recognizes that Senior *does* understand the fundamental principle of capitalism, namely that the capitalist must control the workers' time if he wants to make a profit. The problem for Marx is that Senior does not go far enough. Marx understood that even if the workday is reduced to ten hours, surplus value could still be extracted. The whole point of *Capital* is to argue against the temptation to critique Senior in terms of what he gets wrong, let alone to vulgarly paint him as a corrupt and immoral apologist for the capitalists. Rather, the critique is to be directed at how Senior is not stupid, mistaken, or immoral, but rather quite rational, correct, and even moral in terms of how consistent he is and how he serves the genuine interests of the capitalist class. Capitalism works according to plan, and Senior understood this plan, and he thought and acted in coordination with its logic. The fact that this plan necessarily produces radical inequality, irreparable ecological damage, and severe psychological pain, does not mean that the system as such is failed. It is also not to suggest that other systems have not, or would not, produce similar, if not more miserable, human and natural conditions, but only that there are other systems that can produce less misery and, therefore, would serve different interests, and would not necessarily produce such a metabolistic rift with the natural environment.

Marx recognized that the capitalist maintains his rights as a purchaser of labor when he tries to make the working day as long as possible, and that the worker maintains his right as a seller when he wishes to reduce the working day. This is the great antinomy of capitalism, not wrong against right, but "right against right, both equally bearing the seal of the law of exchange."[79] And Marx goes on to argue that between equal rights it is not the morally right side that decides, but those who wield more power: "force decides."[80] To focus one's attack on Senior, therefore, as being wrong instead of right, and to focus one's struggle on the political level for a shorter workday, is to misrecognize that it is the system itself that requires radical transformation. Which is not to argue that political struggles, concerning, for example, the length of the working day, are not necessary or do not appreciate the necessity of systemic change, but that they often lead to the sacrifice of revolutionary critique and action in the name of practical reform. And this leads us back to the problem of praxis.

If we view *Capital* as Marx's most significant work of praxis, insofar as it forces the problem of revolution to the center of theory and practice, then we need to see how subsequent returns to the text have necessarily staked claims on the problem of praxis itself. Our first point will be that the most important moments of return to the problem of praxis emerge at moments when capitalism and its dominant ideologies undergo structural metamorphoses, beginning with the gradualisms of the British Fabian Society and the influence of Eduard Bernstein on the social democracies of the late nineteenth century, to the Althusserian moment before and after 1968, to the various post-Marxisms of the 1980s, and all the way to the contemporary moment, in which the whole Marxist problematic is up for grabs in the thick of global capitalism's most recent transformations. The question always reduces to two points: whether radical sociopolitical change can emerge from state-managed tactical reforms, and whether the desire for more wholesale economic transformation is itself a debilitating fantasy that effectively reproduces the very systemic logic itself.

It is hard not to recognize in these two reductions the old saw of the reform-versus-revolution debate. When Bernstein argued against the Hegelian influences of the early Marx in order to stress the more scientific economic analysis of the later Marx (of *Capital*, in particular), he opened up two paths: one toward what we can call a vulgar social democracy (Bernstein's own position), in which structural inequalities can be ameliorated by economic revisions within the parliamentary system itself, and another toward a vulgar Marxism, an economism in which all social and political facts are reduced to their economic conditions and any deviation from these conditions effectively supports a nonclass approach (this, in fact, was Karl Kautsky's attack of Bernstein). At stake here is the relation between the economic and the political, which, as we will see, invokes our central problem of the relation between theory and practice. In order to get at the key shifts in the critical investment in one term over the other (either the political or the economic), let us consider the following thumbnail history.

During the nineteenth century, the economic logic of industrial capitalism was transparent, as it relied on the temporal fix of squeezing more surplus value out of its workers by either making them work longer (in a nod to Senior), or by making them work faster (by way of more repression), or by making them work more efficiently (by way of technological advances). From the end of the nineteenth century to World War I, the spatial fix of appropriating cheap labor and resources throughout the global periphery became the dominant form of crisis management and capitalist accumulation. And with this came colonial ideologies of civilizing the natives in the name of capitalist political and cultural ideals. The global economic crash marking the end of the 1920s exposed, once again, the economic realities of the capitalist system. It was at this time, however, that political narratives (from the socialist desires of the Soviet revolution to the capitalist ones of American democracy, from the fascist desires of the National Socialists to the ethnic ones of the Japanese empire) began to overcode the recently exposed economic principles of capitalism. It is precisely these political justifications that persisted following WWII, obscuring the economic logic of capitalism and taking the most powerful form (this time quite progressive) of a liberation politics in the name of decolonization throughout Asia, Africa, and South America. With the trauma of 1968 and the questioned role of the communist party and the betrayal many leftists felt (especially the students involved in the various movements around the world), the relation between the political and the economic returned to the center of debate. Now, the economic stood in for either Stalin or the hypocritical repression and bureaucratization of any number of progressive institutions (from unions to the universities). This backlash against the economic was then abated by the oil crises of the 1970s, and the spotlight directed on the new flexible processes of global production. The hair-trigger geopolitics of the Cold War, however, once again overwrote the cold realities of an emerging transnational capitalism based on post-Fordism.

Louis Althusser attempted to walk the tightrope between these critical investments in either the economic or the political. In his now infamous 1973 work *Reply to John Lewis*, Althusser scrutinized the dominant ideology of the times, driven by both a technocratic economic ideology and a moral-humanist one. For Althusser, this applied to both social democracies and orthodox Marxisms, both of which failed to read *Capital* symptomatically—a way of reading that flashed the structuring absence of Marx's text, which, for Althusser, was precisely that unthinkable and unrepresentable alternative to vulgar economism and moralizing humanism. The famous claim of the "economic in the last instance" (developed over a decade previously in Althusser's essay "Contradiction and Overdetermination," and then again in his and Étienne Balibar's 1968 *Reading Capital*) enabled Althusser to hold the logic of capitalism without submitting philosophy to epiphenomenal status—that is, without submitting philosophy to just another superstructural effect. One problem, as Jacques Rancière pointed out a year later in his *Althusser's Lesson* (1974), is that Althusser's rigorous critique of capitalism as a "structure without a subject," and his absolute rigor around separating theory from politics, blinded Althusser to the question of how power is "localized" in the everyday life of the worker. Rancière writes, "The ideological power of the bourgeoisie is not the power of economism and humanism. It is the power to dispossess workers of their intelligence, to mutilate their capacities, to confront them with a science that has been moved entirely to the side of 'powers of production.'"[81]

Ten tears later, and following the political-economic shifts to a more flexible and global form of capitalist accumulation, Ernesto Laclau and Chantal Mouffe criticized Althusser from the other direction, for clinging to the concept of totality at the expense of the more "multifarious character of contemporary social struggles."[82] For Laclau and Mouffe, Althusser's "last instance" betrayed his stress on the overdetermination of the social formation, and effectively rendered pointless the moment of politics in the name of a homogeneous revolutionary subject. At the beginning of their hugely popular *Hegemony and Socialist Strategy*, Laclau and Mouffe wrote, "What is now in crisis is a whole conception of socialism which rests upon the ontological centrality of the working class, upon the role of Revolution, with a capital 'r', as the founding moment in the transition from one type of society to another."[83]

The moment of neoliberalism's emergence, led by Reagan and Thatcher and their ideological partners in the IMF and World Bank, was perfectly coordinated with Laclau and Mouffe's post-Marxist response, that of a post-structuralist politics of multiplicity in which antagonisms erupt and articulate themselves in ways no longer coordinated with the logic of capitalist crisis. With the concept of totality now wholly discredited, a politics of difference and the championing of the various social movements proliferated—without Althusser's category of the semiautonomous holding things together. This moment of a radical democratic politics, however, lost its momentum after 9/11, and with the antiglobalization movements' recognition that a critique of capitalism cannot be content to only locate and highlight so many human rights transgressions, but must also include a rigorous return to the process of commodification itself and to the logic of the mode of production, perhaps even to the retheorized concepts of totality and structure. It was one thing to criticize sweatshop labor practices throughout the global south, but it was another to provide a more systemic critique of how exploitation occurred even after the corrupt factories were shut down or cleaned up.

What we see in this abstracted narrative is that the most important moments of a return to the problem of praxis stake a claim on the relation between economics and politics. This leads us to the question of the individual subject today, a subject that is necessarily submitted to the economic logic of capitalism (reinforcing the system's reproduction), but also a subject that contains the real political possibility of intervening with this logic on a revolutionary scale. And, again, this takes us to the problem of revolution, to the question of how we might be able to recuperate this term for the present moment. In his *Transcritique*, Karatani Kōjin puts the question like this: "How is a revolution possible in the world where there seems to be no moment for subjective intervention to appear?"[84]

Karatani's response to this contradiction is to read Marx through Kant, and Kant through Marx, in order to hold the realms of economic production and circulation as equally important to the reproduction of capitalism and the exploitation of surplus value. The worker is in the position of both producer and consumer, two positions that are irreducible to each other, and which must not be synthesized. What is important for me is precisely the way this dualism is held, namely through the form of what Karatani calls the parallax.

For Karatani the parallax is like the Kantian antinomy in which "one should renounce all attempts to reduce one aspect to another. . . . One should, on the contrary, assert the antinomy as irreducible."[85] Karatani uses this to read Marx's relation to Ricardo and Bailey, emphasizing how Marx, instead of synthesizing their differences, oscillates between the two, and ultimately brackets one to think about the other, and vice versa—a parallax view that for Karatani accounts for the brilliance of *Capital*.[86] Karatani then uses this parallax view in order to understand the tension between the realms of production and circulation: "Value both is and is not created in the production process."[87]

This rethinking of production and consumption is further developed in Karatani's monumental work *Sekai-shi no kōzō* (*The Structure of World History*), in which he produces an alternative Marxist history based not on modes of production, but on modes of exchange, returning all the way to the gift-counter-gift reciprocal systems of various archaic societies.[88] This move opens up inventive ways of imagining and working toward new forms of associations and exchange in the present and, for Karatani, a more effective way of challenging the trinity of nation-state-capital. Karatani's stress on modes of exchange is cause for small wars within the realm of Marxist political theory; but, unlike other such moves that question the priority given to modes of production, Karatani intervenes without de-emphasizing the economic as such. In this way, Karatani does not collapse the economic into the political, nor does he view them as separate but equal. He is able to hold the parallax between the economic and the political, which leads to both a non-moralizing critique of capitalism and a non-moralizing speculation on revolutionary change. Sometimes his speculations appear absurd (like his call at the end of *The Structure of World History* to transform the United Nations into a new global system that can trigger simultaneous world revolution and realize a world republic), but Karatani's speculations function less as naive fantasies and more as effective exercise regimes for the political imagination.[89] In other words, by speculating on radical alternatives to capitalism (however impossible they may in fact be at any given moment) in such a direct, straight-faced, and methodical way (without the usual rhetorical flourish, opportunistic posturing, or apocalyptic desire), Karatani is modeling for us revolution as form—revolution less as a specific content and more as a theoretically driven practice of engagement . . . more as praxis.

For example, Karatani began his *Transcritique* with a reading of *Capital* that does not accuse capitalism of immorality, because capitalists and workers are only agents of capital's movements (not its subjects). Following the great Japanese political economist Uno Kōzō, Karatani also reminds us that there is no theory of ethical action or revolution in Marx's *Capital*, only a theory of necessary crisis. This leads Karatani away from any kind of ideology critique or liberal consumer movements, and toward the production of new subjects and a new society by way of economico-ethical associations—associations that enable workers to exploit their positions as both workers and consumers, and which allow them to mobilize an ethics based not on good and bad, or happiness and interest, but on freedom. For Karatani, this freedom is based on the Kantian imperative to "be free!"—an imperative that treats others both as an end and as a means. Marx wrote, sarcastically, that the worker is free to either produce surplus value for the capitalist or starve to death. Karatani, in contrast, writes quite earnestly that the worker is free in a third sense: when he or she closes the capitalist circle by buying back commodities as an agent and, therefore, able to break open new exchange communities based on new forms of trade that themselves can potentially revolutionize the whole capitalist system itself.

Karatani criticizes those Marxists who are intent on "teaching" the workers how their dispossession is structurally determined, and who view the overcoming of false consciousness as the royal road to revolution. Karatani even criticizes Jameson's argument regarding the cultural turn (in which a certain materiality of the superstructure—of language, textuality, ideology, subjectivity—not only complicates what was hitherto privileged as the material infrastructure, but also presents genuine territories of revolutionary struggle) as "a form of despair" based on "production-process centrism."[90] In other words, Karatani suggests that it is precisely the project of exposing the workings of ideology and the political-economic system that invariably leads us back to the beginning . . . hoping helplessly for the revolution to come by way of the "natural" developments of the mode of production. And this, for Karatani, overlooks the possibilities for innovative forms of exchange relations that can radically challenge capitalist relations. However, this perspective also misses the point of Jameson's intervention in terms of what we might call an economico-cultural ethics.

Like Karatani, Jameson integrates the same question concerning revolutionary agency into his reading of *Capital*, and asks how to emphasize the inescapable structural logic of the economic without returning to the various vulgar Marxisms, without abandoning any possibility of radical intervention by the subjects of capitalism. Like Karatani, Jameson responds by bracketing the political and focusing on the economic logic of capitalism; but unlike Karatani, Jameson finds an ethics (a kind of anti-anti-ethics) not in Kant, but in the aesthetic act—in the acts of both making and interpreting culture—and in supporting all types of social democratic reform while holding on vigorously to a Marxist critique and its underlying concept of revolution.

In two of his later works, *Valences of the Dialectic* and his short book on the first volume of *Capital*, titled *Representing Capital*, Jameson asks us to consider a thought experiment about exploitation and domination: what if we identified all the dispossession and misery of marginalized populations (of those forced into the no-man's-land of the global system) as a result of exploitation, rather than as a result of domination?[91] For Jameson, this emphasis on exploitation takes us to the central logic of capitalism, and opens up thoughts about an altogether different system, rather than merely reforms of the current one. Ultimately, Jameson argues that when you prioritize the political category of domination, you invariably end up attempting to eliminate or reform the current problems—leading to an emphasis on democracy that almost always functions to reproduce the current system itself, in a social-democratic or even an anarchist mode. Prioritizing the economic category of exploitation, in contrast, leads to a much greater appreciation of the systemic logic itself (that "full employment" is impossible within capitalism).

This is not a vulgar economics (or even an economics familiar to those teaching in North American economics departments), for although priority is given to the economic (to the analysis of structural exploitation rather than sadistic domination), individual and social resistance must still be practiced in the political-ideological realm. One holds on to a more revolutionary economic analysis, while engaging in the more banal political practices, supporting all kinds of single-issue reforms. It is also for this reason that Jameson makes the blasphemous argument that *Capital* is not about politics or labor, but about unemployment, and goes onto argue that unemployment is today the key category for understanding what the particularities of globalization are, and what might lead to the most effective theoretical and practical interventions. This ties in with what we have been calling a non-moralizing critique of capitalism—in which we refuse to personalize the corruption and refuse to feel righteousness when yelling "shame, shame, shame" at the greedy, and in which, instead, we recognize that crisis and dispossession are what happens when the system goes right, not when it goes exceptionally wrong.

Along with crisis and dispossession, revolution, too, is built right into the structure of capitalism. This is Jameson's most enduring theoretical intervention (most explicitly argued in his *The Political Unconscious*, published in 1982): reversing Walter Benjamin's 7th thesis on the philosophy of history ("There is no document of civilization which is not at the same time a document of barbarism"), so that now *all articles of barbarism (from fascist political groups to the most insidious cultural expressions) are simultaneously, and in deep contrast to their intentions, also documents of utopia*. At least, they hold within them a genuine, radical dimension gesturing toward their own destruction and a revolutionary future.

But let's push this idea of the political unconscious even further. A subject, a cultural text, or a collective does not just indicate a repressed ideological or utopian desire, but also future iterations of such desire. In this sense, the unconscious is not just liberated from the subject (so that it does not "exist" in the subject, below consciousness and ready to be uncovered, exposed or brought into consciousness), but it is also liberated from the past and present. Now, the unconscious comes from the future. Jameson's economico-cultural ethics attend to the fundamental logic of commodity capitalism, in which there can be no resolution of capitalism's grounding antinomy (of collectives of workers organized around individual profit) without revolution of the whole system itself, while—and at the same time—cultivating a revolutionary consciousness by way of an incessant attention to utopian possibility. The act of liberating the unconscious from the subject and from chronological time resonates with a Buddhist critique of the subject and positivist history. It also resonates with how we have reclaimed the category of enlightenment, not as a final destination of the subject or of history, but as a killing off of the subject and of history while we (and it) are still alive. We can call this a negative materialism, or the radical nothingness of the future.

FREUD, CURE, AND PRAXIS

This invocation of the political unconscious takes us to our third territory: to psychoanalytic praxis and the category of cure, as well as the question of how this category can be reclaimed today alongside Buddhist enlightenment and Marxist revolution. Every key development within the history of psychoanalysis turns on a similar critique of praxis, in which Freud's clinical practice is either criticized or defended in a way that then shapes how subsequent analysts think about and theorize psychoanalysis. It is argued, for example, that Freud did not listen carefully enough to his patients, and that his clinical skills were dulled by his commitment to theory. Also, that Freud's theoretical speculation was compromised by his capricious experiences with a narrow demographic of patients in the clinic. And from the other direction it is argued that it was Freud himself who was the exemplary practitioner and theorist, and that those who pretend to overcome his ingenious negotiation of the problem of praxis are careerists driven by reactionary ideologies, or a simple desire to kill the father. These critiques are repeated throughout the history of psychoanalysis; younger psychoanalysts accuse the older ones of being too professionally attached to their theories and, therefore, not listening carefully and creatively enough to their patients. Jung, Klein, Winnicot, Lacan, Bion, Fromm, Kohut, Mitchell—each, in turn, not only breaks open a different way of listening in the clinic, but also produces new theoretical terms, and even styles of psychoanalytic writing, that enact this practice itself.

This struggle over the problem of praxis begins with Sándor Ferensci, one of Freud's first intimate colleagues and disciples. Ferensci developed a critique of Freud's lack of "mildness and indulgence," both toward Ferensci himself (who was analyzed by Freud) and toward Freud's other patients.[92] Ferensci's idea of a mutual analysis, in which the analyst freely expresses his or her own emotions to the patient (not only countertransferential material generated by the patient, but all types of personal disclosures of the analyst) so that both the analyst and patient can feel more secure in relation to each other, and focus on the relational dimension of the patient's symptoms, is often recognized as a direct attack on Freud's style, and as the ground zero of Kleinian object relations and all relational and interpersonal schools to follow. What we see with Ferensci, therefore, is the beginning of a pattern in which each plot point within the history of psychoanalysis stakes a claim on the relation between theory and practice.

But we should go back even further, to Freud himself, and to his own critique of psychiatry and that discipline's engagement with the problem of praxis in nineteenth-century Europe. In other words, the coming-into-being of psychoanalysis was generated by Freud's critique of psychiatry, in which the patient was viewed as a passive receptacle of illness that the doctor treated by imposing techniques and procedures irrespective of the patient's specific life history. A hysterical symptom of aphasia, for example, might be treated by speech therapy, or even brain surgery. What Freud realized early on, first with experiments in hypnosis, and then with the more sustained experiments of the "talking cure," is that the patient knows more about his or her symptoms than the doctor, and that it is the doctor's job to figure out how to listen in a way that will open up to the most effective treatment. Of course, to listen to the patient also requires the analyst to listen to him or herself, to call his or her own authority and confidence into question. If the unconscious was the most profound discovery of psychoanalysis, this was because it forced a path right to the center of the new discipline and the analyst's own unconscious . . . necessarily exposing (and then trying to effectively mobilize) the expert practitioner's blind spots and hypocritical motivations.

But the recognition that there is a double unconscious at work in the clinic can be pushed even further: the analyst's and the analysand's unconscious are not altogether separate, but mutually constituting. This not only de-spatializes the unconscious from existing within the subject or underneath an individual's consciousness, but it also links up with how we argued above that the unconscious is de-anchored from the past, now coming from the future as well. This is not to repeat Freud's famous statement about the "timelessness" of the unconscious and all of the wishy-washy mysticisms that flow from that, but rather to argue for a radical temporal quality of the unconscious that returns to the project of psychoanalysis its most profound political and spiritual dimensions. Dimensions that also bear on the concept and desire of "cure," and that we can track throughout the history of psychoanalysis, and connect up with the concepts and desires called "revolution" and "enlightenment."

I write "returns" to the project of psychoanalysis because we can already locate in Freud's early work, namely *The Interpretation of Dreams* published in 1899, this radical temporal quality of the unconscious. For instance, in the sixth edition, published in 1921, there are two key moments, one at the very beginning of the text, and the other at the very end, that provocatively raise this relation between the unconscious and time. In the preface to the sixth edition, Freud explains that there were no alterations to the main text, and then writes, "Thus my assumption that after an existence of nearly twenty years this book had accomplished its task has not been confirmed. On the contrary, I might say that it has a new task to perform. If its earlier function was to offer some information on the nature of dreams, now it has the no less important duty of dealing with the obstinate misunderstandings to which that information is subject."[93] But how can the same text have two different functions at two different times? How can the original text perform a different task twenty years later? Is Freud challenging Marx's argument about historical limitation (that we can only set solvable tasks for ourselves) by arguing *that we can also solve tasks for ourselves that we cannot yet set?* This is, I think, precisely what is at stake in Freud's project.

The Interpretation of Dreams has its own unconscious, one that works in relation to a future that does not yet exist. What better way to figure this unconscious future (and future unconscious), than by collapsing the anticipatory dimension of both the text and its main object of study, the dream itself. And this takes us to the last paragraph of *The Interpretation of Dreams*. Freud writes,

And the value of dreams for giving us knowledge of the future? There is of course no question of that. It would be truer to say instead that they give us knowledge of the past. For dreams are derived from the past in every sense. Nevertheless the ancient belief that dreams foretell the future is not wholly devoid of truth. By picturing our wishes as fulfilled, dreams are after all leading us into the future. But this future, which the dreamer pictures as the present, has been molded by his indestructible wish into a perfect likeness of the past.[94]

I cannot think of a richer sentence in the whole Freudian oeuvre than this last one. It, at once, articulates a radical temporality (in which the past, present and future now exist on the same surface), holding within it a radical philosophy of history (in which this surface of multiple times can be wholly replaced by another surface with a qualitatively different logic) that itself holds within it a radical theory of cure (in which a radical change to the subject is possible in the sense that when history itself somersaults, so do its constituent and constitutive subjects).

The year of publication of this sixth edition of *The Interpretation of Dreams*, 1921, is significant, as it is one year following the publication of *Beyond the Pleasure Principle*, the key text that is usually read as a wedge dividing Freud's project, and forcing him to rethink the dream as wish fulfillment as well as focus on the drives (the death drive, in particular), especially that aspect of the drive that keeps subjects repeating their harmful symptoms and puts the lie to the principle of homeostasis. Beyond the pleasure principle is a beyond that cannot be known and cannot be harmonized, incorporated, or even managed by our present categories of being and analysis. We must always try to hold and give room to the things that do not fit or make sense, just as Freud himself does at the end of *Beyond the Pleasure Principle*, when he writes, with his usual mix of humility and arrogance, that "this in turn raises a host of other questions to which we can at present find no answer. We must be patient," Freud continues, "and await fresh methods and occasions of research."[95] It is this reference to "occasions of research" that stands out, for when we understand these occasions as different historical moments with different limitations and possibilities, we begin to understand Freud's project less as one that practices a bad historicism by tracking the continuity of symptoms throughout the life of a subject (all formed either through oedipal conflicts or at an earlier moment of infancy), and more as one veering on a radical historical materialism that always leaves room for a great rupture or discontinuity of symptoms. Indeed, this materialist psychoanalysis takes its most provocative forms later in the work of Lacan, and then with Félix Guattari, most notably Guattari's two books with Gilles Deleuze, famously subtitled *Capitalism and Schizophrenia.*

Now we have come to the point at which cure merges with revolution and enlightenment. In each discipline, we struggle with the problem of praxis—as meditator and thinker in Buddhism, as actor and reader of *Capital* in Marxism, as analyst and analysand in psychoanalysis. In each discipline, praxis enters into a relation to a future that we cannot yet set or know, especially because the "we" of the future will change so radically by the time we get to the future that we can only hold open a space for this radical change, or death—the death of our former selves and historical times, before our new selves and times are born. This in-between time and space provides another way of understanding the function of enlightenment, revolution, and cure. But it is also this in-between time and space, or radical temporality, that risks being snuffed-out in subsequent psychoanalytic theory and practice.

Cure, like enlightenment and revolution, is nothing other than the radical belief in and fidelity to the possibility that "anything can happen" and that this "anything" has happened numerous times in the past, while recognizing that this possibility is not an excuse to dismiss the limits of our present structures or the pain and suffering (not to mention the delights and pleasures) experienced in the meantime—a meantime that requires the continual engagement with the problem of praxis. Indeed, the ego psychologies of the post–World War II moment attempted to manage the time and space of radical change in the name of strengthening the ego. And when Heinz Kohut writes his final book in 1984, *How Does Analysis Cure?*, he is critical of this ego-psychological focus on management and expansion of the ego. But his self-psychology movement can only go so far as to cultivate the healthy dimension of the patient's narcissism by way of the corrective empathy coming from the analyst. For Kohut, analysis can cure, but only as long as the cure is defined as that moment when a patient's structural defects are rehabilitated, so that the patient is capable of joyfully experiencing life. This is cure as functionality. Cure as radical change is no longer part of the picture.

With his desire not to impose onto the analysand what the analyst considers curative (such as the ego psychologists' value of independence and autonomy), Kohut was intent on criticizing the moralizing and elitist attitude of so much psychoanalytic work. But this was all done within the context of post–World War II North America, in which a reinvigorated liberal humanism defined the limits of philosophical and political thought. Lacan was equally critical of the ego psychologists and their attendant liberal humanism, but his challenge was diametrically opposed to Kohut's, and emphasized that the ego psychologists' fatal flaw was not their championing of autonomy and independence as the cure of psychoanalysis, but rather that they failed to recognize the autonomy and independence of history, that which exceeds the subject and is right inside of it, or that which is "in you more than you," as Lacan famously put it at the end of Seminar XI. This is another way of invoking the Lacanian Real, which we can now argue is nothing else but the condition of possibility of the cure.

When we make our way from the early 1980s to the present, from the restucturings of neoliberal economics to full-blown global capitalism, we are faced with a new challenge for psychoanalysis, namely how to reengage the problems of praxis and cure at a moment when radical change is ridiculed and relegated to the unthinkable, despite the "anything is possible" motto of globalization discourse. One challenge to this enclosure comes from those who identify with relational psychoanalysis. The so-called relational turn is best characterized by the new role of the relational analyst, who no longer functions as a screen or mirror of the analysand, or as an object to be negotiated, but as a subject in his or her own right. As Jessica Benjamin elegantly narrates it, Freud's famous dictum, "where id was, ego shall be," first moves to "where ego was, object shall be" (inspired by the object relations analysts such as Klein and Winnicot), and then to "where object was, subject shall be."[96] This subject-to-subject relational psychoanalysis turns on the diluted Hegelian category of recognition as well as Habermasian ideas of intersubjectivity, in which subjects are mutually constituted. In this case, cure is relegated to mutual recognition, and the ability to repair the inevitable breakdowns that occur within intersubjective relatedness.[97] Once again, cure is only cure within the existing psychological system, something akin to liberal or social-democratic reforms within the existing political-economic system.

Today, some of the most provocative challenges to this enclosure is enacted by those adhering to Lacanian clinical commitments. After decades of Lacan's work being ghettoized within the humanities departments (literature and film studies, in particular) of the North American university (despite still being widely practiced throughout Europe and South America), a new breed of practicing Lacanians has reintroduced the problem of the clinic. Bruce Fink, the translator of Lacan's *Écrits*, is best known among them and we can summarize his position as one that takes Benjamin's move one step further: "Where subject was, id shall be."[98] Unlike the relationalists, Fink sees the analyst not as another subject, whose real relationship with the analysand is front and center and, therefore, the measure of success. Rather, the analyst is here seen as a function of the analysand's desire, which must not be humanized, but rather mobilized, so as to shake loose unconscious fantasies that do not present an available language to be decoded and formalized even though these unconscious fantasies are, as Lacan famously argued, structured like a language.[99] At any rate, there is still the temptation of relating these unconscious eruptions to the analysand's past and present, rather than to an unknown future. Here it might be productive to consider how this temptation is connected to what we generally assume to be the boundaries of the clinic. By stressing clinical technique (listening, asking questions, interpreting, handling transference and countertransference) and reminding us that Lacan was first and foremost a clinician, Fink is performing the admirable and crucial task of reattaching Lacanian theory to clinical practice.

But we are now in danger of reproducing the old notion of psychoanalytic praxis that separates the practice of the clinic from the theoretical essay and extra-clinical speculation. Perhaps, this is as radical as psychoanalysis can be while remaining in the clinic—which is not to long for another escape from the clinic, but for an escape from the usual ways we understand the clinic itself. Two questions arise from this: Where does the clinic begin and end? And if the clinic exceeds the dyad (not in terms of Thomas Ogden's "the analytic third," which still remains in the clinic; nor in terms of Jung's "collective unconscious," which takes the clinic out of history altogether), then must we liberate the unconscious from the clinic, just as we liberated the unconscious from the subject and from the past?[100] My answer is yes. And this leads to a new formulation, and to the mantra that will reconnect us to the problematics of Buddhism and Marxism as well as to the work of Isozaki: Where id was, the future shall be.

THE RADICAL NOTHINGNESS OF THE FUTURE

In its most basic form, the internal contradiction of praxis works as follows: (1) in Buddhism, it is the contradiction between the belief in enlightenment that always exists as possibility and the complacent behavior and destructive ideologies enabled by this belief; (2) in Marxism, it is the contradiction between the belief in the possibility of radically different systems coming into being (as capitalism itself came into being following feudalism) and the structural limits of imagining these different systems within the confinements of capitalist relations; and (3) in psychoanalysis, it is the contradiction between the belief in the unconscious that includes its own radical freedom and the subjective destruction and entrapment caused by this inexorable quality. By tracking how this problem shifts from one historical moment to the next, and from one problematic to the next, and by tracking the returns to the original production of the problem of praxis and the rereadings of the monumental texts that render it, we have come a long way in refining and recentering praxis as the most generative political, psychological, and spiritual issue of our day.

But there is still something missing—namely, the category of nothing. Instead of turning to the various thinkers who engage "nothing" by directly linking psychoanalysis and Buddhism (such as the impressive work of Raul Moncayo, who rigorously pursues the relations between Sōtō Zen and Lacanian analysis) or those who do so by linking psychoanalysis and Marxism (less directly as the important work by Bernard Stiegler, Ian Parker, and Colette Soler, or more directly as aforementioned by the brilliant and indomitable work of Žižek, Jameson, and Badiou)[101], my own intervention here is to turn to the work of Isozaki Arata, whose architectural negotiation of the problem of nothing profoundly flashes the most pressing contradiction of our contemporary moment: how to think and act for a radical break with our current situation (as individuals and as collectives) without reproducing global capitalism's dominant ideological assumption that there is no alternative, only more of the same. Isozaki engages this problem of how to make room for difference from this side of the future, by attempting to unite, at one and the same time, theory and practice.

Ever since the Japanese triple disaster of 2011, there has been a renewed interest in Isozaki's work and ideas. There are three direct reasons for this. The first is Isozaki's connection to the Metabolist architectural movement in Japan during the 1960s, and the current rethinking of this avant-garde experiment following the 2011 publication of Rem Koolhaus' *Project Japan*, a monumental historical endeavor that includes interviews with all of the Metabolist movement's members, including Isozaki.[102] The second reason is that Isozaki has always been associated with ruins, and has organized many of his projects (built and unbuilt) as well as his theoretical and critical writings extensively around disaster, as well as on the relation between past disasters (specifically the dropping of the atomic bombs) and future disasters. The third reason is his creation of "Ark Nova," the portable structure he has built for the victims of the Tōhoku disasters, forming what I will call an architecture of radical nothingness in the spirit of the three problematics that I am reclaiming in this book.

Each of these three reasons for a renewed interest in Isozaki's work is inextricably connected to his long-standing commitment to the concept of *ma* ("negative time-space"). But before examining this concept, let's first set up the context by recalling the heartbreaking events of the great earthquake on March 11, 2011, followed by the tsunami, and then the nuclear meltdown. The earthquake and tsunami directly affected those living in the towns and villages in the Tōhoku region of Japan, and compelled the survivors to cope with the tens of thousands who died (in some cases, nearly entire communities) and the huge rebuilding process. The nuclear meltdown, in turn, has affected not only those in the immediate vicinity of the Fukushima nuclear reactors, but the whole country, in terms of the potential contamination of the water and food supply. Moreover, the temporality of the nuclear disaster is different from the temporality of the earthquake and tsunami—the danger and damage of the nuclear fallout will occur over a much longer term, with fewer immediate effects. These different, yet overlapping temporalities of disaster (short-term destruction and long-term threat) produce fundamental challenges: how, for example, can we directly engage the immediacy of an event (such as the destruction caused by the earthquake to people, landscape, and infrastructure) while at the same time de-emphasizing the concrete damage in order to attend to the various historical, future, and meta contexts of the immediate situation?

The Metabolists, who were themselves inspired by devastated landscapes and persisting atomic fears following World War II, were composed of young Japanese architects mobilized by one of the more well-regarded Japanese architects of the day, Tange Kenzō. The movement, founded in 1960 with the publication of its radical manifesto *Metabolism: The Proposals for New Urbanism*, developed utopian visions of the future, and practices ranging from megastructures to floating cities to artificial land.[103] Critical of Japan's superficial importation of modernism as well as of the nationalist return to nativist ideas of nature, the Metabolists were techno-utopians promoting an accelerated urbanism that could adapt to a changing world. For example, a newly built factory would be designed modularly, so that it could be easily retrofitted or moved to another location, depending on the local economy. Instead of being forced to witness the structure's decay when the industry changes, therefore, the smooth adaptation to new needs ensures its regeneration.

In contrast to modernist desires for an architecture that could survive great catastrophes, as exemplified by Frank Lloyd Wright's Imperial Hotel (one of the few buildings to remain unscathed following the Kantō earthquake of 1923), the Metabolists were interested in impermanence, and drew inspiration from structures such as the ancient Ise Shrine. First established in the fourth century BC, the shrine has been purposely destroyed and rebuilt every twenty years (almost continuously, sixty-two times as of 2013) on an adjacent site, effectively confusing old and new, original and copy, continuity and rupture, stability and instability. The Metabolists found this architectural ideal to be perfectly suited to their own historical present, which was shaken by the huge social movements (leftist students, anti-Vietnam demonstrations, *Ampo* struggles against the US-Japan Security Agreement), and which was, furthermore, still reeling from the apocalyptic realities of World War II. The biological gesture of the group's name was thus no coincidence, since metabolism indicates an organic process of change and adaptation.[104]

Although Isozaki worked in Tange's studio and was a fellow traveler of the Metabolists, he never fully endorsed their project. Specifically, he could not buy into their techno-utopias, and their underlying desire to manage crisis and preempt the great ruptures of history. Isozaki had a more developed sense of break-down and ruins, one informed by his own theoretical commitments to the negative, and by a more trenchant critique of capitalist accumulation and mass production. Whereas the Metabolists still envisioned the future as an extension of the present (an extension that could be continually regenerated by large-scale urban plans and technological fixes), Isozaki figured the future both as indelibly imprinted with the great disaster of Japanese modernity (Hiroshima) and as a total break with the past and present. This divide most importantly turned on a radically different idea of time and space.

Isozaki shared with the Metabolists a theory of architectural time as mere occasion, an unfixable and multifarious spread of phenomenological experience. He returned to Dōgen's *Shōbō-genzō* and the fascicle called "Being Time" as one of the first instances of a sustained development of this architectural ideal of time, which Isozaki deliberately retranslates as "time comes flying," in order to stress that even the ruins of the future are part of the present structures—in this case, time comes flying from the future to the present.[105] But Isozaki goes a step further, thus marking his fundamental critique of the Metabolists: he views not only time, but also space as merely a multifarious occasion. Whereas most of us think of space as fixed and localizable, Isozaki believes "that space appears only in the *time* that humans perceive, therefore it is always specific, concrete flickering, and never fixed."[106] Now time and space are undifferentiated, and need to be reconceptualized as a single concept—as *ma*. Ma (間) makes up the second character in the words *time* (jikan 時間) and *space* (kūkan 空間), and is often translated as space, room, time, pause, interstice. Isozaki settles on "gap," or the original Sanskrit meaning of "an original difference immanent in things."

For the 1996 Venice Biennale, Isozaki curated an exhibit entitled "Architects as Seismographers" that responded to the 1995 Kobe earthquake and returned to an earlier piece of his called *Hiroshima Ruined Again in the Future*, first made for the Milan Triennale of 1969. *Hiroshima Ruined Again in the Future* was an image of a Metabolist-inspired megaproject in ruins overlayed with an enlarged image of Hiroshima photographed immediately after the dropping of the first atomic bomb. Directly referencing the Metabolist's desire for megastructures, Isozaki saw this image "as a *future* scene of urban megastructures in collapse."[107] Referring to his own generation of those who experienced the death of cities during WWII, he writes, "To us, such cities as were supposed now to be built had already decayed."[108] He continues, "The trauma of urban collapse had been so severe for us in Japan that we were uneasy in accepting urban reconstruction put forward in place of the bombastic and pseudo-humanist Greater East Asia co-prosperity Sphere-type proposals of our recent wartime past." And he concludes, "I could only hope to depict the trauma itself."[109]

In this case, the trauma is not only Hiroshima of 1945, but Hiroshima ruined again in the future. Yet by holding the dualistic tension of time and space in the single concept of *ma*, Isozaki is able to liberate the trauma from the past and recognize it as coming from the future as well. This future trauma, however, is not the return of the repressed. It is, rather, what we might call *the repressed of the return*—the future that cannot be contained or managed, and always arrives as something that exceeds our present possibilities, something that cannot be represented and that must always be repressed. It is precisely in this repressed future that freedom exists, and we can therefore detect, in Isozaki's project, something other than a dark pessimism—something that is more radical and enlivening. *Where id was, the future shall be. Ma* is the condition of this future, just as it is the condition of enlightenment, revolution, and cure.

But even this idea of ruin as a future trauma has a history, which Isozaki narrates in his own work, beginning in the 1960s. During that decade, the image of the future city was inspired by the ruins of World War II and, for Isozaki, "professing faith in ruins was equal to planning the future."[110] But following 1968, and throughout the 1970s, ruins ceased to offer inspiration, and reappeared as nostalgia. Then, with the emergence of the computer in the 1980s, the future city resurfaced "as a virtual image from within the ruins."[111] But by the 1990s, and in the context of media-saturated representations of the first Gulf War (in which what really happened and what was rhetorically represented as happening seemed to have merged), the virtual images themselves were hard to place in reality. There was no longer any objective criteria for victory or defeat, let alone right or wrong, and all that could be confirmed was the rubble of destruction. Isozaki writes, "What is dramatically revealed here is the materiality, the thingness, that had been hidden all along. . . . Rubble is thus scattered to the space of the interstice *ma*."[112]

This takes us to the rubble of the Kobe earthquake that killed six thousand people in 1995. Right up until the Kobe quake hit, people refused to fully accept that Japan was in a full-blown recession, and that the sluggishness of the high-growth economy was more than just a momentary stall. The 1995 earthquake, therefore, was immediately turned into a symbol of Japan's economic downfall. In response, Japanese leaders vigorously implemented various neoliberal policies, effectively destroying the Japanese welfare state (now no longer promising lifetime employment or cradle-to-grave health care, and producing an extremely precarious, flexible labor force of young and old alike). In addition to bringing Japan in line with the principles of the global capitalist economy, in 2003 the ruling Koizumi administration also betrayed the postwar pacifist constitution by sending the nation's Self-Defense Forces to Iraq. Despite the neoliberal hope of recovery through privatization and economic austerity measures, by 2010, Japan's growing poverty rate had almost met the extremely high rate of the United States, making Japan the fourth-highest impoverished country among OECD's thirty member nations. As for the recession, it is now moving into its third decade.

Five days after the 2011 earthquake and tsunami, Karatani wrote an essay about the disaster that lays out the narrative above.[113] Karatani stresses that unlike after the Kobe earthquake, the 2011 Tōhoku earthquake did not come as a surprise shock to the economy, and could not be mobilized by neoliberal politicians and bureaucrats. Rather, the recent disaster will only strengthen the already existing tendencies of economic decline, and confirm that such accelerated capitalist growth cannot last—a lesson that China, India, and Brazil will soon learn as well.

Karatani ends his piece thus:

> Without the recent earthquake, Japan would no doubt have continued its hollow struggle for great power status, but such a dream is now unthinkable and should be abandoned. . . . It is not Japan's demise that the earthquake has produced, but rather the possibility of its rebirth. *It may be that only amid the ruins can people gain the courage to stride down a new path* (emphasis added).[114]

In the spirit of this proclamation, and in collaboration with the artist Anish Kapoor, Isozaki produced "Ark Nova"—an impermanent, human heart–like structure that inflates right on top of the rubble of the past, always ready to be relocated and placed on top of the rubble of the future. With this piece, Isozaki does not offer moralizing commentary about how space will shape revolutionary subjects, about how his work will withstand the next earthquake and tsunami, or even about how the concert hall it contains will soothe the traumas of the triple disaster— but neither does he give up on the radical possibility of what can emerge in the meantime and meanspace.

Isozaki's perspective gives us the opportunity to rephrase the diverse issues that have emerged throughout this essay in the form of a single question: *How does one still hold on to the desire for enlightenment, revolution, and cure without this desire turning into a self-satisfied retreat from the world, a sad militancy, a naive optimism, or a nonsystemic critique of local transgressions and individual symptoms?*

Isozaki responds to this question by producing a kind of terminal architecture, one that shape-shifts from nothing to something, and back again to nothing, all the while holding open the space-time for the future to come flying in. It promises to be one of the more successful failures—as these attempts are always destined to fail—at resolving the impossible problem of praxis and breaking free from the smothering logic of our present.

I am reading "Ark Nova" as an intervention into Buddhism, Marxism, and psychoanalysis. Or, more precisely, as Buddhist, Marxist, and psychoanalytic praxis. The work is not an allegory or an application of these three problematics. Rather, it exists right inside of them, and represents as much (and as significant) an engagement with them as any performed by the recognized authorities in these respective domains. "Ark Nova" also functions to reveal how we can think all three problematics invoked in this essay in conjunction—each flashing the blind spots of the others, each already inside of the others. And this, finally, returns us to "critical theory," and to my earlier argument that what distinguishes it from other critical projects is the non-hierarchical mobilization of all thoughts, acts, and materials regardless of their disciplinary boundaries. At the beginning of this piece, I mentioned that Buddhism, Marxism, and psychoanalysis share a commitment to critical theory, an undisciplined rigor, although at the same time they do not fit comfortably within the contemporary university. The reason for this is that they do not submit to the university's grounding (and only half-true) assumption that the truth will set us free.

Psychoanalysis teaches us that even if we know full well why we behave the way we do (even if, in other words, we know how our symptoms work, and what activates them), this knowledge does not keep us from repeating old patterns. In fact, oftentimes it is precisely our accurate knowledge of the truth about ourselves (however humble, elegant, or analytical) that keeps us locked into our harmful symptoms. In this sense, it is precisely the truth of our self-analysis, and the pleasure we take in the force of the narrative itself, that is likely to prevent us from radically transforming it and experiencing personal change. At its best, psychoanalysis gets this paradoxical reality, and centers it with the hope that something creative and nourishing, perhaps even revolutionary, might result from the continuous and routine confrontation with the impossible.

Something quite similar can be said about Marxism. Knowing that inequality and violence are built into the capitalist system itself, that they are objective facts of a mode of production organized around inexorable expansion and a structural rift between those who own the means of production and those who labor under it, will not keep us from reproducing the system, or from feeling that there is no escape from the present configuration of things. No matter how clearly we understand that crisis (or commodification, or dispossession) are the predictable effects of capitalism "going right," rather than the exceptional and avoidable effects of it "going wrong," and no matter how much we recognize that it is tactically counterproductive to moralize against so many bad actors (terrorists, crony capitalists, rogue leaders) or chance events (natural disasters, pandemics, random catastrophes), and blame them for disrupting our otherwise smooth sailing into the peaceful future, we are still no closer to changing the system itself. To resign ourselves to this paradox is not the answer either—not only because such settling strengthens the system and dulls our critical edges, but because the pleasure gained by a spirited and non-moralizing critique of capitalism is enlivening, and radical politics will always require a reclaiming of personal pleasure from the state, and a redirection of erotics away from the dominant order . . . a reclamation project that itself is another name for love.

In the context of Buddhism, finally, we can state that no matter how much we know the limits of our knowledge and of the impermanence of our present desires, pleasures, frustrations, as well as the selves that experience these desires, pleasures, and frustrations, and no matter how awake we are to the four noble truths, or even to the recognition that daily practice must supplement the blind spots of our understanding, the likely possibility remains that these very insights and commitments to Buddhism will function to keep us from the radical core of Buddhism itself. Every beautiful anecdote about a Buddhist teacher, every brilliant *kōan*, every sublime silence functions to take us further away from Buddhist enlightenment, however much they keep us coming back for more. This is for the simple reason that to register the power of Buddhism, or of one's own Buddhist qualities, necessarily ensnares us, and confirms that we are still short of enlightenment. And yet, to give up on enlightenment while remaining a Buddhist, or to give up on cure as a psychoanalytic patient or on revolution as a Marxist, might *seem* to escape the central paradoxes of each problematic, and might indeed make us more moderate, and thus more socially acceptable to others. But this is not the answer either. And even if we go to the hyper-logical extreme and recognize that the very giving up on enlightenment, revolution, and cure might actually generate them as lucky side effects—this is still not the answer. There is no answer. There is praxis.

NOTES

The author gratefully acknowledges the support of the Mellon Foundation's New Directions Fellowship, as well as Martin Zeilinger, Martin Bastarache, Juhn Ahn, and Peter Fitting for their generous assistance with editing and research.

1. Steven Heine's introduction to Abe Masao's classic *A Study of Dōgen*, for example, puts it this way: "Abe has also been strongly influenced by D. T. Suzuki and Hisamatsu Shinichi, and he shares their commitment to Zen as a form of religious praxis over and above philosophical theory." Abe Masao, *A Study of Dōgen: His Philosophy and Religion* (Albany: State University of New York Press, 1992), 3.

2. Here we might want to remember Gilles Deleuze's groundbreaking argument in the last paragraph of book 1 of his two cinema books, that the new image, the one that marked a mutation after the first fifty years of cinema, had to become "truly thought and thinking." Film, in other words, had to think, not just represent thinking or the practice of filmmaking. Gilles Deleuze, *Cinema 1: The Movement-Image* (Minneapolis: University of Minnesota Press, 1995), 215.

3. Fredric Jameson, *Valences of the Dialectic* (New York: Verso, 2010), 372.

4. Ibid.

5. Sigmund Freud and Joseph Breuer, *Studies in Hysteria*, trans. Nicola Luckburst (New York: Penguin, 2004), 306.

6. Ibid.

7. Jacques Lacan, "Intervention," in G. Favez, "Le rendez-vous avec le psychanalyste," *La Psychanalyse* 4 (1958): 305–14.

8. I thank one of this manuscript's anonymous reviewers for stressing this point about the way that Buddhism has historically negotiated the contradictions of enlightenment.

9. See Hakamaya Noriaki's *Hongaku shisō hihan (Critique of the idea of Original Enlightenment)* (Tokyo: Daizō Shuppan, 1989), and Paul Swanson's "'Zen Is Not Buddhism': Recent Japanese Critiques of Buddha-nature," *Numen* 40 (1993): 115–49. In English, also see *Pruning the Bodhi Tree: The Storm over Critical Buddhism*, ed. Jamie Hubbard and Paul L. Swanson (Honolulu: University of Hawai'i Press, 1997), Jacqueline I. Stone's *Original Enlightenment and the Transformation of Medieval Japanese Buddhism* (Honolulu: University of Hawai'i Press, 2003), and James Shields' *Critical*

Buddhism (London: Ashgate, 2011). In Japanese, see Matsumoto Shirō's *Zen shisō no hihanteki kenkyū* (*Critical Studies in Zen Thought*) (Tokyo: Daizō Shuppan, 1993) and *Engi to kū: Nyoraizō shisō hihan* (Pratityasamutpada *and Emptiness: Critiques of the Doctrine of* tathagata-garbha) (Tokyo: Daizō Shuppan, 1989).

10. Hee-Jin Kim, *Dōgen on Meditation and Thinking: A Reflection on His View of Zen* (Albany: State University of New York Press, 2007), 55.

11. See Hubbard, *Pruning the Bodhi Tree*, x. This case is explained in more detail in William Bodiford's "Zen and the Art of Religious Prejudice: Efforts to Reform a Tradition of Social Discrimination," *Japanese Journal of Religious Studies* 23 (1996): 1–28.

12. Žižek has been making this point in various lectures ("The Irony of Buddhism," November 26, 2012; and "The Buddhist Ethic and the Spirit of Global Capitalism," August 10, 2012, at the European Graduate School) and in the section entitled "Lacan against Buddhism" in *Less Than Nothing: Hegel and the Shadow of Dialectical Materialism* (London: Verso, 2012), 127–35.

13. On this point, see Jameson's "Lacan and the Dialectic: A Fragment," in *Lacan: The Silent Partners*, ed. Slavoj Žižek (London: Verso, 2006).

14. This statement by the Dalai Lama has been circulated in many different forms. Among the first places I have located it is in the Dalai Lama's *Beyond Dogma: Dialogues and Discourses* (Berkeley: North Atlantic Books, 1996):

> Of all the modern economic theories, the economic system of Marxism is founded on moral principles, while capitalism is concerned with only with gain and profitability. Marxism is concerned with the distribution of wealth on an equal basis and the equitable utilization of the means of production. It is also concerned with the fate of the working classes—that is the majority—as well as with the fate of those who are underprivileged and in need, and Marxism cares about the victims of minority-imposed exploitation. For those reasons the system

appeals to me, and it seems fair. . . . The failure of the regime in the Soviet Union was, for me not the failure of Marxism but the failure of totalitarianism. For this reason I think of myself as half-Marxist, half-Buddhist (109).

15. See Stuart Smithers, "Occupy Buddhism: Or Why the Dalai Lama is a Marxist," *Tricycle* magazine, n.d., accessed June 26, 2014, http://www.tricycle.com/web-exclusive/occupy-buddhism.

16. See my "Japanese Film without Japan: Toward a Nondisciplined Film Studies," in *The Oxford Handbook of Japanese Cinema*, ed. Daisuke Miyao (Oxford: Oxford University Press, 2014), 13–14; and *After Globalization*, cowritten with Imre Szeman (London: Wiley-Blackwell, 2012), 45–46.

17. "The view that practice and enlightenment are not one is a non-Buddhist view. In the Buddha-dharma they are one. Inasmuch as practice is based on enlightenment, the practice of a beginner is entirely that of original enlightenment. Therefore, in giving the instructions for practice, a Zen teacher should advise his or her disciples not to seek enlightenment apart from practice, for practice itself is original enlightenment. Because it is already enlightenment of practice, there is no end to enlightenment; because it is already practice of enlightenment, there is no beginning to practice." Quoted from Kim, *Dōgen on Meditation and Thinking*, 23.

18. "Both exoteric and esoteric Buddhism teach the primal Buddha-nature [or Dharma-nature] and the original self-wakening of all sentient beings. If this is the case, why have the buddhas of all ages had to awaken the longing for and seek enlightenment by engaging in ascetic practice?" Quoted from Abe, *A Study of Dōgen*, 19. Some scholars question whether or not Dōgen actually traveled to China, thus engaging this *hongaku* paradox and considering the entire narrative a late fabrication. See Carl Bielefeldt's *Dōgen's Manuals of Zen Meditation* (Berkeley: University of California Press, 1990); Steven Heine's *Did Dōgen go to China? What He Wrote and When He Wrote It* (Oxford: Oxford University Press, 2006); and William Bodiford's article "Remembering Dōgen," *Journal of Japanese Studies* 32, no. 1 (2006): 1–21.

19. Again, Steven Heine clarifies this point in his *Did Dōgen Go To China?*

20. Regarding Kamakura new Buddhism, see *Re-visioning "Kamakura" Buddhism*, ed. Richard K. Payne (Honolulu: University of Hawai'i Press, 1998).

21. "From the very moment when a disciple comes to meet face-to-face with the one who is to be his spiritual friend and knowing teacher, there is no need to have the disciple offer incense, make prostrations, chant the names of the Buddhas, do ascetic practices and penances, or recited Scriptures: The Master just has the disciple do pure meditation until he lets his body and mind drop off." Dōgen, *Shōbōgenzō*, trans. Hubert Nearman (Mount Shasta: Shasta Abbey Press, 2007), 4. On Dōgen's trip to China, see Henrich Dumoulin, *Zen Buddhism: A History*, vol. 2, *Japan*, trans. James W. Heisig and Paul Knitter (Bloomington: World Wisdom, Inc., 2005), 56.

22. I thank Juhn Ahn for alerting me to this issue. For more on the Daruma-shu, see Bernard Faure's "The Daruma-shu, Dōgen and Sōtō Zen," *Monumenta Nipponica* 42 (1987): 25–55; and Bielefeldt's *Dōgen's Manuals of Zen Meditation*. Since Eisai distanced himself from the Daruma-shu and Dōgen was in need of followers, Dōgen accepted the Dauma-shu disciples as his own.

23. Here I am following Steven Heine's argument about Ju-ching's influence on Dōgen. Heine argues that Dōgen's emphasis on Ju-ching's influence was not immediately expressed following Dōgen's return from China, but began in subsequent periods as a means to contrast his positions from rivals. See Heine's *Did Dōgen Go To China?*, 3. Bielefeldt also makes this point in *Dōgen's Manuals of Zen Meditation*, 28.

24. For more on the discursive struggle over the *Shōbōgenzō*, see Steven Heine, "Critical Buddhism and Dōgen's *Shōbōgenzō*: The Debate over the 75-Fascicle and 12-Fascicle Texts," in *Pruning the Bodhi Tree*, 251–85.

25. Heine calls Dōgen's style a Sino-Japanese "proetic" (prose-poetic) style of writing "replete with ingenious punning and word-play between languages as well as philosophical nuances embedded in lyrical imagery." Heine, *Did Dōgen Go To China?*, 2.

26. Here I am relying on Kim's translation, taken from *Dōgen on Meditation and Thinking*, 23.

27. Abe, *A Study of Dōgen*, 25.

28. Ibid., 29.

29. See Matsumoto Shirō, "The Doctrine of *Tathagata-garbha* Is Not Buddhist" in *Pruning the Bodhi Tree*, 165–73.

30. Kim, *Dōgen on Meditation and Thinking*, 24.

31. Dōgen, *Shōbōgenzō*, *Zen Essays*, trans. Thomas Cleary (Honolulu: University of Hawai'i Press, 1986), 5.

32. Hakamaya Noriaki, "Ideological Background of Discrimination," in *Pruning the Bodhi Tree*, 344.

33. Ibid., 347–48.

34. See Matsumoto Shirō, "Comments on Critical Buddhism," in *Pruning the Bodhi Tree*, 161.

35. See Jacqueline Stone's *Original Enlightenment and the Transformation of Medieval Japanese Buddhism* (Honolulu: University of Hawai'i Press, 2003).

36. Hakamaya, "Ideological Background of Discrimination," in *Pruning the Bodhi Tree*, 346–48.

37. Harry Harootunian, *Overcome by Modernity: History, Culture, and Community in Interwar Japan* (Princeton, NJ: Princeton University Press, 2000), 250–61.

38. "Before touching on the personality and thought of Dōgen the monk, first I would like to make the reader aware that I am a layman with regard to Zen, and that I express nothing but admiration for Dōgen. I can only write my impression of his admirable qualities. If by doing so I can arouse interest in some people in one of the great religious masters born to our country, and if I can clarify that the essence of our own culture cannot be properly understood without taking such religious figures into consideration, then I'll be satisfied." Watsuji Tetsurō, *Purifying Zen: Watsuji Tetsuro's Shamon Dōgen*, trans. Steve Bein (Honolulu: University of Hawai'i Press, 2011), 25.

39. This leads to Watsuji's argument about the absolute truth of religion and the historicized expressions of this truth. Watsuji

argues that it is precisely because he has not attained the absolute truth, but is authentically on the search for it, that provides him special access to the particularized truth of Japanese culture and, therefore, protects him from falling into what he condemns as Buddhism's faulty mysticism. It is here that Watsuji invokes the dialectic, and a conservative appropriation of Hegel: "For Dōgen, creative self-activity of absolute spirit does not simply appear as a natural consequence of the dialectic, but appears as the dialectical development present in one's own life, including all its impurities, and moreover, each step of that development also appears as something driven by illogical reasons" (111).

40. On Nakano Shigeharu see Miriam Silverberg, *Changing Song: The Marxist Manifestos of Nakano Shigeharu* (Princeton, NJ: Princeton University Press, 1990); on Tosaka and Miki see Harootunian, *Overcome by Modernity*; and on Kamei see my *The Flash of Capital: Film and Geopolitics in Japan* (Durham, NC: Duke University Press, 2002).

41. Harootunian, *Overcome by Modernity*, 258.

42. Naoki Sakai, "Return to the West/Return to the East: Watsuji Tetsurō's Anthropology and Discussions of Authenticity," in *Japan in the World*, ed. Masao Miyoshi and Harry Harootunian (Durham, NC: Duke University Press, 1993), 235–70.

43. Ibid., 269.

44. See Robert H. Scharf, "Whose Zen? Zen Nationalism Revisited," in *Rude Awakenings: Zen, the Kyoto School, and the Question of Nationalism*, ed. James W. Heisig and John C. Maraldo (Honolulu: University of Hawaiʻi Press, 1995), 40–51; and "The Zen of Japanese Nationalism," in *Curators of the Buddha: The Study of Buddhism under Colonialism*, ed. Donald S. Lopez Jr. (Chicago: University of Chicago Press, 1995), 107–60; also Bernard Faure, "The Kyoto School and Reverse Orientalism," in *Japan in Traditional and Postmodern Perspectives*, ed. Charles Wei-hsun Fu and Steven Heine (Buffalo: State University of New York, 1995), 245–81; as well as my "Uses and Abuses of the Nation: Toward a Theory of the Transnational Cultural Exchange Industry," in *Social Text* 44 (1995): 135–59.

45. D. T. Suzuki, *Introduction to Zen Buddhism* (New York: Grove, 1964), 88.

46. Ibid., 46.

47. Ibid.

48. This raises the long-standing issue of sudden versus gradual enlightenment, in which sudden enlightenment is associated with the unmediated recognition of one's true nature, while gradual enlightenment is associated with cultivated practice. Dōgen, although often associated with the latter, is quite sophisticated in relation to this problem, not unlike the way, as I argued above, that he subtly negotiates the problem of dualisms. See Bielefeldt's chapter "The Sudden Practice and Ch'an Meditation Discourse" in *Dōgen's Manuals of Zen Meditation*, 78–108.

49. Nishida Kitarō, *An Inquiry into the Good*, trans. Abe Masao and Christopher Ives (New Haven, CT: Yale University Press, 1987), 35.

50. Ibid., 3–4.

51. Ibid., 5, note 3.

52. William Haver's "Introduction" to Nishida Kitarō's *Ontology of Production: Three Essays*, trans. William Haver (Durham, NC: Duke University Press, 2012), 1–33.

53. Masao Miyoshi, *Off Center: Power and Culture Relations Between Japan and the United States* (Cambridge, MA: Harvard University Press, 1998); and *Learning Places: The Afterlives of Area Studies*, ed. Masao Miyoshi and Harry Harootunian (Durham, NC: Duke University Press, 2002).

54. "Although the Meiji constitution designated the emperor as sovereign, he is essentially a 'being of nothingness'; similarly, in the context of the Greater East Asia co-Prosperity Sphere, he does not rule over all from above, as in the case of the Soviet Union, but rather exists at the foundation as a 'transcendental apperception' (zero sign) that unifies the various autonomous countries of Asia." Karatani Kōjin, "Buddhism and Fascism," in *History and Repetition*, trans. Seiji Lippitt (New York: Columbia University Press, 2012), 184.

55. Nishida, "Human Being," in *Ontology of Production*, 166.

56. Aristotle, *Nicomachean Ethics*, trans. Robert Bartless and Susan Collins (Chicago: University of Chicago Press, 2012).

57. Ibid, 147–48.

58. Nishida, "Human Being," 148.

59. Haver, "Introduction," 31.

60. Ibid., 31.

61. See Hakamaya's "Critical Philosophy versus Topical Philosophy," in *Pruning the Bodhi Tree*, 57.

62. Ibid., 58.

63. I will develop Karatani's idea of the parallax later in this essay. For more on this see Karatani Kōjin, *Transcritique: On Kant and Marx*, trans. Sabu Kohso (Cambridge, MA: MIT Press, 2003), 5–7. Also see Žižek's excellent review of Karatani's *Transcritique*, entitled *The Parallax View* (the same title as his later book), which first appeared in *New Left Review* 25, January–February 2004, 121–34.

64. Martin Puchner, *Poetry of the Revolution: Marx, Manifestos, and the Avant-Gardes* (Princeton, NJ: Princeton University Press, 2005), 12.

65. Ibid., 12.

66. Ibid., 22.

67. Karl Marx and Fredrich Engels, *The Communist Manifesto*, trans. L. M. Findlay (Buffalo: Broadview, 2005), 81.

68. Ibid., 77.

69. Ibid., 64.

70. Karl Marx, *Capital*, vol. 1, trans. Ben Fowkes (New York: Vintage, 1977), 138.

71. Ibid., 150.

72. Ibid., 151.

73. Ibid., 151.

74. Ibid., 152.

75. Ibid., 152.

76. Ibid., 152.

77. See Marx, "Preface" of *A Contribution to the Critique of Political Economy*, ca. 1859: "Mankind thus inevitably sets itself only

such tasks as it is able to solve, since closer examination will always show that the problem itself arises only when the material conditions for its solution are already present or at least in the course of formation." Available at http://www.marxists.org/archive/marx /works/1859/critique-pol-economy.

78. Marx, *Capital*, 333.

79. Ibid., 344.

80. Ibid.

81. Jacques Rancière, *Althusser's Lesson*, trans. Emiliano Battista (London: Continuum, 2011), 99. Rancière continues by arguing that the problem is that of "the compatibility between the absence of power at the level of labour processes, and power at the level of the state" (101).

82. Ernesto Laclau and Chantal Mouffe, *Hegemony and Socialist Strategy: Towards a Radical Democratic Politics* (London: Verso, 1985), 2.

83. Ibid., 2.

84. Karatani Kōjin, *Transcritique: On Kant and Marx* (Cambridge, MA: MIT Press, 2005), 19.

85. Ibid., 121.

86. Ibid., 5–7.

87. Ibid., 20.

88. Karatani Kōjin, *The Structure of World History* (Durham, NC: Duke University Press, 2014).

89. Ibid., 305–7.

90. Karatani, *Transcritique*, 21.

91. Fredric Jameson, *Valences of the Dialectic* (London: Verso, 2010), 565–82; and *Representing Capital* (London: Verso, 2014), 150–51.

92. Judith Dupont, ed., *The Clinical Diary of Sándor Ferenczi*, trans. Michael Balint and Nicola Zarday Jackson (Cambridge, MA: Harvard University Press, 1988), xiii.

93. Sigmund Freud, *The Interpretation of Dreams*, trans. James Strachey (New York: Avon Books, 1965), xxix.

94. Ibid, 660.

95. Sigmund Freud, *Beyond the Pleasure Principle* (New York: Norton, 1961), 77–78.

96. Jessica Benjamin, "Recognition and Destruction: An Outline of Intersubjectivity," in *Like Subjects, Love Objects: Essays on Recognition and Sexual Difference* (New Haven, CT: Yale University Press, 1995).

97. Ibid.

98. See Bruce Fink, *Fundamentals of Psychoanalytic Technique: A Lacanian Approach for Practitioners* (New York: Norton, 2007), and *A Clinical Introduction to Lacanian Psychoanalysis: Theory and Technique* (Cambridge, MA: Harvard University Press, 1997).

99. This is what Lacan meant when arguing that the unconscious is structured like a language; not that it is a language to be interpreted and deciphered, but rather that unconscious signification is not totally random—it has a logic that works, like linguistic languages, through the differential relations of its component parts.

100. I write about Jung's understanding of history as it differs from Freud's in *The Already Dead: The New Time of Politics, Culture, and Illness* (Durham, NC: Duke University Press, 2012), 190–93.

101. In particular, see Bernard Stiegler's *What Makes Life Worth Living: On Pharmacology* (Cambridge, Polity, 2013); Ian Parker's *Lacanian Psychoanalysis: Revolutions in Subjectivity* (London: Routledge, 2010); and Colette Soler's *Lacan: The Unconscious Reinvented* (London: Karnac, 2014).

102. Rem Koolhaas and Hans Ulrich Obrist, *Project Japan: Metabolism Talks . . .* (Koln: Taschen, 2011).

103. Reprinted in ibid., 207–21.

104. One reason why architects and urban planners are currently returning to the Metabolists is related to the growing interest in radical ecological studies, such as John Bellamy Foster's argument that there is a metabolistic rift between the social system of capitalism and the non-human natural system. For Foster, Marx had already recognized this rift in *Capital* when he criticized

capitalism's relation to soil fertility. The Metabolists, themselves inspired by Marxist theory, were trailblazers in incorporating these concerns into their urban plans and structures. John Bellamy Foster, *Marx's Ecology: Materialism and Nature* (New York: Monthly Review Press, 2000).

105. Isozaki Arata, *Japan-ness in Architecture*, trans. Sabu Kohso (Cambridge, MA: MIT Press, 2006), 89.

106. Ibid., 89.

107. Ibid., 84–88.

108. Ibid.

109. Ibid.

110. Ibid., 100.

111. Ibid.

112. Ibid.

113. Karatani Kōjin, "Jishin to Nihon," trans. Seiji Lippit, March 16, 2011. For an English version, see Karatani Kōjin, "Earthquake and Japan," http://www.kojinkaratani.com/en/article/earthquake -and-japan.html.

114. Karatani Kōjin, "Jishin to Nihon."

BUDDHAPHOBIA

NOTHINGNESS AND THE
FEAR OF THINGS

Timothy Morton

It's awfully considerate of you to think of me here
And I'm most obliged to you for making it clear
That I'm not here

SYD BARRETT

From 1962 to 1963 Jacques Lacan gave his tenth seminar. Its final hours are preoccupied with a rather searching and sensitive
assessment of Buddhism. Lacan had recently returned from Japan, where he visited a Buddhist shrine. It is illuminating to
observe Lacan translate Buddhism into his own terms. From
the standpoint of someone who has studied and practiced Buddhism extensively, Lacan is at the very least generous and illuminating.

Lacan takes the attitude of a careful guide. He explains how
Buddhist practitioners go through a number of phases of study
and practice. He distinguishes concepts such as *emptiness* from
Western mistranslations such as *nothingness*. (His discussion
of the Zen *kōan* on Joshu's Mu, for instance, is particularly at-
tentive.) He teases out distinctions between Buddhism and the
mindset that divides the world into monotheism and polythe-
ism. He thinks aloud about the multiplicity of Buddhas as mani-

festations of enlightenment—why this infinite mirroring? He knows fairly well what a bodhisattva is—a being who has taken on relieving all sentient beings of their suffering until they attain ultimate Buddhahood. He discusses his colleague Paul Demiéville's work on sudden versus gradual enlightenment.[1]

Then Lacan settles on an episode in the Japanese shrine concerning a Buddha statue:

> I enter the little hall where this statue is and I find there on his knees a man of thirty to thirty-five years old, a sort of very low-grade employee, perhaps a craftsman, already really very worn out by existence. He was on his knees before this statue and obviously he was praying . . . after having prayed, he came very close to the statue . . . he looked at it in this way for a time that I could not measure, I did not really see the end of it, it was superimposed itself on the time of my own look. It was obviously an overflowing look whose character was all the more extraordinary because it was a matter there, not I would say of an ordinary man—because a man who behaves in this way could not be such—but of someone that nothing seemed to predestine, if only because of the evident burden that he was carrying on this shoulders from his work, for this sort of artistic communion.
>
> You have seen the statue [Lacan is showing slides], its face, this expression which is absolutely astonishing because of the fact that it is impossible to read in it whether it is completely for you or completely inward looking. I did not know then that it was a Nio-i-yin, Kan-ze-non but I had heard tell for a long time of the Kuan-yin. I asked in connection with this statue and in connection with others also, "Is it a man or a woman?" I will skip over the debates, the detours of what happened around this question which is full of meaning, I repeat, in Japan, given that the Kannon are not all in a univocal fashion in a female form. And it is there that I can say that what I collected is a little bit like a survey at the level of the Kinsey Report, the fact is that I acquired the certainty that, for this cultured young man . . . the

question before a statue of this kind, as to whether it is male or female, never arose for them.[2]

This is a very rich narrative on the significance of the experience of beauty: on the look of statues, and the look of people who look at statues—and the voyeurism of people looking at people looking at statues, in particular from the sidelong, distorted (anamorphic) position of Lacan, and the paradox thereof: is the voyeur inside or outside the scene? Narrative form necessarily invites identification, fantasy, a certain sliding of anticipation and memory: the play of desire. And a certain gap between the subject of enunciation and the subject of the enunciated, a gap that Lacan detects in what is known as the Liar sentence: *This sentence is false.*[3]

Of particular note is Lacan's astonishment at the gaze of a Buddha statue: is it inward or outward? More pointedly, is it "for you" or "completely inward looking"? And further—is this a female or a male? There appear to be wavering ambiguities, even contradictions. Lacan sees the statue as a Rorschach test or even as a Kinsey Report on gender. Notice that the Kinsey Report reference turns the seeing of a man or a woman—or a gay man or a straight man?—in the statue into a test for queerness. And notice that despite Lacan's insistent questioning, no one seems concerned. There is something ambiguous, something queer about the statue—something that might awaken anxiety, but in the Buddhist context in which the statue is viewed, no one seems anxious. As I shall argue here, this queerness is precisely correlated to the irrational fear of Buddhism.

Indeed, many of the coordinates of what is here called *Buddhaphobia* overlap with those of homophobia: a fear of intimacy, a fear of ambiguity, a fear of inwardness and introversion, a fear of theory rather than praxis.[4] This is a fear that ultimately affects even those Marxian schools that most frequently correlate theory and praxis. Some kind of phobia certainly seems to affect the intellectualist and scientist "non-Buddhism" that claims to be above (and superior to) the sectarianism of what it patronizes as "X-buddhism." Indeed, the stance of non-Buddhism is quite sectarian in an unconscious manner, as it implies dismissing what in several esoteric schools is the most important cognitive state: devotion. For these schools, devotion is not simply devotion to a particular (human) person who transmits the teachings, though it may start there. Devotion is a nonconceptual intimacy of mind with itself. Heaven forbid that one have nonconceptual intimacy! It would ruin the sense of intellectual superiority.

As we proceed we shall find that the kind of syndrome exemplified here is not accidental. Indeed, François Laruelle, the avatar of non-Buddhism, provides a way of asserting that one's assertions are not philosophical, the sort of paradox that Lacan himself swept away in his critique of metalanguage. Non-philosophy provides non-Buddhism with a way of being above (meta) Buddhism while still making Buddhist assertions that claim to be more correct than what it calls "X-buddhism." How this fails to be a "decision" (a philosophical truth claim, in effect) eludes this author. It is patent enough that this decision about decision accepts uncritically the Western appropriation of Buddhadharma as an ism among isms, and reduces whatever Buddhism might be to a style (an ism) of thought, allowing non-Buddhism the typically modern consumerist gesture of disavowing consumerism, of trying to find an ism beyond ism. The decision of no decision ignores the symbiotic relationship between meditation experience and institutionalization: yogis and yoginis and the monasteries that spring up around the shrines that spring up around the caves or other spaces in which they have practiced. Siddhārtha Gautama was, it should be remembered, a heretical Hindu yogi.

Alongside predictable fascination-anger with the language of addiction (because it short circuits the idea of a subject being able to jump outside its phenomenological system), a symptom of the "anything you can do, I can do meta" of non-Buddhism is the pervasive critique of mindfulness, whose contemporary Western practice non-Buddhism denigrates as "relaxationism" and which Žižek denigrates as "Western Buddhism." Naturally the critique of mindfulness is not surprising to an "X-buddhist": Buddhist texts are full of critiques of mindfulness. Moreover mindfulness, calm attention on something or other (breath, statue, a chicken one is murdering), is not in fact Buddhist, but rather common to numerous spiritual practices. The fatuous reduction of Buddhism, even New Age Buddhisms, to "relaxationism" is less intelligent than . . . Buddhisms as such, which in none of their forms claim that calm attention is the point. *Awareness* might be the point, or a point—but it's what one is aware of that is the real point: impermanence, suffering, emptiness. Mindfulness might be a way to achieve awareness, or not.

The critique of mindfulness is immanent to Buddhisms. So much so that one might say that to critique mindfulness is . . . to be a Buddhist. Indeed, the Buddhist critique is far more searching, insofar as it does not suggest that mindfulness is evil or complicit with oppression, as if running around screaming and hitting one another were a path to realization (how's that been working out?). Rather, Buddhisms suggest that mindfulness is a helpful way to induce a state of relaxed attentiveness necessary for most people to notice some basic facts.

Queerness is, in Buddhaphobia at any rate, predicated on a fear of things, or of a certain feature of thingness, conjured up in the idea of fetishism, which has long been associated with homosexuality since the inception of the term in the later nineteenth century. That is to say, queerness has to do with what Judith Halberstam examines as an inverted fear of being buried alive—that something, some thing, is buried in me.[5] There is an entity in me that is not me. As we shall see, this idea compresses a central tenet of Mahāyāna Buddhism concerning Buddha nature—it is an entity in me that is more than me. For specific forms of Western thought, this entity has an intolerable object-like quality. Buddhaphobia assumes the form of an allergic reaction to this quality. The allergic reaction maps onto the always-already presence of Buddhism, and of what we shall call nothingness, within Western thinking.

I shall call it *nothingness* here, despite Lacan's careful parsing of nothingness versus emptiness. The term *nothingness* is pervasive. Furthermore, it cuts to the heart of the matter—it is a term with feet in Western and Eastern thought. Indeed, philosophers such as Nishitani, inspired by Buddhism and Western philosophy in equal measure, deploy the term. And, perhaps most significantly, nothingness evokes the specter of nihilism, the specter that haunts modernity.

In what follows, I shall be following the viewpoint of what in the esoteric Buddhism called Mahamudra is known as "the analytic meditation of a pandita."[6] I use this approach because as a proud "X-buddhist" member of the Drupka Kagyü sect of Tibetan Buddhism, I am most familiar with it. This sect regards the teachings of Mahamudra ("Great Symbol") and Dzogchen ("Great Perfection") to be practically identical. In those teachings, the Buddha nature is not to be sought anywhere outside of one's regular mentations (philosophizing, asserting, loving, hoping, hating, fearing, desiring, and so on). It is not to be striven for at all, but rather appreciated for what it already is— the essence of one's mind. And yet there is a sharp difference between such mentations, which are confused, and the basic default state, which manifests all the aspects of Buddha mind: unchanging, open, lucid, compassionate, suffused with renunciation and devotion. It is just that the Buddha mind is discovered to be the default state of mind as such. The analytic meditation of a pandita is intended not to produce concepts but to allow one to appreciate the default state.

Yet some reckoning with concepts must happen in a scholarly essay. The intellectual approach I adopt in this case is that favored by Mahamudra and Dzogchen, namely that of the Prāsaṅgika Madhyamaka exemplified by Chandrakīrti.[7] This approach is most similar to the destructuring of thought common to Heidegger and Derrida. In this thought, nothing (reified or conceptual) is posited. Instead, all reified positions are deconstructed until their inherent paradoxes and aporias are unloosened. Thus Prāsaṅgika is used as a tool to exhaust conceptual mind, allowing the default state (known in Dzogchen as *rigpa*) to become obvious. This default state knows itself as such as a possibility condition for its existence. We shall return to this idea of self-knowing as not outside and "meta" but as inherent to what mind is. This is because it is the grounding feature of the default state that I claim Buddhaphobia finds so uncomfortable.

In short, the goal is to appreciate what is already the case (Buddha mind), rather than to produce axioms, which non-Buddhism appears to be doing about what it construes Buddhism to be doing. Appreciation is what is known as the aesthetic experience in Western philosophy, and it is the best translation I can think of for *gom*, which is the Tibetan for *meditation*: it literally means "growing accustomed to," without applying a prefabricated technique. Which is why, *pace* non-Buddhism, it is referred to by Mahamudra and Dzogchen as *non-meditation*. It is the role of the aesthetic that is key to understanding Buddhaphobia, which appears to regard it as an optional extra, often unpleasant.

Meditative appreciation is *of itself*, in this case—there is, claims the esoteric view, an awareness that knows itself as such without an infinite regress of meta-ness. To this extent it is "secret," not only because the instructions for this meditation are orally transmitted under special circumstances, but because they depend upon actualization to be appreciated, and because what is appreciated is vivid but unspeakable. There is no way to figure out what the view is about in advance. Thus doing or making (as Latour might say, *assembling*) has ontological priority over thinking or understanding, which is what differentiates this lineage of Buddhism (often called the *practice lineage*), headed by the Karmapas, from more scholarly lineages such as the Gelugpa, headed by the Dalai Lamas.

The best reason to use Mahamudra and Dzogchen is that the self-appreciation they evoke is a key irritant to Buddhaphobia. Yet the paradoxical cut between understanding and actualizing suggested here evokes the paradoxical differences between theory and praxis in critical theory.

NOTHINGNESS AND ANXIETY

The sexual ambiguity of the statue coupled with its seeming coy inwardness evoke anxiety, the topic of Lacan's seminar. As in Heidegger, from whom Lacan learned much, anxiety is the one emotion that never lies.[8] Anxiety is fear without an object—fear as such, fear as one's inner space, opened and opening, strung out in temporality, in a shifting, ill-defined shadow zone.[9] Anxiety awakens the disturbance of nothingness. Western Buddhisms— for instance, the one promoted by Tibetan émigré Chögyam Trungpa—weave this existential insight into their view. The point of meditation, argues Trungpa, is to cut through the emotional babble down to the basic affect, the bedrock "basic anxiety" of existing as such.[10] Thus meditation is correlated with a certain variant of the psychoanalytic project, and indeed with the "Daseinanalysis" that Heidegger pioneered with Medard Boss.[11] Lacan appears to have intuited that there might be a Buddhist approach to subverting—literally passing beneath—anxiety.

Lacan recounts how the statue has been stroked, perhaps for centuries, as if the Buddhist nuns who stroked it were wiping away imaginary tears. The statue "represents in its polish this unbelievable something of which the photo here can only give you a vague reflection of what is the inverted radiation onto it of what one cannot fail to recognise as something like a long desire borne throughout the centuries by these recluses toward this divinity of psychologically indeterminable sex."[12] The object has become a fetish, a thing that shimmers with a weird not-quite-agency, "an inverted radiation."

Consider the distortion Lacan narrates—looking sidelong at someone looking at a statue not looking at either, unable to see the man directly. And observing the shiny trace of fetishistic touching rendered in the slide by "the inverted radiation onto it." The breathless, unpunctuated hypotaxis of the prose also does something anamorphic, like Deckard in *Blade Runner* honing in on an implanted memory by rotating and zooming into an image, trying to see it from an impossible point of view oblique to the picture plane. Is this fetishistic gaze like a metalanguage, successfully outside the gravitational field of the Buddhist man's devotion? Or is it an uncanny *doubling* of that devotion, a photographic and grammatical rendering of it, clinical detachment aside, caught in its weird logic? The uncertainty might make some philosophers anxious.

It is indeed a reaction to fetishism that constitutes an essential ingredient in Buddhaphobia. Despite the impossibilities and paradoxes of thinking a subject behind or beyond fetishism, within Lacanian theory; despite its debt to the post-Kantian lineage in which Lacan's thinking of fetishism manifests; when it comes to Buddhism, Buddhaphobia labors to think outside the fetish. It postures itself as demystification.

For Lacan, anxiety is correlated with the "sliding of the signifier": the fact that when I arrive at two doors, one of which says "LADIES" and the other of which says "GENTLEMEN" I supplant the basic anxiety of not knowing which one to enter with a fantasy that I am the kind of person who goes through *this* not *that* door.[13] Is the door with a label on it not uncannily like the statue in a certain respect? It is a physical entity on top of which floats a semiotic one. In the same way, the statue is a piece of porcelain or stone that seems to gaze, that seems to appear as a woman, or is it a man? What the statue and the toilet door evoke is the nothingness of fantasy, the way it oozes around things, filling them in yet undermining them by supplementing them. Buddhaphobia is in a certain sense a fear of fantasy as such.

Lacan employs the Kinsey Reports as a simile for his questioning of Buddhist practitioners concerning the gender of the Buddha statue he has seen. The relevant thing about the Kinsey Reports is that their form replicates precisely this paradox. In personal interviews I discover varieties of possible identities and fantasies. I answer according to my investment in them. Such is the logic of the consumer survey and of the *Cosmopolitan* quiz ("Are you *x*? Take our quiz and find out"), a logic to which we shall return when we examine in more detail the extent to which Buddhaphobia is indeed a certain fear of consumerism. Such a report on fantasy also raises the specter of infinite regress, because I have fantasies about what sorts of fantasy I have. The specter, to be more precise, of an infinite loop in which my fantasy becomes the object of my fantasy. Perhaps there is no way to exit this loop. We shall see how a certain fear of loops is also an essential ingredient of Buddhaphobia.

Why a statue? Why this obsession with an object that looks like a person? Or is it a person transformed into stone or metal? Is that in fact exactly the point: Buddhisms suggesting that what beats at the heart of every sentient being—what makes them sentient as such, even—is an object-like presence? Protestations of being above such things notwithstanding, is a fear of (nonconceptual) physicality the core of Buddhaphobia?

The loop-like self-enclosure of this object, with its ambiguous gaze, brings up the question of narcissism, another component of Buddhaphobia. Narcissism finds the world to be its mirror. Is this not another intimacy with Buddhism at the heart of modern philosophy? Since, that is, for Hegel and Kant, reality appears for a subject—it is opaque until I see it, just as I know the light is on in the refrigerator only when I open it. We have here an anxious doublet: the dark, withdrawn opacity of a thing, and the fact that it reflects me when I apprehend it. The thing in itself disappears, yet it is uncannily "there." This paradox is also intrinsic to Mahāyāna Buddhist theories of emptiness, which play on the theme of mirror reflections.

The ultimate refuge of the narcissistic personality—that is, *someone whose narcissism is wounded*—is the accusation that the other is narcissistic. Like the person who says "I don't like bullies" and then proceeds to bully you, the wounded narcissist is obsessed with pointing out the other's narcissism. Hegel's nightmare of Buddhism is an image he assumes to be deeply narcissistic: a statue of a baby sucking its toe. In actual fact this is a Hindu image, of Krishna Narayan from the *Markandeya*

Purana, a point that underlines the state of orientalist scholarship in Hegel's time, and perhaps also his willingness to see Buddhism a certain way—to project Buddhaphobia onto a conveniently available Indian object. Hegel's fascination with the toe-sucking Krishna exhibits the rather common orientalist racism that "Asians" are "inscrutable."

How dare those Buddha statues not look at me directly? How dare they turn their eyes downward, as if inward? Are they secretly conspiring against me? Are they faceless, desireless automata? Buddha statues are evil insofar as they are passive, like Melville's Bartleby the Scrivener. Bartleby is a significant figure for thinking of a number of issues in contemporary theory, from biopower to political struggle. Yet theory's exasperation with Buddhism reads almost exactly like the exasperation with Bartleby among the characters in Melville's tale: he just sits there, preferring not to. In other registers, however, theory is quite happy with Bartleby, from Levinas, Blanchot, and Agamben (as Thomas Carl Wall has shown) to Žižek's own contribution to the *TRIOS* series.[14] So theory seems to have little space as yet for an explicitly Buddhist Bartleby. It seems evident that in attacking the passive Bartleby-like statue, I am attacking inner space as such, trying to close the gap between what a thing is and how it appears. (In this volume, Eric Cazdyn's essay examines Isozaki's notion of *ma* in a similar vein.)

I now begin to use Žižek as the touchstone for a certain contemporary manifestation of Buddhaphobia. I do this not in the spirit of undermining Žižek's philosophical view, but rather of exploring the coordinates of a structure of feeling that shapes his thought. This structure of feeling has to do with deep and pervasive currents in modern philosophy and social space. In particular, Žižek's explicit pitting of (Hegelian, Marxist, Lacanian) theory against Buddhism will be subject to scrutiny here.[15] What will emerge is the necessity of thinking of Buddhism and theory together.

This thinking, with regard to Lacan, is underway within Lacanianism itself, as the work of Raul Moncayo amply demonstrates.[16] One suspects that his work, albeit stamped with the imprimatur of one of the world's foremost psychoanalytic presses, would still not meet with approval from the Žižekian strain of thought, favoring as it does what it calls a "postmodern" approach that separates "spirituality" (good) from "religion" (bad). That this line of argument has roots in the Frankfurt school, well cited by Moncayo, is ironic, given the school's own indebtedness to a certain Hegelianism of its own.

In Hegel's rage against a static image, there is something uncannily similar to the Taliban assault on the Buddhas of Bamiyan, endorsed by Žižek—along the lines of "at least the Muslims were sticking up for their beliefs!"[17] These assaults are profoundly symptomatic of Buddhaphobia. As Žižek argues in *The Sublime Object of Ideology*, the sadist reduces the other to a malleable, faceless cartoon he can beat up without consequences.[18] Like a statue. Statues cannot take offence. But what if they could? Žižek's equation of Buddhism with capitalist complicity—I can shop and subject myself to capital while I meditate, blissfully detached in a Matrix-like simulation of happiness—has to do with the fear of a certain kind of object, an object such as a statue that appears to have a weird agency. And can't we discern this agency, goes the fantasy, in the aesthetic seduction of the (consumerist) object? In his equation of Buddhism and capitalism, it appears as if Žižek does not credit this part of Lacan's seminar with the seriousness and relevance it might obtain in other hands. Why this disavowal of his father, Lacan? Why his return to grandfather Hegel, who expresses nothing but fascinated horror at the prospect of Buddhas, beings who directly embody nothingness?[19]

It is to Hegel that Žižek looks for his Buddhaphobia. Lacan's discussion eerily echoes Hegel's discussion of another statue in his far less sensitive treatment of Buddhism: "The image of Buddha in the thinking posture, with feet and arms intertwined so that a toe extends into the mouth—this [is] the withdrawal into self, this absorption in oneself."[20] This image provocatively illuminates a self-enclosure commonly associated with the aesthetic. Indeed, Kant's *Critique of Judgment* had specified that the experience of beauty was one of an object-like entity discovered in one's experiential "inner" space, insofar as the beautiful thing cannot be dissected or analyzed further: it is just there, yet it is ungraspable.[21]

Since Kant is definitely in Lacan's lineage, I now bring him into the conversation. Lacan names an experience of "artistic communion" in his discussion of his apprehension of the "look" of the man in the Japanese temple, regarding the statue:

> It was obviously an overflowing look whose character was all the more extraordinary because it was a matter there, not I would say of an ordinary man—because a man who behaves in this way could not be such—but of someone that nothing seemed to predestine, if only because of the evident burden that he was carrying on this shoulders from his work, for this sort of artistic communion.

The man's apparent inner state differs from his appearance to Lacan. It is as if Lacan is noting the phenomenon-thing gap in the man himself, and without doubt this underscores how the man's experience is being seen through a Kantian lens. For Kant beauty just is a "thing" I find in my inner space, a thing that is not conditioned by me, or by the thing from which I seem to have obtained the experience (such as the statue). The experience of nonconceptual beauty underwrites the transcendental aesthetic with which Kant begins the *Critique of Pure Reason*. There are raindrops, but I cannot apprehend them directly: I only perceive raindrop phenomena, these wet splashes on my head (Kant's own example).[22] Raindrops are raindrops—they are raindroppy, not gumdroppy. Yet I can't tell beforehand where raindrop phenomena end and the "actual" raindrop thing starts. I cannot specify in advance a metaphysical dotted line that decisively separates phenomenon from thing. Thus ends the lineage of scholasticism, where I can make ontological statements without referring to the strange, loop-like way in which the subject is already "there" in some kind of relation with the object, always-already. The self-enclosure of a raindrop depends upon a disturbing gap between raindrop as phenomenon and raindrop as thing, a gap that I cannot locate in advance in ontically given, phenomenal space.

Hegel resolves this tension by arguing that since I, the subject, can know the phenomenon-thing gap, there is no (actual) gap. Kant's delicate "correlationism" collapses into Hegelian idealism.[23] What Hegel manages to avoid here is precisely *nothing* or rather *nothingness*, a nothing that is not absolutely nothing at all, which Paul Tillich calls an *oukontic* nothing, but rather what he calls a *meontic* flickering, a-ness that is unlocatable yet real and palpable. This nothingness Hegel associates with the Fichtean I and with A=A, the ground of logic that seems to have one foot, or perhaps a toe, disturbingly outside the dialectic. And he associates both the transcendental I and A=A with a certain primitive form of consciousness, a form that he calls *Buddhism*.[24] In other words, Buddhaphobia is a condition for thinking: Buddhism is what must be rejected in order to have logic at all.

What Hegel wards off is the nothingness that plagues philosophy in modernity. One could imagine the whole of philosophy (at least Continental, if not the anxious police work of analytic philosophy against phenomena such as self-reference) as a family of stances regarding meontic nothingness. And one could readily correlate these stances to thoughts about Buddhisms, the "religion of nothingness."[25] Schopenhauer, for instance, far friendlier to Kant and actively hostile to Hegel, ended *The World as Will and Representation* with the word *nothing*, a word that appears explicitly as a reference to the Prajñāpāramitā Sūtra, the great Buddhist Mahāyāna text concerning nothingness (or emptiness, *shunyatā*), the Sūtra of the Heart of Transcendent Knowledge.[26] Nietzsche was evidently concerned by the soft, passive nihilism he finds in Buddhism. Heidegger was fascinated by possible connections between emptiness and the nothingness that he sees as a necessary way stage on the journey out of modernity, and his conversations with the Kyoto School (Nishida, Nishitani, and others) bear this out.

So despite Lacan's sensitivity to the differences between emptiness and nothingness, we might usefully find affinities. Such affinities are, after all, one reason why Lacan finds it necessary to tease them apart. The basic argument of the essay will be that nothingness is always already installed within Western philosophy. It is this intimacy to Western thinking that some philosophy finds allergenic. The nothingness is the basis for the Jesuit misrecognition of Buddhism in Tibet, a miscrecognition that influenced Hegel powerfully:

Sie sagen, dass das leere oder Nichts, dere Unsang aller Dinge sen; dass aus diesem Nichts und aus der Bermischung [Vermmischung] der Elemente, alle Dinge hervorgebracht sind, und dahin wieder zuruct sehren mussen; dass alle Wesen, sowohl belebte als unbelebte, nur in der Gestalt und in den Eigenschaften von einander unterschieden sind: in Betrachtung des Ubwesens oder Grundstoffs aber, einerlen bleiben.[27]

They say that mere Nothingness is the basis of all things; that all things are brought out of this Nothing and out of the mingling of the elements, and must tend back there again; that all phenomena, both living and non-living, are only different from one another in form and in superficial properties: upon examination/ contemplation of phenomena or basic elements, however, nothing besides remains.

"Der Nichts" (the Nothing) evidently resonates with Genesis 1:2 ("without form and void") and with Neoplatonic Christian doctrines of the infinite void, doctrines made compulsory in 1277 and strangely repeated in the Newtonian and Cartesian consensus.[28] Yet it is couched here as disturbing: how can a whole society think like that? Thanks to Alexander, Pyrrho had been influenced in his radical skepticism by Mahāyāna Buddhist doctrines of emptiness—or was it the other way around? The undecidability on the direction of the transmission speaks to a philosophical miscegenation that many Western philosophers have found disturbing. In particular, by the time we get to the modern age with its Kant and its Hegel, philosophy is supposed decisively not to be religion. Kant was supposed to have placed philosophy safely beyond metaphysics. Yet here we have the possibility that Western philosophy has religious DNA—the DNA of a non-Western religion, to boot.

Pyrrhonian skepticism is akin to the Prāsaṅgika Madhyamaka, insofar as it abstains from positive statements. Nothingness is wedded to the unspeakable: a mountain, a tree, a stone is beyond concept—there is an irreducible gap between what we say it is and what it is. But . . . isn't this just Kantianism? A nervous Hegelian might blanch. The installation of nothingness deep in Western thought is disavowed in the Buddhaphobic imaginary. For instance, consider the loop-like quality of this encyclopedia entry: "They say that mere Nothingness is the basis of all things; that all things are brought out of this Nothing and out of the mingling of the elements, and must tend back there again." A profound anxiety about self-reference extends through modernity from Hegel to Russell. Yet does this language not evoke the loop-like zeugmas of Genesis 3:19 ("Dust thou art, and unto dust thou shalt return") and the "ashes to ashes" and "dust to dust" of the Anglican burial service? Yet the loop form of coming from and returning to nothing is precisely what the Jesuit missionaries—the source for this encyclopedia entry—hold up for suspicious inspection.

NOTHING AND THE PHYSICAL

Meontic nothing is disturbing because it is palpable—it is not absolutely nothing at all. Imagine the universe according to Spinoza, in which there is absolutely nothing apart from substance, or the Deleuzian realm in which there is no lack: there is "not even nothing" in such a world. On the other hand, a world in which there is nothingness is a world in which I can detect that things are not as they seem. And the trouble with this is precisely what Lacan says about pretense: "What constitutes pretense is that, in the end, you don't know whether it's pretense or not."[29]

What this means is that nothingness is strangely *physical*. It is not physical in the way that metaphysics, and the metaphysics of presence in particular, specify: I cannot grasp the raindrop in itself, whereas for standard Aristotelian ontology, I can absolutely do this. Likewise in post-Kantian eliminative materialism, I can also do it: I can strip away appearances and end up with the thing. The way the thing exists, for Aristotle and for eliminative materialism, is as a presence that constantly subtends the (illusory or accidental) appearance of a thing. Thus we might see eliminative materialism as a falling away from Kant, another reaction to him, sharing something with Hegel's idealism insofar as it disavows the anxiety of the phenomenon-thing gap.

What we are dealing with here is what we know familiarly as the metaphysics of presence: for something to be real, it must be constantly present. The metaphysics of presence is strikingly similar to the Buddhist Mahāyāna ("Great Vehicle") concept of *eternalism*: the idea that there exists a single, independent, and lasting entity (or more) beneath appearances. And it is also weirdly similar to what this doctrine calls *nihilism*: the idea that there is absolutely nothing underlying appearances at all. Both these views are held to be mistaken extremes in the Mahāyāna. The correct view lies "between" them, not as a compromise but as a radical transcendence of both: this is what is called *emptiness*, or what this essay calls meontic nothingness.

Let us consider the ways in which Western avoidances of the Kantian gap are ways of foreclosing nothingness. For instance, consider the scientistic idea that the mind is totally reducible to the brain. I call it *scientistic* because, strictly speaking, science can't make metaphysical assertions about what is real. Scientism should be rigorously distinguished from science, and not all scientists are scientistic. Indeed, scientism finds its most hospitable welcome outside the science departments, with some exceptions. Unlike theoretical physics, psychology is currently prone to scientism. The reduction of mind to brain has some support among psychologists such as Wilfrid Sellars and some scholars who themselves draw on Buddhism for support—for instance, Thomas Metzinger, whose *Being No One* asserts that the mind is simply an epiphenomenon of the brain.[30] This argument closely resembles some forms of Theravadin Buddhist "atomism" and the exiled Dalai Lama (head of the Gelugpa lineage of Tibetan Buddhism), eager for support, is prone to endorse it with a verve that sometimes seems uncomfortably like Stockholm Syndrome. And yet, any Buddhist would note that such a view as Metzinger's lacks the sense in which Buddhist "atoms" are phenomenological. Buddhist "dharmas" ("atoms" in this case) are somewhat sophisticated correlations of subject and object. To have a raindrop, there must be a drop of rain, eyes to see it, a field of vision ("eye consciousness dhatu") and a capacity of sight, a mind to know that it's a raindrop, and so on. This applies to each sense organ. A raindrop is more like a rainbow, on this view: a viewer is intrinsic to it.

Yet for eliminative materialism, there is no subject at all, no need for senses or sense fields or consciousness. The Buddhist concept is being used as window dressing, as if scientism were insufficient in itself, or as if scientism had more in common with religion than with science—both of which are true statements.

Since according to materialist reductionism one can say everything about minds in terms of brains, then there is no such thing as mind. That is why the most extreme version is known as *eliminative* materialism. Such a move reduces or collapses the phenomenon-thing gap, since the mind is taken as less real than the brain. Mind is just how a brain appears. There is nothing in particular to worry about: brains are more real than minds, or minds are totally unreal. The view that brains subtend minds upgrades the metaphysics of presence with a post-Kantian twist. But raindrop appearances are not less real than raindrops: when a raindrop splashes on me, I detect a raindrop, not a gumdrop. One might surmise that the eagerness with which eliminative psychology embraces Buddhism is in part an unconscious attempt to stuff the genie of nothingness back in the bottle, by accommodating Buddhism to a form of materialism that even Theravadin schools might balk at. To say that there is no mind whatsoever, but that there are neurons, is not the same thing as saying that entities are phenomenological constructs, which is more like what even the earlier Buddhist schools argue.

Something is "there." There are raindrops. There is mind. Yet how? Fear of nothingness is fear of a certain *physicality*, a physicality whose phenomena I cannot predictably demarcate from its reality in advance. We can guess, then, that this physicality has the quality of *givenness*—it is just "there" yet not in a way I can grasp conceptually. Nothingness, as Levinas argues, has to do with the "there is" quality of givenness.[31] It forms the necessarily disturbing substrate of my phenomenal experience, disturbing precisely because it is not "just stuff" just some kind of neutral stage set on which I strut and fret my hour. Since there is a gap between phenomenon and thing, I experience such a givenness as a distortion of my phenomenal world.[32] Something is wrong, out of joint, glimpsed out of the corner of my eye, a slight flickering. There seems to be some correlation between this idea, which is housed in phenomenological theology, and the Buddhist Prajñāpāramitā Sūtra's notion of emptiness: "Form is emptiness, emptiness is form."[33] Eliminative materialisms and idealisms have little trouble with the first formula (*form is emptiness*). Scientism takes this phrase to mean that it is vindicated. It is the second one, *emptiness is form*, that disturbs.

This trouble is ironically also common to the experiential etiology of a Buddhist meditator. As Trungpa puts it, "Form comes back."[34] Reductionism and elimination make one feel clever, but what happens when the meditator drops her fixation on feeling clever? Or consider the frequently repeated slogan of the Sōtō Zen master Dōgen: *first there are mountains, then there are no mountains, then there are mountains.* Is it not the case that what appropriations of Buddhism within eliminative psychology ward off is precisely the third statement? What on earth could it mean?

Nothingness is not nothing at all, so it is physical, but not in the sense of constant presence. Nothingness is disturbing. It is there, in a mind-independent sense; it is part of what is given. But I cannot see it directly. There is a weird crack in my world. Perhaps there is only one crack—the one between subject and nonsubject: this is how Kantians (and others including Heidegger) police the gap, by putting some kind of copyright control on it. Or perhaps there are as many gaps as there are things, and relations between things. This is what object-oriented ontology has begun to think about the phenomenon-thing gap.

Let us distinguish this nothingness from the Neoplatonic void established in 1277 by the Bishop of Paris and underwritten by Papal edict, and not really challenged, even in physics, until Einstein's idea of space-time. Space-time is much more congruent with nothingness because space-time is *form*: an aesthetic (in an expanded sense) rippling that emanates from things, rather than the blank smooth container of things. It was postulated in the thirteenth century that it would be heretical to consider God powerless to have made anything at all; therefore he could have made an infinite void; therefore he did.[35] The Neoplatonic void is just a metaphysically present something or other, constantly there, surrounding things. Nothingness, by contrast, is far closer to esoteric concepts in medieval theology such as the cloud of unknowing or the dark night of the soul.[36] Such concepts have periodically been condemned . . . as forms of Buddhism.

Schopenhauer made the nothingness in Kant explicit by positing a gigantic ocean of Will that lies behind appearances, or as he calls them, "representations." Raindrops, flowers, Buddha statues and humans are all manifestations of Will. Will is a surging machination behind appearances, such that when you strike me, that is Will striking itself.[37] In every action, Will is looping into itself. This loop-like, self-devouring presence is not merely a blank, constant opacity. Will is more like an oceanic whirl, a modern version of any number of ouroboric beings that delimit the universe. Such a whirl is not unrelated to the historical moment of *The World as Will and Representation*. The nineteenth century witnessed the discovery and manufacture of entities (such as evolution) of a scale sufficient to allow the phenomenon-thing gap to become manifest, opening up the conditions under which Schopenhauer glimpsed Will in operation behind this gap.

Reading Schopenhauer makes it plain that this thought occurs at the exact moment at which science discovers vast machinations such as geological time. Will far outstrips the human subject, although Schopenhauer regards the human subject is its most perfect representation to date. Schopenhauer talks of seeds that have lain dormant for thousands of years, waiting to sprout in the right conditions.[38] Seemingly inert things take on a weird life—weird, because it operates outside the domain of those beings we metaphysically posit as "alive," such that "life" in this case has more in common with the undead. Indeed, as the phenomenon-thing gap begins to be thought it eats away at rigid boundaries between life and nonlife, such that more and more beings inhabit a spectral realm in between the worn-out categories of animate and inanimate. Darwin's argument in miniature is that there are no species as such, yet there are ducks and worms; yet it is next to impossible to specify exactly when a proto-duck evolves into a duck. Evolution pulsates with nothingness, riven from within by uncanny gaps that proliferate everywhere. In the same way, Marxian capital cannot be seen or touched directly, but rather it is a spectral "vampire" eating away at the seemingly solid world: "All that is solid melts into air."[39] In evolution and capitalism, nothingness gains a disturbing actuality. It can be exhilarating, refreshing, erotic, horrifying, strange. The Derridean term for these weird beings is *hauntology*, a term similar to *différance* insofar as it contains a silent difference from itself, enacting nothingness in language.[40] From Freudian dreamwork to Derridean *différance*, nothingness pervades theories of how language, meaning, and thought interact.

Nothingness is thus firmly installed in contemporary Western philosophy, thanks to a confluence of events in social and ecological space, and of events in the realms of thought. It is precisely this installation of nothingness, always already, that causes a reaction to Buddhism, a reaction that takes the form of an allergy: an autoimmune response in which thought goes into a self-destructive loop concerning something already present within it.

NOTHINGNESS AND ENJOYMENT

What drew Hegel to the image of Krishna Narayan? Was it perhaps because the classic image of a meditating Buddha, with crossed legs, appeared to lack the crucial element of self-pleasuring, of auto-affection? After all, Krishna-Vishnu is actually sucking his big toe, wondering why the liquid that it touches tastes so sweet. The way the image is quilted onto Buddhism is precisely the "intertwining" which Hegel says applies to "feet and arms."[41] Krishna-Vishnu only holds one foot with one hand. If you want intertwined arms, and intertwined feet, look at a classic Buddha image. It is as if Hegel blends the intertwining of the Buddhist image with the self-pleasuring of the Hindu one.

There is indeed a kind of enjoyment in a Buddha image. The pervasive prejudice that Buddhists are all about transcending pleasure and pain is somewhat correct, at least as regards Theravadin Buddhisms. But is the Buddha in the classic image enjoying his lack of enjoyment? His enigmatic, Mona Lisa–like smile might suggest something like a perverse inner state of bliss that he is not quite giving away, like the cat that got the cream, or the Hindu god who got the cream from his toe.[42] Sucking is a heightened form of breathing, as if meditators were not simply respiring but ingesting—taking in flesh, not air. Hegel is fascinated and horrified by blissful experiences of infantile pleasure, pleasure available to ordinary mortals like Siddhārtha Gautama. This is, after all, the polar opposite of Christ on the cross (a tortured, dying god). This image is alarming more in the eyes of the Hegel than in itself: babies gleefully suck their toes all the time, and indeed Krishna Narayana is the form of a toe-sucking baby.

Though the image is Hindu, it does indeed capture something some non-Buddhists find disturbing in Tantric Buddhist images of sexual union (Tibetan, *yab-yum*). In these images, a female Buddha copulates with a male one. Yet both are aspects of the "same" thing, existing in inseparable union (Sanskrit, *yoga*)—the knower and what is known. It is here that we could turn to Luce Irigaray for an explicitly anti-Hegelian argument that at least one entity (woman) cannot be reduced to a one, or subdivided into a two.[43] What Irigaray is describing is in a sense a *fractal* entity, a being who exists in a transfinite space between one and two. Fractal things are made by loops in which functions are iterated by being fed back into themselves.

Hegel's image of the toe sucker rather wonderfully transmutes the image of appearance and essence in union (but also in duality) that is too easy to see as a perfect harmony. Harmony would require some medium in which the harmony could occur, and there is no such medium, for there is only appearance and "essence." Hegel morphs the *yab-yum* into its rightly disturbing double of sensual passivity: the penile toe penetrating the vaginal mouth, the vaginal mouth sucking in the penile toe. Since Krishna-Vishnu is sucking the toe to see how it makes things taste so sweet, the toe is also a nipple, so there is indeed a polymorphous, queer sexuality here that Hegel finds impossible to contain. His own prose repeats ungrammatically, as if lubricated, enacting the looped disturbance: "This [is] the withdrawal into self, this absorption in oneself."[44]

Let us not forget the "intertwined" arms and feet. It is somewhat strange that the feet and arms intertwine "so that a toe extends into the mouth." *So that?* Why would intertwining have to take place before a toe could go in a mouth? It is as if there is already an embrace of the body by itself as another. Moreover, it is as if, in the "so that" the toe has taken on a horrifying life of its own, wiggling away from the life of totalizing spirit. The toe "extends" it wants to thrust itself down the throat, like a penis, or like one of Francis Bacon's figures disappearing into a keyhole or a washbasin.[45] Would it have been less disturbing if the mouth had (actively) tried to swallow the toe? The translation captures something of the Cartesian view of matter as sheer "extension" so that we find ourselves unable to tell whether there is a willing subject "behind" the toe's descent into the mouth's wet cavity. The extension of the toe (willed or not? by the mind, or by the toe itself?) is precisely self-annihilating, and pleasurably so. The mixture of sexuality and death could not be harder to miss. Or is it asexual pleasure? Or presexual?

THE THINKING POSTURE

The toe sucker is physically introverting. The body turns round on itself and disposes of itself down one of its own holes. Being loses its spiritual or ideal aspect and actually *becomes* this very image, as in Hegel's telling syntax: "The image of Buddha . . . this [is] the withdrawal into self." Hegel repetitively adds "this absorption in oneself" as if he himself is incapable of getting away from the fascinating, sucking loop—he sucks his own language. There is a swirl of enjoyment, a sucking backwash that is not a standstill, but rather an entirely different order of being. This Buddhist being is only recognizable in Hegel's universe as an inconsistent distortion, at once too insubstantial and too solid. Buddhism is nothingness in all its palpitating weirdness. The circle of the toe sucker is a blank zero that is not utterly nothing, but rather becomes heavy and dense, unable to shift itself into dialectical gear. The body circulates its touching everywhere—arms and feet, as well as toe and mouth.

Meditation is tantamount to reducing the body to a horrifying inertia, a *body without organs* in the Deleuzian-Guattarian terminology.[46] The nearest approximation is a black hole, a physicality so intense that no information escapes from it. On the other hand, the image is made of organs rather than a single, independent body. If Hegel is terrified of the static body without organs of the meditating ascetic, in which the inside of the body threatens to swallow all trace of working limbs, perhaps the description also evokes an even greater panic concerning the possibility of *organs without bodies*. As one starts to examine the image, nothingness proliferates into a veritable sea of holes. The zero of the open mouth, stuffed full of the body of which it forms a part, while the body curls around in a giant, fleshy zero too, like a doughnut: this is the inconsistent, compelling image, the fascinating kernel of Hegel's fixation.[47] (How many times has one heard that doing yoga is bending oneself like a pretzel—something one puts in one's mouth?)

Buddhisms do indeed assert that physical posture not only supports meditation, but also embodies it, as in yoga and mudra (gesture), where postures enact forms of enlightenment, and not only symbolically. According to the scriptures, these postures straighten the channels (*nadi*) and allow the energies (*prana*) to flow smoothly in their loops. For the energy circulates in all kinds of loops that can be debilitating or energizing: loops upon loops, multiplying what Hegel takes to be the pathological symptom of a stunted belief. As any Buddhist meditator could have told Hegel, meditation is indeed a highly physical process. This idea of "posture" is disturbingly between categories of mind and body. It resembles the asanas of yoga, postures that induce the "subtle body" to become smooth and pliable. A glance at the reception (or lack thereof) of Irigaray's work on yoga and in particular on prana betrays the still-operative orientalism and intellectualism that can cope (in the modern academy) with meditation as long as it seems clean and abstract or like a sport, but wants little to do with channels and loops of energy.[48] One of the disturbing things about this subtle body is that it blatantly defies the Law of the Excluded Middle, the logical rule that underwrites default Cartesian dualism of body and mind; or more accurately, and more drastically, soul and extension. Western philosophy still remains all too comfortable with this dualism. The Law of the Excluded Middle derives from the Law of Noncontradiction, which we will also see violated as we proceed.

Meditation as yoga is indeed a set of "thinking postures" to use Hegel's phrase, the textual ambiguity brilliantly (accidentally?) betraying his anxiety about the idea that a *posture* could *think*. Buddhaphobia wants there to be an infinite distance between *posing* a philosophical proposition, conceptually *positing*, and this *posturing* thought, this thinking that postures and postures that perform thinking. It is perhaps the sclerosis of resisting the weird physicality of posturing that leads Heidegger to assert that he wishes to replace "cogitating attitude" with "thinking comportment."[49] Thinking, on this view, is already a kind of gesture or posture, since it is an orientation to a preexisting world of equipment, of physical things—some of which are toes and mouths.

What is the pretzel logic of the thinking posture? Deleuze and Guattari imagine the body without organs as a looping flow of energy within a sealed container, a flow that is not different from a certain eroticism:

> The BwO: it is already under way the moment the body has had enough of organs and wants to slough them off, or loses them. A long procession. The *hypochondriac body*: the organs are destroyed, the damage has already been done, nothing happens anymore. . . . The *paranoid body*: the organs are continually under attack by outside forces, but are also restored by outside energies. . . .

The *schizo body*, waging its own active internal struggle against the organs, at the price of catatonia. Then the *drugged body*, the experimental schizo. . . . The *masochist body*: it is poorly understood in terms of pain; it is fundamentally a question of the BwO. It has its sadist or whore sew it up . . . to make sure everything is sealed tight.

Why such a dreary parade of sucked-dry, catatonicized, vitrified, sewn-up bodies, when the BwO is also full of gaiety, ecstasy, and dance? . . .Is it really so sad and dangerous to be fed up with seeing with your eyes, breathing with your lungs, swallowing with your mouth, talking with your tongue, thinking with your brain, having an anus and larynx, head and legs? Why not walk on your head, sing with your sinuses, see through your skin, breathe with your belly: the simple Thing, the Entity, the full Body, the stationary Voyage, Anorexia, cutaneous Vision, Yoga, Krishna, Love, Experimentation. Where psychoanalysis says, "Stop, find your self again" we should say instead, "Let's go further still, we haven't found our BwO yet, we haven't sufficiently dismantled our self."[50]

Beyond the self-concept there lies this entity, this weird embodiment. "Yoga, Krishna, Love, Experimentation": precisely. From this viewpoint, signification, the sign over the toilet, the look of a statue, the question in the Kinsey Report, is being put into a loop, sewn up back into objectal status—like what Gödel does to Russell and Whitehead, in logic. Is this sewing up of the orifices, this closing of the body in on itself, not remarkably like the Tantric text, "Centering":

4. When breath is all out (up) and stopped of itself, or all in (down) and stopped—in such universal pause, one's small self *vanishes* . . . .
12. Closing the seven openings of the head with your hands, a space between your eyes becomes *all-inclusive* . . . .
14. Bathe in the centre of sound, as in the continuous sound of a waterfall. Or, by putting fingers in ears, hear *the sound of sounds.*[51]

The sound of sounds is called *anahata nada* in Sanskrit. It means "unstruck sound," a sound pervaded with nothingness, a sound that lies at the basis of all other sounds. The loop-like recursion of *sound of sounds* suggests this weird, transcendental yet physical entity.

As well as being disturbingly feminine, Hegel's version of Buddhism is disturbingly infantile. For Hegel, the Buddhist constantly equates form with mere accident, which in itself is "indifferent" nothing. "Human holiness consists in uniting oneself, by this negation, with nothingness, and so with God, with the absolute."[52] Union with God is embodied in extending one's toe into one's mouth in an impossible, fantastic act of self-swallowing, a precise figuration of the paradoxical impossibility (for Hegel) of "will[ing] nothing . . . want[ing] [nothing], and . . . doing nothing" (the sneer in the tricolon is almost audible). Again, the image of *willing nothing* is at once vacuously negative and disturbingly positive.

The idea of willing nothing may have seemed impossible to Hegel, but it precisely what Schopenhauer advocates, in his Buddhist literalization of Kant. Since the Will is the thing in itself, it cannot be destroyed, because destroying is itself an act of Will. Will may only be suspended. Suspension *plays* with nothingness, in something like the same way in which evolution or capital or dreamwork play with nothingness. There is a strange in-betweenness that these concepts exemplify, neither one thing nor another, but rather the suspension of solid, stable constancy. Another term for this suspension is *the aesthetic*: the world of representation that is capable of suspending the will in phenomena such as music. Such ideas had precedents in the "darkness mysticism" of medieval apophatic theology, which played with the idea that thought and language could negate themselves.[53] The kinds of privation and sensual training that contemplative Christianity enjoins as a means to attune to the divine find uncanny, mass cloned versions of themselves in forms of consumerism. For instance, vegetarianism as a form of mystical access to the divine in the later seventeenth century gradually became a readily available lifestyle choice by the early nineteenth.[54] Let's proceed by investigating this phenomenon.

Suspension of the will might remind one of the suspensions that in the Victorian period began to be mass produced and sold back to people in the form of consumer products.[55] For consumerism is about moving beyond the satisfaction of needs, and playing precisely with representations (style). The ultimate consumerist product then is that suspension itself, which is why seemingly high aesthetic states and drug-induced bliss became the benchmarks for consumerism—why the most refined form of consumerism was a Romantic or bohemian kind that was self-reflexive, consuming consumerism itself. Consumerism is shot through, then, with nothingness and enjoyment, and it disturbingly exemplifies in social space the ramifications of some of the philosophy we have been studying. Small wonder then, that part of Buddhaphobia is a fear of consumerism.

FEAR OF CONSUMERISM

We now embark on a series of more detailed reflections on the components of Buddhaphobia: fear of consumerism, fear of narcissism, fear of passivity, fear of loops, fear of things. This is not a progressive sequence, but rather a knot of fears, like beads strung on a rosary. Throughout this sequence, the reader will note a deliberately iterative style, a circulation like someone "telling" prayer beads, a telling as counting or computing—as automated process—that is not irrelevant to the content of these small, globular sections. For if meditation is always "practice" (as in the common phrase *mediation practice*)—a doing that is a suspension of achievement in a subjunctive mode—then it necessarily assumes a loop form. It is the encounter, over and over, with itself. This is not dialectics at a standstill (Benjamin)—it is dialectics in a loop. Such a looping traverses, while necessarily not reducing, an intrinsic difficulty of thinking nothingness. As

Eric Cazdyn argues in this volume, an engagement with Buddhism necessitates a refreshing of notions of theory and practice.

Consumerism appears to be "wrong" on two counts. First, there is the fact that it has a weird, mass spirituality about it. One could see New Age as a recursive form of this spirituality-as-consumer-product. A recursion not unrelated to the role of crystals, beads, incense, diet, and other physical things in New Age forms. Such "useless" consumer objects are taken as tokens of spirituality and as possessing healing or energizing powers. Second, there is the appropriation of meaningless, useless enjoyment. It is crass, yet contemplative. It riots in products and shopping, yet it withdraws from social action. Indeed, contemporary Buddhist thought in the West strives to distinguish itself from what has been called *spiritual materialism*, a consumerist attitude to religion as such, in which I am free to choose what I like, thus debasing the very idea of religion as intimacy and binding.[56]

Yet it is not easy to distinguish consumerism and a certain religiosity. This difficulty is precisely the cause of the immense energy expended on differentiating them. Consider again Krishna's insouciant tasting of his toe, and its relation to nothingness. Nothingness is threatening because of its inertia as well as its blankness, its "indifferent" refusal to lift the body into the spirit world. For while toe disappears into mouth, what also happens is that sensations multiply all over the body's surfaces. And, of course, the toe never actually disappears—it is held gently in the mouth, in a state of suspension not unlike Schopenhauer's solution to the machination of Will, which is to put it in a recursive loop through art (and in particular music).

Now actually to put one's foot in one's mouth would involve all kinds of delicate nudging and coaxing, not the sudden (aggressive?) "extension" and sucking that Hegel seems to imagine. The image is a Buddhaphobic one, because it imagines the body's intimacy with itself as a violent, self-canceling act. Elsewhere Hegel describes pure subjectivity as "the night of the world" in which float "a bloody head" and a "white ghastly apparition."[57]

By a stark contrast, the toe sucker is a body integrated into a circular form, manifesting ongoing periodic waves of intertwining and sucking. The violence and sudden flashes of appearance in the night of the world conceal a far more threatening nonviolence and constant rhythm: life in its pulsating inertia. And it suggests that what Buddhaphobia really fears is not being swept up into some unknown other. What is really feared is *the intimacy of life*—the way one can put one's toe in one's mouth, at any moment. Buddhaphobia thus exemplifies Bataille's argument about religion, which is that it is a search for a lost intimacy.[58] In this respect the poetic image of *nirvāṇa* celebrated in nineteenth-century English literature—the drop absorbed in the ocean—is aptly *physical* as well as nihilating.[59] Think of all those droplets, merged.[60] They have been "drunk" by the ocean, which is just themselves, yet not themselves. Nietzsche detects the joyfulness in this self-cancelling existence in his concept of the Dionysian.[61]

The "drop in the ocean" topos links to consumerist absorption in the other: participation in mass rituals of style, succumbing to the directives of fashion, taking psychoactive substances that flood the brain with strange neurochemical soups. Lacan correctly perceives the threat to heteronormative masculinity that the Buddha statue evokes. Its passivity is coded as feminine or queer. Hegel exemplifies the phobic response that Žižek only repeats. It is something disturbing about Buddhism's view of the subject that Žižek evidently finds provocative. In particular, it is an object-like entity that withdraws from access: Buddhism calls it Buddha nature. Fear of this object-like entity is akin to homophobia: a horror and fascination combined that is particularly acute when the writer is a closeted Buddhist. Some of Žižek's most frequently employed Lacanian concepts such as "subjective destitution" and indeed his insistence on the necessity of the void approach Buddhist ideas about emptiness.[62] Žižek's evident interest in loop-like phenomena, in which the subject is entangled with an object, is also very close to Buddhist styles of thought. Some evidence is available in Žižek's admission to Glyn Daly in *Conversations with Žižek* about how closely his view resembles that of the principal Buddhist philosopher of emptiness, Nāgārjuna.

Nevertheless, in this assertion, Žižek bends Nāgārjuna into a form of Hegelian perspectivism: "Objectively nothing exists, and entities only emerge as the result of perspectival differentiation in which every differentiation is a partial distortion."[63] Notice the visuality of the language, versus the haptic enjoyment of the absorbed droplet. In this visuality might there be a resistance to consumerism? And also to Kant? On this view there is no radical phenomenon-thing gap, only the necessary distortion of a "partial" or "perspectival" view. Because I can think the gap, there is no actual gap—this is the Hegelian solution to Kant—and what remains are the ways in which my subjectivity, my total attitude, distorts reality in a particular way. Thus philosophy is necessarily the history of philosophy, since ideas and the havers of those ideas are inseparable: hence Hegel's narrative of phenomenological styles of thought (Skepticism, Unhappy Consciousness, Beautiful Soul, and so on). But Buddhist emptiness means more than that. Theravadin emptiness is the lack of a (single, lasting, independent) self. Mahāyāna emptiness is the lack of a (single, lasting, independent) being *tout court*: raindrops, humans, and even Buddha nature arise from emptiness.

Manifestly, Žižek dislikes Buddhism insofar as it gives one a good reason not to be a Marxist. A Marxist does not allow herself to be suspended in consumerism, which is the way Buddhism appears in this argument. The notion of socialist sacrifice might necessarily enjoin a postponing of enjoyment. According to this view, consumerism turns one into an object, in the worst way: inert, passive, a head full of products. Consider, for instance, the approval that Adorno heaps on Hegel when he describes genuine self-reflection, the subject meditating upon "its real captivity" as opposed to Buddhist meditation. Adorno approvingly cites the notion of Hegelian "involvement," suppressing the association with *Insichsein*, the loopy being-within-self that for

Hegel just is Buddhism.[64] Or consider the way in which Adorno castigates the materialistic consumption of an easily available form of Zen as a "corny exoticism," the decoration of a vacuously uncritical form of modern subjectivity.[65] This corniness surely has a consumerist resonance. The *corny* is what distinguishes the kitsch from the truly critical high modern art product.[66] The corny evokes a worn out form of enjoyment, a product whose use is somehow a stain on its integrity, a nothingness. And yet, *corny* also suggests the weird presence of the corn-fed: feeding on a sweet, buttery *substance*. Buddhism is commodity fetishism. There is indeed a corniness in cultures that have been Buddhist for some time. Consider only the fact that in Taiwan, Buddhist shrines are decorated not only with statues of Buddha—small cute ones, in the spirit of sentimentality as a social bonding force—but also of Snoopy, Hello Kitty, and other cute fantasy creatures. The softness, the sweetness, the "lameness" of much Buddhist culture is one of the most threatening things about it, in the eyes of Buddhaphobia.

If political economy is the transcendental signified, it seems as if Buddhism just can't win. Feudal structures likewise come under attack as if Buddhism were intimately their product, in Wang Lixiong's Marxist critique.[67] Likewise Adorno and Horkheimer make a childishly elementary blunder when they assume that "son of a noble family" (a phrase often heard in Buddhist sūtras) means "aristocrat."[68] It's a term for "bodhisattva," someone who has taken on the liberation of all sentient beings, the "noble family" in question being the Buddha family—to which even worms belong.

Recall, however, that the Hegelianism that underwrites Marxism is a covering over of the nothingness opened up by Kant. Geist, or History (with a capital H), or (human) relations of production, or will to power, or Dasein (and so on) become the "decider" that opens the thing in itself for (human) inspection. A metaphysically present entity (Geist, the subject, production) subtends the phenomenon-thing gap, reducing its disturbing shimmer. What results is something like the logic of the Freudian "borrowed kettle": Buddhism has too much hierarchy, and too little; it is fundamentally capitalist, and fundamentally feudal, and . . .

The correlation between consumerism and Buddhism is as deep as the nineteenth century. Consumerism is castigated as a machine that turns people into machines. The Western anxiety about Buddhism is in particular concerned with the machine-like, nonhuman quality of Buddhism seen, for instance, in Tibetan prayer wheels. I can turn the prayer wheel without having to change my attitude—the prayer wheel is like canned laughter, insofar as it renders my subjective input unnecessary. It is "interpassive" to use Žižek's brilliant term for the Internet.[69] Such objects seem to automate religion in a way that perturbates Western thinking. Yet in a perhaps more disturbing sense, we can see how such objects are not simply adjuncts to human meaning, but entities in their own right: the prayer wheel itself prays. Buddhism promises a greatly expanded social, psychic, and philosophical space in which nonhumans are accepted as equal participants. Yet the automation subsequent upon this promise has been associated with the distinguishing features of industrial capitalism. There is a century-long lineage of associations, perhaps starting with the Sanskrit scholar Monier Monier-Williams, who concludes his study of Buddhism with a catalog of automated forms of prayer; it continues today.[70] As Marcus Boon has shown, Buddhism is a powerful ally in thinking the strangeness of automation in such phenomena as copying, phenomena that undermine even as they promote ideas such as property, copyright, and authenticity.[71] Automation has also been associated with fascist war machines. Christopher Hitchens repeated the oft-cited (automated, ironically) idea that the Japanese used Zen to train kamikaze pilots to turn their planes into suicide bombs.[72] If one has ever seen a kamikaze plane up close, with its minimal size and tiny fins, there is a genuinely threatening sense in which the pilot becomes only the steering mechanism of something that could hardly be said to transport a human from one place to another. There is a contour of consumerist abandon even here: a drop in the ocean is a suicidal drop, from a certain standpoint.

What disturbs about the image is precisely the thought of an army of faceless, fascist robots, clones with a single purpose—to wipe out life. The orientalist Buddhaphobia is not hard to detect. Yet beyond this, the Marxian critique is not of automation per se, but of automated ideology: the notion that capitalist ideology functions just like a prayer wheel, insofar as it is located in things, not in people. What is troubling about criticisms of automation and copying is not only that they seem well within anthropocentric modernity. What is also troubling is that such criticisms do not seem to take into account the way in which the Marxism from which they emerge strictly blocks off regressive exits from the consumerist machine age, the exit, for instance, of a "return to nature" that can only look like fascism. Indeed, Žižek insists that the journey from alienation within commodity fetishism must be a journey *through* this fetishism, not despite it or away from it.[73]

The journey is strictly correlated with the path through, not in spite of, nihilism and nothingness. Commodification establishes an irreducible gap between what a thing is (in Marxist terms, its use value) and how it appears (its exchange value). Consumerism is shot through with nothingness. There is no good reason why I should choose to consume this rather than that: it is a matter of establishing a performative rather than a pregiven identity.[74] I am not being dictated to by other humans (king, pope) so much as by the compelling power of things and advertising. And I am not concerned, as a consumerist, with the use value of a thing—I even begin to doubt whether such a use value truly exists. I am concerned rather with how consuming a thing fashions me as a particular kind of consumer. I am a Mac person. I am a PC person. I am a vegan. I am a foodie. Abstinence and boycotting are also forms of consumerism in this regard: I boycott fur, you boycott sugar in protest against the slave trade. Predictably, drug culture is the ultimate expression of this: *I am an opium fiend; I am an acidhead*.

This culture of consuming substances that change the mind is correlated with what Colin Campbell calls bohemian consumption—the self-reflexive *consumption of consumption* we now know as window-shopping.[75] It is a style that emerged within Romanticism—think de Quincey and his opiated sojourns among London's East End workers, but also Wordsworth, who vicariously "enjoys" the experiences of the pastoral other. Bohemian or Romantic consumer performance styles are not emulative: I am not looking up to some higher-status person when I perform them. In the sense disconcertingly recognized in the Freudian PR tactics of a Bernays, democracy implies that there is no guarantee that my style is a good one. Democracy is thus caught up in a certain pretense, and the line from Lacan again becomes handy: "What constitutes pretense is that, in the end, you don't know whether it's pretense of not."[76] In other words, democracy is caught in the aesthetic and in nothingness. There is something disturbing about Buddhism akin to the pejorative language of "lifestyle choice." The dreaded term "spirituality" (as opposed to religion and also as opposed to reductionist scientism) begins to rear its ugly head. By the nineteenth century, the possibility that a Christian might convert to Buddhism was a real threat—only consider Schopenhauer.[77] And in part this was a threat that someone might drop religion altogether in favor of something more up-to-date. The very "ism" that forms the last two syllables of *Buddhism* is, somewhat pejoratively, a marker of the emergence of Buddhadharma in Western culture in the age of the consumer.[78] The label arose during the Romantic period: the *Oxford English Dictionary*'s first citation is from 1801.[79] What I am arguing is that this "ism," far from distorting Buddhadharma, brings out something inherent in it—and that, pace Buddhaphobia, this is a good thing.

The phenomenology of Buddhism and of consumerism do

indeed overlap somewhat.[80] Is it not the case that consumerist identity is already a disturbance of a single, solid self, a disturbance that precisely takes the form of a loop? In this loop I constitute myself in relation to some object, or as Lacan writes in his pithy matheme, $ ◊ a: a stands for *petit autre*, a little "thingy" that is not me, which advertising calls *the reason to buy* and psychoanalysis calls *the object-cause of desire*. In turn, ◊ stands for "is constituted in relation to." I am constituted in relation to an object-cause of desire. I find myself in a loop. I am not self-contained, but rather I am what I desire: I am a circulation around some object, based in psychoanalytic terms on the more physical circulation of libido around its object, *drive*. Thus arises the delicious paradox of Brillat-Savarin, early in the history of modernity: *Tell me what you eat and I shall tell you what you are.*[81] Or Feuerbach's formula: *Man is what he eats*, a formula that arose almost at the same time as Brillat-Savarin's.[82] We see in this not-quite-overlap of desire and drive the disturbing duality of nothingness: it is nothing—just circling, without attainment (desire); and a weird something, insofar as drive always attains its object, like the way lips swallow a toe.

In consumerism, I have become my own fetish—in a sense, *I have become my own Buddha statue*, wiping away my own imaginary tears, as in Lacan's account of the Buddhist nuns.

It is not difficult to detect the gaps, the nothingness, in such loops. A related gap exists between "the consumer," that ideal subject of contemporary economics, and actual consumers, humans who eat things and wear things. There is the I who I think I am, and the I qua consumerist subject, and the I qua this instance of "the consumer." Has an original, natural me been conned or painted over? Is this really what is wrong with capitalism—that it is a crime against nature? Or does capitalism reveal something true about reality—that *there is no nature*, that nature is always a regressive, retroactive construct applied to things after I have realized that I am in the new kind of social space?

And does this idea that there is no nature mean that there

is nothing at all—that all appearances are merely illusions? Or does it mean something more like meontic nothing, shimmering presence apart (to use *shimmer* transitively)? A shimmering that has to do with enjoyment? Return to the image of Krishna Narayan. Baby Krishna sticks his toe in his mouth because it has been dipped in the Milk Ocean. He is surprised to find how sweet his toe tastes. The "anything goes" of the consumerist product—whatever floats your boat, whatever "little other" (*objet petit a*) turns you on, is good. Is this not the reason for Žižek's cleaving to the curmudgeonly stiffness of Pope John Paul II, against the flexibility of the Dalai Lama, on homosexuality, for instance?[83] For Žižek, the Dalai Lama's pliancy betrays a lack of commitment, a softness that is the hallmark both of excellent kitchen paper towels and of consumerist subjects. Whatever floats my boat is fine: it is not difficult to detect within this maxim the dreaded narcissism, that object of scorn in the Buddhaphobic lineage. It is to narcissism that we now turn.

FEAR OF NARCISSISM

There is a lineage of links between psychoanalytic thought and Buddha statues, in which Lacan's engagement makes sense. The fifteen-year-old Schopenhauer enjoyed the look of porcelain Buddhas in a shop window: "their smile is so friendly." In 1856 he bought one, a Tibetan *rupa* (Sanskrit, *form* or *body*), a form of the Buddha Shakyamuni, and had it gilded.[84] He enjoyed how it glinted into the apartment of a local priest, as if to threaten or challenge him.[85] Freud owned several Buddha statues, many of which he displayed quite prominently in his consulting room at 20 Maresfield Gardens, London. An entry in his diary of October 6, 1931, talks about one of them. It was a small jade Kannon, a Japanese Kuan Yin, made in the nineteenth century.[86] Kuan Yin is the Buddha that Lacan thinks about in the tenth seminar. Moreover, Freud bought other Kannons, including a bronze Buddha bust in 1909 from Tiffany's as a birthday present.[87] To buy oneself a Buddha statue for one's own birthday—how bohemian, how narcissistic. Freud displayed it in the front window of his consulting room.

It is "Western Buddhism" that Žižek mainly attacks, but the assault leaks into "proper" Buddhism, thus betraying its Buddhaphobic core.[88] This corrupt form of Buddhism—or is it Buddhism altogether that is corrupt? Žižek is unable to decide— disturbingly emphasizes unconditional, narcissistic forms of pleasure: self-soothing. Paternalistic Jeremiads on the supine self-actualization culture of 1970s America spring to mind, Jeremiads whose endless reproduction almost looks like a deeply pleasurable compulsion to repeat. What if 70s spiritualities, Esalen perhaps the foremost among them, were indeed the truth of Buddhism? And that indeed, the reason why Buddhism is intriguing is that it locks into a growing acceptance of narcissism since 1945? The trouble with trying to step outside of narcissism is the same as the trouble with trying to step outside of language. We could see the assault on narcissism as itself a kind of narcissism.[89] We are likely to call someone a narcissist who is in fact suffering from *wounded narcissism*—that is, a kink or two in his or her loop. In a sense, a wounded narcissist isn't narcissistic enough. Therefore, she or he attacks or withdraws from the other—from the loop that is the other, that is—precisely because the other loop is provocatively efficient and closed. Wounded narcissism most often goes on the offensive against narcissism as such, projected into the world. "Narcissist" is the accusation that narcissistic woundedness deploys against the other. Far from lofty critique, a Buddhist would perceive a perfectly elementary reason for Žižek's hostility to Buddhist self-soothing: a narcissistic woundedness so painful that it seems better to paint the whole world with its raw colors than examine itself in all its halting lameness.

Thus anything that looks like self-pleasuring is suspect for Žižek. It is better to have an empty ritual than one suffused with (the wrong kind of) meaning, because that would betray something "narcissistic" about that meaning. This assault on autoaffection has so spooked actual Buddhists that it is common to defend oneself against it: "Yes, I am a Buddhist, but not one of those New Age Western Buddhists, I assure you." A robust defense of Buddhist against Hegelianism must therefore commence with a shameless occupying of the dreaded narcissistic position. There are numerous propositions within post-Hegelian Western philosophy that we might use for this occupation. For instance, consider Zarathustra's "Love your neighbor as yourselves, but first be such as love yourselves" which sounds like it comes straight out of a Buddhist manual on what is called *maitri*, or even "worse" from a self-help book.[90] Then there is Derrida:

> Narcissism! There is not narcissism and non-narcissism; there are narcissisms that are more or less comprehensive, generous, open, extended. What is called non-narcissism is in general but the economy of a much more welcoming, hospitable narcissism, one that is much more open to the experience of the other as other. I believe that without a movement of narcissistic reappropriation, the relation to the other would be absolutely destroyed, it would be destroyed in advance.[91]

Buddhaphobia is a fear of nothingness that is precisely the fear of an uncanny presence, a presence that is the starting position of Hegelianism itself, A=A. A presence that is me but I disavow it, "destroy [it] in advance" (Derrida). There is something homophobic about Hegel's deployment of the image of Krishna sucking his toe. Hegel goes on to deplore the fact that lamas (Tibetan incarnate teachers) are brought up in a feminine passive way. It is as if what is being warded off is that phobic sequence popular in nineteenth-century sexology and diet: narcissism → masturbation → excess energy → more masturbation → homosexuality. This is why Cornflakes was invented. It was believed that young boys who eat too much meat are prone to an excess of psychic energy which results in this pathologized narcissistic loop. Homosexuality, in medieval theology, is called self-love, which is what it is also called by Kellogg, the inventor of Cornflakes, that homophobic cereal that was designed to stop boys from going into a self-pleasuring loop, a kind of medicine that by ingestion would work better than just chaining boys to the bed.

The subtle body is a concatenation of loops that can have kinks and knots. Meditation is a yoga that causes these knots to loosen. If Buddhism is to be defended within "theory" then it is precisely this most "demonic" aspect, its New Age, spiritual-consumerist "narcissistic" incarnation that should be taken as the core. This means that consumerist Buddhism really does betray something deep about Buddhism, as Žižek argues pervasively. It is not to be peeled away from Buddhism as a bad appearance that has nothing to do with Buddhism's essence. It is, rather, evocative of what precisely disturbs theory about Buddhism. This disturbance is the result of a confluence between consumerism, automation, narcissism, and nothingness.

Wounded narcissism is a damaged loop. The wounded narcissist accuses the other of narcissism precisely insofar as she or he is disturbed by a loop whose echo is found within himself or herself. Philosophy can be narcissistically deaf to how it sounds in the ears of the other. And a symptom of this is its overuse of the term *narcissistic* to describe opposing views. The horror of narcissistic self-absorption is a horror of an incomplete, fractured narcissism seeing a reflection of itself seemingly whole, projected into that enigmatic smile, Buddha as the Mona Lisa, those lowered eyelids that suggest that the other could, but does not care about me. . . . To this extent, Buddhaphobia itself is a philosophical form of wounded narcissism.

FEAR OF PASSIVITY

There is a strange overdetermination in leftist critiques of Buddhism. On the one hand, Buddhism sinisterly softens you up for the capitalist workforce. On the other hand, it makes you unfit for work. This latter anxiety is also found in capitalist critiques of Buddhism.[92] What seems to disturb is something useless, something coded as passive. A smile is provocative insofar as it is passive—it is just a curve on a surface, yet it is rich with meaning. This brings us to a still deeper consideration of the allergy to the aesthetic common in Buddhaphobia. Consider the slightly wicked glint of Schopenhauer's Buddha statue. There is a physical thing yet there is an expression, some kind of gleam. There is something like agency in this aesthetic effect, and something unlike it. The statue does something to me—but it is not doing anything in particular. Indeed it glints at me, this glint being precisely the gaze in psychoanalytic terms, an object-like entity that just stares blankly, rather than looking at me per se. It is as if the statue is saying not only *There is another, non-Christian religion*, but also *There is another, non-efficient causal realm*. Like the Mona Lisa's enigmatic smile, the Buddha statue's glint affects me, but in a nonconceptual way. It provokes me with direct, experiential evidence that there is at least one other thing in the universe. Thus whatever we may think about narcissism, and this essay's attempt to recuperate it, it appears that *solipsism* is quite different, and that one reason for refuting solipsism is found precisely in the results of self-absorbed, aesthetic experiences such as meditation or beauty. For ironically it is in those experiences that I find the most intimate evidence that I am not alone. The evidence is disturbing to the exact extent that I cannot analyze it further: it is a quantum, it is of a piece, incapable of being subdivided.

The placement of the statue is gestural—something like an insulting gesture toward the priest into whose window it shone. Yet this gesture is achieved without movement, without action. There is something one might now call *passive aggressive* in Schopenhauer's glee at his angling the statue just so. Schopenhauer, a good Kantian, thinks that causality is part of the phenomenal realm, not the noumenal: it exists in a possibility space that includes what is called the aesthetic dimension.[93] How a painting or a statue affects me is, on this view, remarkably similar to how a kick affects me—or rather vice versa: what we think of as causality does not happen behind or below things, but rather out in front of them, as it were, where art happens. The trouble with the effects of Buddha statues is the trouble with art in general, from the standpoint of a popular Western philosophical conception. Art is strange or evil, because it affects me without touching me, without moving me it moves me in another sense: a philosophical idea that goes back at least to Plato's *Ion*.[94] It seduces me and holds me without my will, and in some accounts it subtends or is always-already given, before my intention or willing.[95] For Schopenhauer, this quality of the aesthetic enables it to suspend will, in the same way that the clutch in a car disengages the gears from one another—they keep spinning, but do not interact. Thus in music I experience pure willing, in which one note leads to another one, one phrase to another, but not in such a way that it would be better to listen to it much faster, since the point is not to reach the end as efficiently as possible.[96] Music puts me into a state of suspended animation.

It is not total, opaque inertia that Buddhaphobia seems to fear. If it is opacity, then it is a strange opalescent opacity, the way a precious stone glitters or a statue glints. It is something more like what Freud first called *the nirvāṇa principle*, otherwise known as the death drive: the way in which a lifeform, down to a single-celled organism (for Freud) and quite possibly below that, is an inconsistent entity that is trying to wipe out that inconsistency. This attempt at self-cancellation (*nirvāṇa* means *extinction*) ironically creates a loop, in which the lifeform produces more of itself: more of a barrier between itself and the external world, for instance, or simple cloning or sexual reproduction. We shall explore loops in the following section, but the next logical step is to consider the anxiety about passivity expressed in Buddhaphobia.

Freud describes this passivity as *quiescence*, in James Strachey's quite beautiful translation of *Beyond the Pleasure Principle*.

Without violating the Law of Noncontradiction, how could the aim of life be death? Unless, of course, there is an object-like entity at the core of human being, an entity felt as an object precisely because it is inhuman, a-human: what is called *Buddha nature*, elegantly embodied in Buddhist statuary. Are they dead or merely sleeping, "quiescent"? Lifeforms yearn to return to "the quiescence of the inorganic world," to become like statues.[97]

Moreover, the inverse is yet more disturbing. It is the idea, now quite unexceptionably part of quantum theory, that nonhuman beings, even "inanimate" things, vibrate with a life of their own without being pushed mechanically. If there is an ontological reason for this, it is that the appearance dimension of a thing (its aesthetic dimension, in fact) is glued to what it is inseparably, rather than being some kind of candy sprinkled on a featureless extensional lump. Yet this ontology is just what Western philosophy has mostly been designed to ward off. The common Western philosophical fear of art is a fear of nonhuman and nonanimate agency. The aesthetic dimension is quiescent: it pulsates with a strange agency yet it does not act. "Thou still unravished bride of quietness": Keats expresses a provocative wonder at the opacity and weird secrecy of a product, a Grecian urn most likely to have been the Portland Vase, the source for the Wedgwood facsimile made before Keats wrote the poem, a facsimile made using one of the original industrial scale division-of-labor production methods, and to which he would have had easier access. The vase remains a consumerist object right now.[98] In Keats's poem, the urn seems to rotate. It circles, still yet moving, like the images plastered on it: a musician piping silent tunes, a sacrifice that never arrives. The provocation of the urn is the provocation of suspended animation, which just is the aesthetic in its most disturbing guise: unreasonable pleasure, unreasonable happiness, unreasonable existence. Quiescence is weird life, life as death. Life as an object rather than as a subject. Moreover, beauty in the Kantian sense seems to be a signal from the realm of death, in the sense that it is a part of a quiescent world of things that impinges on me, which I find furthermore in my inner space, on the inside of me. Quiescence is evocative of the shimmering "silence" of the drive, how this thing in me always finds its target and sucks at it. Or as the Buddha himself was said to have put it, referring to his enlightenment:

> Deep, peaceful, perfectly pure,
> luminous, uncompounded, and like nectar
> is the Dharma I have obtained.
> Even if I were to teach it,
> it could not be known by another.
> Certainly, I must remain silent in the forest. (Lalitavistara
> Sūtra)[99]

The esoteric Buddhism of Dzogchen puts it this way: how does a mute describe the taste of sugar?

Substantiality underlies nothingness. Shimmering agency underlies substantiality. Žižek brilliantly and frequently observes that the "No" of the superego injunction hides a much more primordial and disturbing injunction to enjoy, an injunction of "Yes."[100] He argues that this injunction to enjoy is what now fuels capitalist ideology. The injunction to *take it easy* is pervasive in contemporary culture, and thus one might easily become suspicious of it. Indeed, the term *chill out* derives from the drug cultures of opium, cannabis, and ecstasy: in the sophisticated opium dens of the 1920s New York, chilled fruit was served in spaces in which suspended animation was a daily occurrence, life reduced to stasis rippling with strange dreams, the Deleuzian Body without Organs. Does one not talk of *quiescently frozen* popsicles? Yet as Adorno again remarks, utter peace is a powerfully evocative of utopia: "'Being, nothing else, without any further definition and fulfillment.' . . . None of the abstract concepts comes closer to fulfilled utopia than that of eternal peace."[101] Adorno imagines an exhausted consciousness, staring blankly—the kind of gesture one finds in Buddhist meditation instruction, in which the meditator is enjoined not to make an effort, but to allow experiences to take place simply, without blocking. One might indeed accuse the maniacally repeated injunction to take it easy of being the precise opposite, as an injunction to feel anxious even about the moments when one is not working, in the same way that the injunction Žižek notes coming from a can of Coca-Cola (*Enjoy!*) makes life quite irksome.

Yet there is not a thin bright line between the commodity's injunction to be passive and the call of utopian quiescence. There cannot be, simply because both are modalities of the aesthetic. The aesthetic is profoundly ambiguous, and in this sense, modern philosophers are still Platonists afraid of art. In the end, in the last instance, art should be good for you, and this goodness should consist in telling you what and how to think and act. The lack of a definite difference between what this bottle of Coca-Cola says and what Adorno says is a cause of anxiety: how will we know when we are relaxing correctly? Am I being duped? How can I know in advance? Another Lacan slogan springs to mind: *les non-dupes errent*. Those who think they have seen through delusion are participating fully in that delusion.

Fear of passivity is how Nietzsche became susceptible to Buddhaphobia: Nietzsche who, in other respects, might be more sympathetic toward Buddhism than others in his era. For Nietzsche, Schopenhauer's idea of the will's suspension was akin to a refined form of slave morality: "*beyond* good and evil," yes, but nevertheless resigned to the inevitable.[102] Nietzsche saw in Buddhism a religion of joyless, faceless clones, the emerging mass of the nineteenth century. Against this he asserted the exuberant acceptance of the flux of becoming. Yet as Heidegger argues, this flux is another kind of metaphysically present constancy.[103] Nietzschean "life" could be one of the last gasps of the metaphysics of presence, submerged in the ocean of nothingness opened up within reason itself, and therefore opened up within the physical, biological, and social sciences.[104] Yet there is more than a trace of Buddhism in Nietzsche's doctrine of eternal recurrence, in which one learns to dance joyfully with the inevitability of existence, in the manner immortalized in *Groundhog Day*.[105] This might be evidence of the way Buddhism itself forms a strange loop within Western philosophy, such that the more one tries to pull away from it, the more one finds oneself repeating it. This brings us to our next topic.

FEAR OF LOOPS

What is to be feared? Not absolutely nothing, not the nothing of, say, Spinoza, *oukontic* nothing. This nothing is "not even nothing": apart from substance, for Spinoza, there is absolutely nothing at all. What is to be feared, by contrast, is a *meontic* nothing that is not absolutely nothing, but rather a spectral, shifting presence of absence: shimmering substantiality.[106] This nothing is best referred to as *nothingness*. One might call it nihiliation, or "nothing-ing." Absolute oukontic nothing does not disturb, because it is totally nonexistent. Nothingness, however, is peculiar because it defies the metaphysics of presence that asserts that to exist, you must be constantly present, yet nothingness does "exist" in a paradoxical way. Nothingness defies the (never formally proved) Law of Noncontradiction, which section gamma of Aristotle's *Metaphysics* straightforwardly delineates.[107]

The Law of Noncontradiction (LNC) has been the touchstone of Western philosophy. The touchstone, that is, until Georg Cantor and nineteenth-century mathematicians discovered all kinds of entities that defied it. Such discoveries are congruent with evolution, capital and other entities discovered in that era, insofar as they glaringly indicate gaps between what a thing is and how it appears. A set of infinities can contain members that do not sum to that set, the dreaded Russell paradox. Thus a person can be a set of things that do not sum to a single, constantly present self. Nevertheless, we see things like people and pencils scuttling around all over the place. We see meadows and clouds, yet they cannot truly exist unless we allow "exist" to mean "be a fuzzy paradoxical set."[108] This is because meadows and clouds are made of things that are also fuzzy, and if we keep on subtracting those things, we are left with nothing at all (the Sorites paradox). Either reality is not logical, or the Law of Noncontradiction is not congruent with reality and thus *not logical enough*. It is this second view that Buddhism espouses, along with a choice few Western philosophers. In Dzogchen, for instance, reality is nothing at all, yet it sparkles with the appearances of . . . everything.

The Law of Noncontradiction is invoked by Russell and Alfred Tarski in their attempts to rid the world of self-reference, loops in the form of sentences such as *This sentence is false*, sentences that are both true and false at the same time (*dialetheic*). The very concept of metalanguage was invented by Tarski specifically to police such sentences, to police them by specifying, for instance, that "*This sentence is false* is not a sentence." We have already seen a hint of how the trouble with the idea that there is a place outside of language is the same as the trouble with the idea that there is a place outside of narcissism. The war on self-referential loops brings these two themes together. The trouble for the logic police who use metalanguage to restrain loops is that for every metalinguistic rule one can invent a viral sentence that undermines it. For instance, for the rule concerning what counts as a sentence ("A true sentence is not like *This sentence is false*") I can invent the following virus, just by putting the rule itself into a loop: *This is not a sentence*. In a way I have just made the self-reference much more virulent, because I am no longer referring to truth and falsity, but to the existence of sentences as such. Note again that I can do this by bending the rule into a loop, folding it into a pretzel like a meditator sitting cross-legged or Krishna sticking his toe into his mouth. Or like a statue that may or may not be looking at me; that may or may not be male.

I can make a metalanguage into an object language. Gödel

takes on that giant police station of logic, Russell and White-head's *Principia Mathematica*. The *Principia* promises mathematics and logic without self-reference. Precisely because it is so successful on its own terms, Gödel forces it to say the very thing that it tries not to say, a self-referential sentence, and a highly virulent one at that: *This sentence cannot be proved*. The *Principia* was designed precisely to exclude such sentences. Gödel puts Russell and Whitehead into a loop. This is weirdly because their work so coherently provides a logical foundation for mathematics. Since the *Principia* allows mathematical statements to be defined using logical propositions, the reverse can be done: one can assign a specific number to any statement (the Gödel number). And so I can make a thing that is both a string of numbers and a statement. Precisely because of this feature, I can put the text into a loop, because it has already begun to talk about itself.[109] That is what Hegel cannot stand about the "Buddhist," a-logical A=A: it is already in a loop. In its obdurate refusal of dialectical motion it *is* moving.

Lacan sums up the whole tradition from Cantor to Gödel, and the lineage of phenomenology, in the line "No metalanguage can be spoken."[110] This is the potent sense in which it is not the case that a sentence just collapses into its context, but precisely the other way around: when I look for a context that might supply meaning, all I find is a host of other sentences. This host includes the very rules out of which sentences are made. Or, as Heidegger puts it, evoking A=A, "Language is—language."[111] There is a necessary exasperation in Heidegger's phrase, as well as the tip of the iceberg of a mystery. A circle is both maddeningly closed and maddeningly self-devouring. My very attempt to define language is itself an instance of language, in such an all-encompassing way that I cannot speak about it without making more of it to speak about. (Recall that for Heidegger, language means things like car indicators as well as words: it is everywhere.)[112] It is strange because we think language is a useful tool for referring to things—but when I open my mouth to talk about things, out comes another thing. And speaking at all depends upon listening, such that quiescence underlies speech—thus the basis of language is, in a certain sense, silence. Rhetoric, as Heidegger argues, is actually the art of listening, which is why the second part of Aristotle's *Rhetoric* is an exhaustive account of the different moods in which an audience might find itself.[113] Having meanings is a long way down the line of language. This line includes physicality, quietness, and listening.

In the same way, I can make my mind into a loop by meditating. I can use my mind, that prodigious generator of concepts, in the same way that Gödel uses the *Principia*. I can turn all that generation into a kind of object, in the Keatsian or Kantian sense, an unravished bride of quietness that is palpable yet withdrawn, opaque yet sparkling, quiescent. Whenever I have a thought, there is my mind, in the same sense in which "Language is—language." To put one's mind in a loop means to experience it as a thing—a disturbingly (for the conceptual mind) ungraspable thing, like beauty.

Meditation, Gödel's Incompleteness Theorem, and loopy self-reference all evoke nothingness. A meditating mind is thinking and not-thinking at the very same time. A coherent logical system must be able to talk nonsense in order to be true on its own terms. A sentence can say two opposed things at once. It appears that in each case there is a gap—between mind and thoughts, between coherence and nonsense, between p and not-p. Yet at the very same time, it is strictly impossible to locate this gap anywhere in particular. There is no point at which *This sentence is false* starts to lie. There are no fuzzy, ambiguous parts in *Principia Mathematica*. There is no separation between thoughts and mind just as, to use the traditional Buddhist analogy, there is no difference between the ocean and its waves. Loops are *nonorientable*, in the language of topology. A Möbius strip does not "start" to twist anywhere in particular.

There are precedents in Western Continental philosophy for thinking contradictions in a logical way. Schelling proclaimed that there was a contradiction at the heart of things. Ironically, Hegel himself also often departed from the supposed Law of Noncontradiction. Consider what he says about motion. An object can move because it is both here and not-here at the same time. Graham Priest analyzes this idea of Hegel's. Suppose that an object really is displaced from itself by some length. Given the surprising features of the quantum world, one wonders whether the length might be empirically measurable, and related to the Planck length; but this is not relevant to the discussion here.[114] One might suppose that movement consists simply of the fact that "contradictions arise at the nodal points of certain transitions." Thus "motion is a continuous state of contradiction." When I am leaving a room I am both in and out of the room. When a cup shatters, it is "a cup and not a cup" at that instant.[115] To be a thing at all is to defy the Law of the Excluded Middle, and the Law of Noncontadiction that underwrites it.

A thing is inherently unstable, argues Hegel, because the reality of the thing stems from the subject's apprehension of it, which develops in a spiraling, dialectical fashion as the apprehension modifies the thing, which modifies apprehension, and so on. The state of mind that does not grasp this cleaves to what for Hegel is the false immediacy of A=A. Yet in a further irony this "immediacy" is in itself contradictory, despite Hegel's dismissal of it, according to a Buddhist analysis. A=A is the lynchpin of Buddhaphobia. Although Hegel attributes contradiction to motion, he seems unable to tolerate the contradiction-in-stasis of A=A. Without a subject, an object shimmers. Or, without an object, a subject floats—and in that sense, is "reduced" (for Hegel) to being just another object. A=A indicates a disturbing universe of objects without subjects. Or at any rate, entities existing without the need for decider-like beings (subject, history, Will, human economic relations, will to power, Dasein) to make them real.

Hegel is disturbed by A=A because it insults the way in which his philosophy papers over the gap between phenomenon and thing opened up by Kant. Kant had shown how there is an irreducible gap between what we think we know and our reason. For instance, I can count, but I cannot show you what number is, without resorting to counting (for instance, on my fingers); but number is a condition of possibility of counting. Thus there is a gap between phenomenon and thing. Yet since I can think the gap, there is no gap: this is Hegel's reasoning. If you do not appreciate how the phenomenon-thing gap is not really a gap, you have fallen at the first hurdle in the game that ends with becoming a true Hegelian. What you have ended up with, in Hegelian, is the disturbing "narcissism" of A=A, the night in which all cows are black, that famous Hegelian condition.[116] What you end up with, in other words, is a moment at which the search for the Absolute *has not even begun.*

A=A is the nadir of "not getting it," of "falling at the first hurdle"—or of not even trying to jump over the hurdle. Of simply sitting down and "occupying" the racetrack as it were, staging a sit-in against this stupid preprogrammed race. Hegel dismisses A=A as a parasite that finds a host in a primitive form of consciousness that he calls Buddhism.[117] The dialectic is under orders to disavow A=A, to discover that A=A, like a little ball under a certain cup, is always already caught in the dialectic that will propel the story forward to the self-realization of the Absolute. A=A is thus both inside and outside of Hegelian thought, a parasite that does not sit well in its Hegelian host.

Hegel images A=A as a stultifying blank:

Hence was derived the second definition of the Absolute: the Absolute is the Nought. In fact this definition is implied in saying that the thing-in-itself is the indeterminate, utterly without form and so without content—or in saying that God is only the supreme Being and nothing more; for this is really declaring him to be the same negativity as above. The Nothing which the Buddhists make the universal principle, as well as the final aim and goal of everything, is the same abstraction.[118]

What in A=A is Hegel afraid of, if we think like Freud for a moment that all philosophies are forms of paranoia, attempts to explain the world to defend against—what? A gap, a void, precisely the Kantian gap between phenomenon and thing. Moreover, a gap that prevents the dialectic from taking place. And, weirder, a gap that enables a thing to perform itself—for an algorithm to look like it might be thinking, for instance. To return to A=A is to have exposed Hegelianism for what it is: a preprogrammed ruse that knows in advance that A=A must be disavowed or sublated, and the exact procedures of that disavowal or sublation. A=A is the logic of the uncanny "liveliness" of a thing, without me.

The phenomenon-thing gap is not absolutely nothing at all. Hegel flattens out this something or other into the opacity he denigrates. Why? Because there is a more basic fear of a weird *presence* in and as nothingness. In other words, an automated dialectic that takes place without a subject: dialectics in a loop. Behind the fear that the dialectic is prevented by the inertia of the Nothing is the more basic fear that *the dialectic has already started, without me*. A=A is already sufficient unto itself. As we have seen, the idea that something is functioning without my input is feared as a basic feature of capitalist ideology. Žižek argues pervasively that capitalist ideology resides in the commodities and their exchange networks, not in people's heads: it functions without our needing to believe, without us.

The phrase A=A contains something. "Equaling A" is something that happens to "A" as it were. There is a slight distortion or movement of trace within that very formula, a happening of something.[119] A=A has something of the flavor of a contradiction that is already present, a strange loop or spectral, plasmic entity. Again, this differs from the Hegelian contradiction in the thing, insofar as I do not know in advance that A=A is simply an opaque blindness in me to this contradiction, but rather that *A=A is already contradiction*, or rather a double-truth (dialetheia), both true and false simultaneously. This is what the Hegelian narrative forecloses.

A loop is a circle, and a circle is not necessarily merely an image of harmony. Circles are intrinsically rather shocking, not soothing, because they are palpable evidence of a reality that does not fit neatly into the universe of integers and fractions, the rational numbers. There is something disturbing about the total smoothness of a circle, a smoothness that can only be thought, never represented by algorithmic plot or by charcoal on bark. Circles live in a dimension that I can think, but that I cannot see or touch. There is no smooth bridge between pi and the nearest rational number. There is a gap that makes the set of real numbers (rational plus irrational) into a paradox. Loops make this thought "worse" because they are circles that circle—they *encircle*, they are doing, performing, circling. They always get around to themselves, and they never do: no wonder the Indians chose the circle to represent zero—that heretical number needed for double-entry bookkeeping, hence the creation of Jewish ghettos during early commercial capitalism.[120] Zero is a number with a Buddhist lineage, as Marcus Boon's essay in this volume demonstrates.

What is disturbing about this image for a certain kind of logic? It is that there is a minimal difference, a circulation, within the perfect identity of the circling loop. It's not just A, it is A=A: some kind of invisible movement is taking place, like the track of a bird in a clear blue sky or black cows pressing against me in the night. It is self-contradiction: the loop remains the same, yet different from itself. It is an Ouroboros, a self-swallowing serpent. The minimal image of contradiction is thus a circling, which is perhaps why Pythagoras had Hippasus strangled for insisting on the existence of irrational numbers such as pi. The circle deviates from itself, yet this deviation is itself.

A night in which all cows are black still has cows, if we take the image as hiding in plain sight something on its own face—it is not absolutely nothing at all. There are these cows everywhere, these ungraspable cows. It's a universe of entities—I can think them, but I cannot directly perceive them, yet they are (physically) real: the Kantian universe where there are raindrops that are raindroppy, I can think them, they are not popsicles, but I cannot access the raindrops in themselves.

To acknowledge a necessary paradox concerning identity, which thinking Buddhism might aid, is to differ from existing appropriations of Buddhism within Western philosophy, in a direction that might indeed look more like "theory." Eliminating paradox by eliminating anything like a self at all has been the way to go. Consider the case of Derek Parfit, who tests self-interest theories of ethics within utilitarianism to destruction, in the name of thinking the necessary disposition of humans toward the very large temporal scales of radiation and pollution. It is remarkable that Parfit, at the heart of *Reasons and Persons*, comes clean about how good the no-self view is for his inner state. In transcending self-interest theories we need not throw the baby of intimacy out with the bathwater of self. Quite the opposite, in fact: dropping self-interest theory immediately involves us in what Parfit himself refers to as a more intimate contact with other life forms and with future selves. Parfit embraces something like Buddhism, derived from an encounter with the thought of Steven Collins.[121]

In a moving passage in the very middle of *Reasons and Persons*, a passage that is startlingly personal compared with the blisteringly rational mode of Oxbridge utilitarianism that his work exemplifies, Parfit writes:

> Is the truth [of no-self] depressing? Some may find it so. But I find it liberating, and consoling. When I believed that my existence was [a "deep further fact, distinct from physical and psychological continuity, and a fact that must be all-or-nothing"], I seemed imprisoned in myself. My life seemed like a glass tunnel, through which I was moving faster every year, and at the end of which there was darkness. When I changed my view, the walls of my glass tunnel disappeared. I now live in the open air. There is still a difference between my life and the lives of other people. But

that difference is less. Other people are closer. I am less concerned about the rest of my own life, and more concerned about the lives of others.[122]

This is the rhetoric of simplification: something is let go, resulting in a greater intimacy and care. Analytic philosophy thus seems to have been more hospitable to Buddhism than the continental lineage we have been studying. Parfit's words themselves exemplify the intimacy and openness to the future that a no-self view bestows. His prose is inimitably lucid and spare:

I find the truth liberating, and consoling. It makes me less concerned about my future, and my death, and more concerned about others. I welcome this widening in my concern.[123]

Parfit puts himself on the line. He is saying that a view, achieved the hard way—by thinking about things in one's study, on one's own, without the peer pressure and situational validation of a monastery, for instance—can be good for one. This intimacy without ego is precisely what Buddhism is about, though Parfit would hesitate to describe himself as a Buddhist. The fact that such tender language appears in super-hardcore Oxford philosophy, however fleetingly, is remarkable. It is a devastating moment in the argument, not a biographical aside. Utility, which is precisely happiness, emerges here not out of self-interest but from the opposite impulse. Indeed, Parfit's project is to show how self-interest theories of ethics are self-defeating, especially when we subject them to the stress test of thinking them on sufficiently large timescales. In a sense, translating from Analytic to Continental for a moment, self-interest theories are autoimmune, in the way that Schopenhauer's Will scavenges on itself when it tries to fulfill itself.

What Parfit's language misses is that to let go of the self-concept might also be to put oneself into a loop. This loop would imply a more intimate relationship with . . . "oneself." Simply to insist that the self-concept be dropped is rather schematic, as if one were looking at the problem from a high altitude. From the somewhat more "personal" viewpoint of a meditator, the words of Dōgen at the start of the *Shōbōgenzō* apply: "To study the Way is to study the self. To study the self is to forget the self. To forget the self is to be enlightened by all things of the universe."[124] *Study* here does not mean schematic examination, but rather what in Tibetan is called *gom* (the term for meditation), *becoming familiar with*, a necessarily aesthetic appreciation.

Notice that for Dōgen, to drop the self is to coexist with *things*. Let us flesh this out.

To exist is to be ever so slightly different from yourself, which is the secret of "narcissism"—autoaffection in the end is equal to heteroaffection. Hegel's phobic image of A=A is an image of a loop in many respects. Hegel calls this loop "withdrawal into self" a phrase that uncannily resonates with Heidegger's notion of the withdrawal of objects: when a thing just functions, it is withdrawn-into-itself (*Entzug*).[125] And Buddhism is the religion of this "being-within-self" (*Insichsein*). This withdrawal is not unrelated to a certain thingliness. When I meditate, when I "practice" I encircle my mind with my mind, putting it in a loop wherein its semiotic, ideational, mentative qualities (its appearance) are folded like droplets into the ocean of its thingness. So now our argument veers toward the fear of things.

FEAR OF THINGS

It is reasonably evident that idealism is anxious about the status of the thing. Let us return for a moment to another kind of anxiety about things, the anxiety expressed in eliminative materialism. Recall that this anxiety is preoccupied with nothingness, whose symptom is an irreducible gap between appearance and reality that I nevertheless cannot locate anywhere in reality as such. It would reduce this anxiety to eliminate the gap, and certain forms of materialism are one way of doing so. Yet elimination is plagued by the very self-reference and ambiguity it seeks to abolish. Eliminative psychology claims that thoughts are actually brain firings. Yet as Husserl argued, this implies an infinite regress. Since the idea *All thoughts are brain firings* is also a brain firing, there is no way to check its truth. This insight provides the basis for phenomenology.[126] Thoughts have as it were a kind of logical DNA that is independent of the mind that is thinking them, especially of its wetware. Ideas somewhat resemble parasites such as viruses that cannot exist outside a host (bacterium, mind), yet are not reducible to that host. In this sense, an idea is a thing, just as a virus is a string of (DNA or RNA) code.

Thus my mind is full of entities that are not me (thoughts), just as my brain is full of entities that are not me, or not even my brain: symbionts such as *Toxoplasma gondii*, for instance, DNA with its kludge-like properties, reptilian and mammalian brain parts. As ideology theory demonstrates, ideas have a certain agency: human subjects become vectors for them. These things that are not-me, even the ideas, are agents that might affect me, or kill me, or drive me insane, or cause me to be more introverted.[127] Ecological awareness seems ripe for a Buddhist interpretation. The world teems in a claustrophobic manner.

Yet this teeming world is underwritten by nothingness. Differences between and within me and not-me are what provide the fuel for the world to function. The problem of nothingness is not the problem of a blank, inert void, but the problem of things tout court: they are here, within and without. They are thoughts. They are statues.

What could be more evocative of this problem than a statue? To put it another way, what is more evocative of the fear of the thing in Western thought than the famous *res intellectus* of Descartes, the thinking thing—out of which Žižek gets quite a lot of mileage, a mileage that might seem ironic at this point in our analysis?[128] For the Cartesian cogito depends upon a certain paranoia that I might merely be a puppet, an animated statue: a thing, driven around by forces that are demonic precisely insofar as they are not-me, and not under my control. The idea that I might be a puppet is the very idea via which I discover my existence. Do we not encounter in this formula the strange level-crossing self-referential loop that we have encountered throughout this essay, a loop that some Western philosophy is trying with all its might to cancel out?

And is it not to the credit of Lacan that he does not cancel out this loop, but rather expands it into a baroque, even more disturbing version of itself? "I am not wherever I am the plaything of my thought. I think of what I am where I do not think to think."[129] I am I insofar as I do not coincide with myself—yet I am myself, as Lacan's use of the Liar (*This sentence is false*) in the essay from which I quote here bears out. Or to put it in Douglas Hofstadter's terms, *I am a strange loop*.[130] To be at least one thing, the (human) subject, is to be not that thing at the same time: an intolerable (for some) inconsistency or ambiguity, or downright contradiction. It is apparent in Lacan's use of *plaything*, which rather elegantly encapsulates the issue of thingliness, and the issue of play, which is also an issue of negation and ambiguity, the Batesonian bite that is not a bite.[131] This sense of play is perhaps closer to the strangeness of Buddhism than the avowedly Buddhist-inspired Parfit's hilarious attempt, within utilitarianism, to smooth out the contradictions in the cogito: "This is the thinking of a thought, so at least some thinking is going on."[132]

In this sense, Badiou is not a Lacanian, since for him to exist is to be consistent. Nor is Badiou a Cantorian. Rather he cleaves to the Zermelo-Fraenkel interpretation of Cantor, an interpretation that precisely removes the wrinkles of inconsistency such as sets that contain members that are not members of themselves. The infamous Russell set paradox is a glaring example of the kind of self-reference implied in the idea of transfinite sets, sets that contain infinities that lack a smooth continuum between them, the kinds of infinity upon which circles depend; the kinds of infinity that make real circles different from ones drawn with pixels or pencils. The set of real numbers contains the set of rational numbers, but without a bridge between these sets: there is a striking paradox.

It is a short hop from considering the I as not-me—a thought that already happens in Kant's distinction between the *subject* and the phenomenally situated *self*—to considering mountains as not-mountains (Dōgen), or sets of things as not-sets of things (not members of themselves), and so on. To be a thing on this view is an unbearable, impossible contradiction. And contradictions must be eliminated, according to an idea—an idea-virus, so to speak, whose virulence is still operational: the Aristotelian Law of Noncontradiction. So much Aristotle has been shed in modernity: the kind of substance ontology pejoratively called scholasticism since Kant; teleology, dead since Darwin. But the Law of Noncontradiction persists, notwithstanding the mathematical lineages of Cantor and Gödel. In holding a thing to be consistent in order to exist, Badiou shows himself susceptible to this virus.

Yet a Buddhist meditator is supposed to hold, if only for her progress along the path, that a mountain might not be a mountain. Indeed, she is expected to *see* a mountain as a not-mountain. Otherwise she would be back to square one, in which mountains are just (her concept of) mountains, or square two, in which there are no mountains (but there are atoms, or mountain-thoughts, and so on). Emptiness is form. A Buddhist meditator does something totally illogical from the standpoint that to be a thing is to be consistent. Yet this thought that a thing is consistent in order to exist flies in the face of mathematics since Cantor, and also of ontology since Kant—in other words, it flies in the face of modernity. Fear of Buddhism is a fear of things, insofar as things turn out to be no-thing, as in the famous *kōan* of Joshu's Mu: when asked whether a dog has Buddha nature, Joshu replied *Mu*, a privative prefix that might, or might not, mean *not* or *no-thing*, but perhaps more basically *non-* or *un-*.[133] A prefix waiting for a word, let alone a sentence, to complete it. An organ without a body. A little bit of viral code, waiting for a host.

Furthermore, from the standpoint of the Mahāyāna, from which the Prajñāpāramitā Sūtra emerges, the Buddhist meditator is trying to evoke or otherwise realize what is already the case—that she is not who she is, not a confused being, but rather a Buddha. As one progresses along the path there are ever more paradoxical ways of asserting this—for instance, in the Tantric view of Dzogchen one has never strayed "a hair's breadth" from this Buddha nature, despite one's perception of oneself as a necessarily confused sentient being. This is patently absurd if one cleaves to the Law of Noncontradiction. There is a thin bright line between a sentient being and a Buddha, and this line is intrinsic to Dzogchen. Confusion just isn't enlightenment. Yet the intrinsic nature of the confused mind is totally and already enlightened, always-already. There is a disturbing gap between this nature of mind (Tibetan, *ngowo*) and how it appears as confusion: disturbing because it seems so categorical, yet at the same time, I cannot locate it anywhere, since confused mind's essence is totally enlightened.

Buddha nature (Sanskrit, *Thatāgatagharba*) is a not-me that is in me. Indeed, this not-me is more "me" than myself, which is only a confused perception. So progress along the Buddhist path is on this view a matter of faith in an entity—a *thing* insofar as a minimal definition of a thing is that it is a not-me—whose realization is also the understanding that I myself am a thing, insofar as "myself" is also a thing-like construct, an idea with its own logical genome, its own weird determinateness. I am beset from both sides: a not-me (confused, sentient being) realizes that it is also a not-me (totally enlightened Buddha).

We could call this realization a process, but that would be a way, albeit quite fashionable and upgraded, to preserve some kind of presence, insofar as the process itself, happening "in" time, can be taken as a sort of constant thing, though a fluid one. And this popular process philosophy way of understanding Buddhist realization does not really do justice to the idea that right now, in my very confusion, at this very moment, the confusion itself is nothing other than Buddha mind. Process thinking is a way to domesticate the profound contradictoriness of this idea, to bring it within the purview of the Aristotle virus, LNC. Whitehead, grandfather of process philosophy, was after all Russell's collaborator on the loop-suppressing *Principia*.

I come from nothing not only insofar as I am made of other things such as DNA and memories, but also insofar as there is an irreducible gap between me and actuality, Buddha nature, a gap that is intrinsic to being me, and that is located as it were "inside" me in my inner space. This is the gap between relative and absolute truth (Tibetan, *kundzop* and *döndam*) in the Yogacharin Mahāyāna, a gap that generates another gap between "confused" and "real" relative truth. This other gap is based on the fact that Buddha nature is not nothing at all, but rather has all kinds of phenomena (such as compassion and equanimity) that are inseparable from it. Yet they are inseparable in the same way that a crystal ball and the shapes and colors that appear in it are inseparable: there is still a gap, even here, between what in Dzogchen is called *ngowo* (nature) and *salwa* (clarity, appearance). All phenomena (*nangwa*), from the most confused to the most enlightened, are empty. This emptiness is *why they exist*, not why they fail to exist.

Thus any phenomenal, experiential "state," including an enlightened one, must have a quality of tentative, wavering inconsistency, an illusion-like quality that is celebrated in the Sūtra and Tantra traditions. In other words, both confused and realized phenomena are shot through with what this essay has been calling nothingness. Consider, for instance, the traditional analogies of Nāgārjuna: life is like a mirage, an image in a mirror, an echo, a dream, a shadow, empty space, a magical display, a reflection of the moon in water, the heavenly cities of the *gandharvas* (the musicians of the gods).

Are these not also weirdly similar to the descriptions of William Blake's character Thel, a character invented at the very start of modernity? Thel is a teenage girl, suicidal and self-absorbed, unable to cope with the life-and-death cycles of existence: she is, in other words, a kind of Buddhist, at least in the eyes of Buddhaphobia. Thel describes herself as various tricksterish forms of environmental anamorphic shape:

> O life of this our spring! why fades the lotus of the water?
> Why fade these children of the spring, born but to smile & fall?
> Ah! Thel is like a watry bow, and like a parting cloud,
> Like a reflection in a glass, like shadows in the water,
> Like dreams of infants, like a smile upon an infant's face,
> Like the dove's voice, like transient day, like music in the air.[134]

It is almost as if Thel had heard of Nāgārjuna's analogies for emptiness (reflection, dream, hallucination . . .): the resemblance is uncanny. She does not understand why she is so transient and illusory, along with the phenomena in her world, and she refuses the moral lessons of the beings with whom she speaks (a flower, a cloud, a worm, a clod of clay). These beings seem more than happy to be recycled. It seems as if Thel wants to get off the wheel altogether. The moral lessons of the entities with whom Thel speaks are Christian in tone. One dies, but to a greater glory, as part of God's plan. For Thel this is just metaphysics, and in this sense she is more advanced than her interlocutors, precisely insofar as she seems more regressed than them. This might remind us of what Adorno says about true progress, which might look like decadence precisely because it does not fit the surrounding paradigm. Adorno takes as his example Nietzsche weeping at the sight of a horse being whipped.[135] Unconditional compassion for another sentient being's suffering is expressed, rather than a moralizing sense that pain is part of a divine scheme.

Thel is like the Beautiful Soul, a stage in Hegel's history of phenomenological styles, whose certainty he brilliantly describes as "changed immediately into a sound that dies away"—a phrase that resounds with the Hegelian contempt for Buddhism we have been exploring.[136] To study Hegel's Buddhism is to call for a reexamination of issues in Hegel's aesthetics that would take his fascinating, abject image of the Buddha into account. On the one hand, "the primitive artistic pantheism of the East" appears to jam together the two halves of art, nature and idea, as "unsuitable" and opaque to one another. Thus are produced forms that cannot adequately bear their content, either becoming "bizarre, grotesque and tasteless" (rather like Hegel's view of the proliferating dreams of Hinduism), or turning "the infinite but abstract freedom of the substantive Idea disdainfully against all phenomenal being as null and evanescent," rather like his view of Buddhism.[137] In the *Introductory Lectures on Aesthetics* Hegel was keen to criticize the idea of God as merely "*One*, the supreme Being as such": in this formula "we have only enunciated a lifeless abstraction of the irrational understanding."[138] On the other hand, the inwardness of the Romantic art form is analogous to a pure "consciousness of God . . . in which the distinction of objectivity and subjectivity is done away."[139] Could the inwardness with which Hegel characterizes Buddhism have anything to do with this, or is it merely to be construed as marginal to Hegel's thought? Hegel appears disturbed by the notion of irony: a sense of "the nothingness of all that is objective" which gives rise to a "sickly" form of "quiescence and feebleness—which does not like to act or to touch anything for fear of surrendering its inward harmony." Hegel here offers what could later be used as a critique of Schopenhauer, whose fusion of Buddhism and the aesthetic presents just such a "morbid saintliness and yearning," based on an "abstract inwardness (of mind)," a "retirement into itself."[140] Surely there is an echo of this in the Buddhism of *Insichsein*? And could what Hegel says about irony, that most Romantic of tropes, be isometric with his view of Buddhism and in particular, Buddhist meditation practice?

Thel is all dressed up with nowhere to go. And is not Thel herself also accused of a certain narcissism insofar as *The Book of Thel* is often read as Blake himself wanted it not to be, as a "moral hymn" in reverse about how young girls should stop being so narcissistically absorbed and start having sex with men as soon as possible? Is not Thel, in other words, a *figure for theory*?[141] Buddhism and theory are not so distant, in the figure of Thel.

"Like a reflection . . . like music in the air." Like something that is like something. Thel's self-description is in a loop. This loopy quality also aligns it with Buddhism, in which reality is *like* an illusion. If one knew that it was indeed a complete illusion, like a Hare Krishna, one would be in a sense protected from what is disturbing about illusion, since as Lacan has argued (and this essay has already quoted), "What constitutes pretense is that, in the end, you don't know whether it's pretense or not." Talk about illusion is talk about phenomena. The phenomenality of things is evidence that there are things, but since Hume and Kant it might be impossible for Western philosophy to think these things without thinking their strange withdrawal from phenomenality.

An idea encapsulated in a sentence (an *ideologeme* in Althusserian) or a code encapsulated in a strand of DNA is a strange loop that is both physical and semiotic. What if this strange loop quality came about because of a deeper, more pervasive loopiness in which things and their appearances were separate, yet irreducibly glued to one another? A thing is not its appearance. Yet it appears just this way. When we follow appearance we never find the thing, because there is a thing. It is like following a Möbius strip, a non-orientable surface on which it is impossible to specify a front or back, inside or outside. The twist in the Möbius strip cannot be constrained to one particular part of that shape. Yet there appears to be a strange level-crossing loop in which one side of the strip magically flips into the other as we trace it. Is this not reminiscent of the strange loop between *sentient being* and *Buddha* that we have just explored?

It is peculiar, then, at least in this light, that Žižek should be so interested in loops and Möbius strips. That a certain idea takes the form of a Möbius strip is one of his very favorite formulations.[142] Since the fear of self-referential loops is what activates Buddhaphobia, it is as if Žižek's philosophy is afraid of that with which it is most intimate.

A statue, and perhaps in particular a Buddha statue, exemplifies the weird thingliness I am describing here. I use *weird* with the weight of its etymological resonance from the Old Norse, *urth*, which means *twist* or *turn*, as in *a twist of fate* or *a funny turn* or *a strange turn-up for the book*.[143] A statue is a thing that is also an appearance, an appearance that is inseparable from it. It is also an embodiment of a person—hovering uncertainly (and thus threateningly) between representation and simulation. It does look at me, insofar as the gaze is (in Lacanian and thus Žižekian) a kind of object that holds me in its gravitational field. What is disturbing about a statue is not that it might be looking at me, but that *I might be one too*. I might be an object among objects. Yet is this not at least the partial lesson of the phenomenological lineage that passes through Hegel to Husserl, then to Heidegger and his followers, from Lacan to Althusser? A statue, like Thel, is also a figure for theory: a seemingly inert, passive set of texts and thoughts that nevertheless possesses a weird agency, that "looks at me" and undermines my place in the supposedly natural order of things. It is inert, yet this very inertia has a strange fascination about it.

A strange wonderment that is passive, yet this passivity has its own disturbing activity, an activity that undermines the difference between doing and thinking: theory. "Wonder, a most philosophical affect": *thaumazein mala philosophikon pathos* (Plato, *Theaetetus*). Theory flickers with nothingness. Thinking Buddhism is a way to think theory beyond certain deadlocks. Consider the firewall that some theory draws between East and West, as if even talking about Eastern philosophy, let alone (heaven forbid) thinking it or actually practicing it were always a kind of imperialist orientalism. This firewall is enabled by Buddhaphobia, in which the most interesting discovery of modernity, nothingness, is projected onto non-Western philosophy and practice. A less phobic encounter with nothingness is

thus a less phobic encounter with Buddhism. Such an encounter, enabled by some kind of philosophical allergy medicine, is a
way to imagine the future of theory outside of modernity.

It would be an encounter that took the Marxist foreclosure
of the regressive "back to nature" exit seriously. To start with
the "bad new things" rather than yearn for the illusory good
old days was what Brecht recommended.[144] Adorno preferred
Schopenhauer's and Wagner's darkness to Nietzsche's relentless
light. Yet this sounds remarkably like the First Noble Truth of
Buddhism: life is suffering, and forms of denial about this Truth
are also forms of suffering. The encounter would not be in the
name of some delicious synthesis of Buddhism and Western
theory. Such an affair would not be an encounter, but rather an
emulsion in which the two streams were not changed. Instead
of this possibility, there might be a disturbing, perhaps at times
horrible, and certainly *weird* encounter. It might not be the case
that Buddhism completes theory, or that theory completes Buddhism. But it is certainly the case that thinking is incapable of
un-thinking, and that in this sense thought has no reverse gear,
which is not quite the same thing as saying that progress is inevitable. It is in a sense only to acknowledge that the strange meeting between Western theory and its Buddhist doppelganger is
already happening—has been happening since 1750, when Je-
suits evoked the horror of The Nothing. Since the zero degree of
political praxis is taken to be Bartleby's "I would prefer not to"
from Žižek to Occupy, theory knows already that passivity is not
inherently apolitical.[145] Yet the specter of hundreds of "passive"
people, sitting like statues, their bodies in a loop, is haunting the
Hegelianism that underpins Marxism: the specter of Buddhism.
Engaging this specter would entail a meaningful encounter with
commodities and consumerism, and thus with those unloved
things we call *objects*.

Within Left theory there is something of a taboo on the notion of interior life, a taboo not dispelled by the rise of technocratic approaches to the management of feelings (self-help).[146]

The current anxiety about subjectivity is Buddhaphobic at its core. This elegance doesn't rule out the possibility that there are other explanations, but it challenges them to be as concise. For example, we could point to the rise of technocratic utilitarianism, obsessed with "objects" and "outcomes," in the culture at large and in the academy in particular. Or we could trace the development of antihumanism (students of Heidegger such as Lacan, Foucault, Derrida) as it morphed into forms of posthumanism that espouse much more radical breaks with anything like the inner life, a phrase that now sounds absurd in many ears. We could explain, as Adorno did, how bourgeois culture gave up on this inner life toward the start of the Second World War, eschewing it for an emerging consumerism that fixated on luxury products. Romantic poetry, art, and music went out of fashion because it disturbingly reminded people of their inner space.[147] The way the humanities regularly express contempt for subjectivity as a mere construct, and a dangerous one at that, might be a classic instance of Stockholm Syndrome.

Buddhaphobia means being afraid that there is something within us: not us, yet extremely intimate, perhaps even more intimate than our sense of being ourselves. As the theologian George Morrison said of God, this something is "nearer than breathing, closer than hands and feet."[148] Or as American wing mirrors say: OBJECTS IN MIRROR ARE CLOSER THAN THEY APPEAR. Buddhaphobia is nothing but a fear of subjectivity as such. Yet this fear is based on the awareness that we are not who we think we are—that the core of subjectivity is actually a kind of *object*.[149] This awareness is disturbing only insofar as it meets resistance from the narcissistically wounded subject of modernity. What is necessary, then, is a reappropriation of what is called narcissism within "Western" theoretical discourse, much as Derrida enjoined. Taking one's cue from what Adorno says of Proust—that he demolishes the aristocracy with "remorseless gentleness"—critical theory might then look and feel quite different, might indeed wither away at least in the eyes of some.[150]

Yet perhaps this might precisely result in something far more effective than basing one's arguments on aggression and fear. The extent to which the previous sentence will encounter filthy looks from many of its readers is an index of its truth.

NOTES

1. Probably in Paul Demiéville, "Le mirroir spiritual," *Sinologica* 1.2 (1947): 112–37.

2. Jacques Lacan, *The Seminar of Jacques Lacan, Book X: Anxiety (1962-1963)*, trans. Cormac Gallagher (n.p., n.d.), 208–9.

3. Jacques Lacan, "Analysis and Truth or the Closure of the Unconscious," in *The Four Fundamental Concepts of Psychoanalysis: The Seminar of Jacques Lacan XI*, trans. Alan Sheridan (New York: Norton, 1998), 136–48.

4. This was recently argued by Roger Corless in "Towards a Queer Dharmology of Sex," *Culture and Religion* 5, no. 2 (2004): 229–43.

5. Judith Halberstam, "An Introduction to Gothic Monstrosity" in Robert Louis Stevenson, *The Strange Case of Dr. Jekyll and Mr. Hyde: An Authoritative Text, Backgrounds and Contexts, Performance Adaptations, Criticism*, ed. Katherine Linehan (New York: Norton, 2003), 128–31.

6. See Thrangu Rinpoche, *Vivid Awareness: The Mind Instructions of Khenpo Gangshar* (Boston: Shambhala, 2011), 43–109.

7. The most comprehensive account in English is C. W. Huntington, Jr., with Geshe Namgyal Wangchen, *The Emptiness of Emptiness: An Introduction to Early Indian Madhyamika* (Honolulu: University of Hawai'i Press, 1989).

8. Heidegger, *Being and Time*, trans. Joan Stambaugh (Albany, NY: State University of New York Press, 1996), 316.

9. Ibid., 304–6, 310–11, 312, 321–22.

10. Chögyam Trungpa, *The Path Is the Goal: A Basic Handbook of Buddhist Meditation* (Boston: Shambhala 1995), 56–57, 106–7; "Basic

Anxiety Is Happening All the Time" *Shambhala Times* April 3, 2009, http://shambhalatimes.org/2009/04/03/basic-anxiety-is -happening-all-the-time-by-chogyam-trungpa/, accessed April 28, 2013; *The Truth of Suffering and the Path of Liberation*, ed. Judith Lief (Boston: Shambhala, 2010), 9–10.

11. Martin Heidegger, *The Zollikon Seminars: Protocols— Conversations—Letters*, trans. Franz Mayr (Evanston, IL: North-western University Press, 2001).

12. Lacan, *The Seminar Book X*, 210.

13. Jacques Lacan, "The Agency of the Letter in the Unconscious," *Écrits: A Selection*, trans. Alan Sheridan (London: Tavistock, 1977), 146–78 (151–52).

14. Thomas Carl Wall, *Radical Passivity: Levinas, Blanchot, and Agamben* (Albany: State University of New York Press, 1999).

15. Most recently, in "Lacan against Buddhism," in *Less than Nothing: Hegel and the Shadow of Dialectical Materialism* (London: Verso, 2012), 127–35.

16. For instance, Raul Moncayo, *The Signifier Pointing at the Moon: Psychoanalysis and Zen Buddhism* (London: Karnac, 2012).

17. Slavoj Žižek, "Passion in the Era of Decaffeinated Belief" http://www.lacan.com/passion.htm, accessed January 2, 2013.

18. Slavoj Žižek, *The Sublime Object of Ideology* (London: Verso, 1991), 134.

19. Žižek's hostility to Buddhism is pervasive. See for example "I Plead Guilty—But Where Is the Judgment?," *Nepantla: Views from South* 3, no. 3 (2002): 579–83; "Nobody Has to Be Vile," *London Review of Books* 28, no. 7 (April 6, 2006), 10; "Self-Deceptions: On Being Tolerant and Smug," *Die Gazette* Israel (August 27, 2001); "Revenge of Global Finance," *In These Times*, May 21, 2005, http:// www.inthesetimes.com/article/2122/.

20. Georg Wilhelm Friedrich Hegel, *Lectures on the Philosophy of Religion*, ed. Peter C. Hodgson; trans. R. F. Brown, P. C. Hodgson, and J. M. Stewart; assisted by H. S. Harris, 3 vols. (Oxford: Claren-don, 2007), 2:252.

21. Immanuel Kant, *Critique of Judgment: Including the First Intro-*

duction, trans. Werner Pluhar (Indianapolis: Hackett, 1987), §4 (49), §22 (90, 92), §58 (221–22).

22. Immanuel Kant, *Critique of Pure Reason*, trans. Norman Kemp Smith (Boston and New York: Bedford/St. Martin's, 1965), §8 (84–85).

23. Quentin Meillassoux, *After Finitude: An Essay on the Necessity of Contingency*, trans. Ray Brassier (New York: Continuum, 2009), 5, 119–21.

24. Georg Wilhelm Friedrich Hegel, *Hegel's Logic*, trans. William Wallace, foreword by J. N. Findlay (Oxford: Oxford University Press, 1975), 119–20.

25. Roger-Pol Droit provides an extensive account in *The Cult of Nothingness* (Chapel Hill: University of North Carolina Press, 2003).

26. As it is known in Shambhala, a major current of Western Buddhism.

27. *Allgemeine Historie der Reisen zu Wasser und zu Lande; oder, Sammlung aller Reisebeschreibungen* (Leipzig, 1750), vol. 6, 368.

28. Edward Casey, *The Fate of Place: A Philosophical History* (Berkeley: University of California Press, 1997), 106–16.

29. Jacques Lacan, *Le seminaire, Livre III: Les psychoses* (Paris: Editions de Seuil, 1981), 48.

30. Thomas Metzinger, *Being No-One: The Self-Model Theory of Subjectivity* (Cambridge, MA: MIT Press, 2004). See also Michael Kurak, "The Relevance of the Buddhist Theory of Dependent Co-origination to Cognitive Science," *Brain and Mind: A Transdisciplinary Journal of Neuroscience and Neurophilosophy* 4, no. 3 (December, 2003): 341–51; "Buddhism and Brain Science," *Journal of Consciousness Studies* 8, no. 11 (November 2001): 17–26. For an opposing view see Graham Harman, "The Problem with Metzinger" *Cosmos and History* 7, no. 1 (2011), 7–36; and Eleanor Rosch, "Reclaiming Concepts," *Journal of Consciousness Studies* 6, nos. 11–12 (November–December 1999): 61–77; "Is Wisdom in the Brain?," *Psychological Science* 10, no. 3 (1999), 222–24.

31. Immanuel Levinas, "There Is: Existence without Existents,"

in *The Levinas Reader*, ed. Seán Hand (Oxford: Blackwell, 1989), 29–36.

32. Jean-Luc Marion, *In Excess: Studies of Saturated Phenomena*, trans. Robyn Horner and Vincent Berraud (New York: Fordham University Press, 2002), 37–40.

33. I quote from the version of the sūtra in twenty-five lines, translated into Tibetan by Lotsawa bhikshu [monk] Rinchen De with the Indian pandita [scholar] Vimalamitra. Translated into English by the Nalanda Translation Committee, with reference to several Sanskrit editions.

34. Chögyam Trungpa, *Cutting Through Spiritual Materialism* (Boston: Shambhala, 1987), 189.

35. Casey, *The Fate of Place*, 106–16.

36. Anonymous, *The Cloud of Unknowing and Other Works*, trans. A. C. Spearing (London: Penguin, 2002); St. John of the Cross, *The Dark Night of the Soul* (New York: Dover, 2003).

37. Arthur Schopenhauer, *The World as Will and Representation*, trans. E. F. J. Payne, 2 vols. (New York: Dover, 1969), 93–165.

38. Arthur Schopenhauer, *The World as Will and Representation*, trans. E. F. J. Payne, 2 vols. (New York: Dover Publications, 1969), 1:137n13; §26.

39. Karl Marx, *The Communist Manifesto*, in *Selected Writings*, ed. David McLellan (Oxford: Oxford University Press, 1977, 1987), 12; William Shakespeare, *Macbeth* (New York: Washington Square Press, 1992), 19.

40. Derrida elaborates hauntology in *Specters of Marx: The State of the Debt, the Work of Mourning, and the New International*, trans. Peggy Kamuf (London: Routledge, 1994).

41. Hegel, *Lectures on the Philosophy of Religion*, 2:252.

42. On the enigmatic quality of Buddha statues, see the account of Ezra Pound's use of Kuan Yin in the *Cantos* in Britton Gildersleeve, "'Enigma' at the Heart of Paradise: Buddhism, Kuanon, and the Feminine Ideogram in the *Cantos*," in *Ezra Pound and China*, ed. Zhaoming Qian (Ann Arbor: Michigan University Press, 2003), 193–212. William Empson was likewise moved by Buddha statues:

see "Faces of Buddha," in William Empson and J. Haffenden, ed., *Argufying: Essays on Literature and Culture* (Iowa City: University of Iowa Press, 1987), 573–76. The book has never surfaced although there are recent rumors that a manuscript has been found. See Richard Pollott, "The Poet's Response: William Empson and the Faces of Buddha," *PN Review* 167 (2006): 54–56. Northrop Frye also took an interest in Buddhism. See Robert D. Denham, "Frye and the East: Buddhist and Hindu Translations," in Jean O'Grady and Wang Ning eds. *Northrop Frye: Eastern and Western Prespectives* (London: Toronto University Press, 2003), 3–18.

43. Luce Irigaray, *This Sex Which Is Not One*, trans. Catherine Porter and Carolyn Burke (Ithaca, NY: Cornell University Press, 1985).

44. Hegel, *Lectures on the Philosophy of Religion*, 2:252.

45. See Gilles Deleuze, *Francis Bacon: The Logic of Sensation* (Minneapolis: University of Minnesota Press, 2005), 18–19, 50, 146–47.

46. Gilles Deleuze and Félix Guattari, "November 28, 1947: How Do You Make Yourself a Body Without Organs?," *A Thousand Plateaus: Capitalism and Schizophrenia*, trans. Brian Massumi (Minneapolis: University of Minnesota Press, 1987), 149–66.

47. The proper Lacanian term is *sinthome*, a pun on the Apostle Thomas, who had to insert his fingers into the gaping wound in the side of the risen Christ, who had returned to convince Thomas of His reality. For Lacan, the sinthome is neither symptom nor fantasy but "the point marking the dimension of 'what is in the subject more than himself' and what he therefore 'loves more than himself.'" (Žižek, *Looking Awry: An Introduction to Jacques Lacan through Popular Culture* (Cambridge, MA: MIT Press, 1991, 1992), 132.

48. Luce Irigaray, *Between East and West*, trans. Stephen Pluháček (New York: Columbia University Press, 2002).

49. Martin Heidegger, *Contributions to Philosophy (From Enowning)*, trans. Parvis Emad and Kenneth Maly (Bloomington: Indiana University Press, 1999), 65.

50. Gilles Deleuze and Félix Guattari, *A Thousand Plateaus:*

Capitalism and Schizophrenia, trans. Brian Massumi (Minneapolis: University of Minnesota Press, 1987), 150–51.

51. "Centreing," trans. Paul Reps, in Paul Reps and Nyogen Senzaki, eds., *Zen Flesh, Zen Bones* (Harmondsworth, UK: Penguin, 1980), 153–54.

52. Hegel, *Lectures on the Philosophy of Religion*, 254.

53. Eugene Thacker, *After Life* (Chicago: University of Chicago Press, 2010), 264.

54. Timothy Morton, *Shelley and the Revolution in Taste: The Body and the Natural World* (Cambridge: Cambridge University Press, 1994), 13–56.

55. Timothy Morton, *Ecology without Nature: Rethinking Environmental Aesthetics* (Cambridge, MA: Harvard University Press, 2007), 111–13.

56. See, for instance, Trungpa, *Cutting Through Spiritual Materialism*. Trungpa invented the phrase.

57. "[H]ier schießt dann ein blutig[er] Kopf, dort ein[e] andere weiße Gestalt plötzlich hervor und verschwinden ebenso." Georg Wilhelm Friedrich Hegel, "Jenaer Realphilosophie" in *Frühe politische Systeme*, ed. Gerhard Göhler (Frankfurt: Ullstein, 1974) 201–89 (204).

58. Georges Bataille, *Theory of Religion*, trans. Robert Hurley (Cambridge, MA: MIT Press, 1992), 57. The view that religion is about intimacy contrasts with the more common assumption that it is about "feeling part of something bigger." For the "something bigger" motif, see William James, *The Varieties of Religious Experience* (London: Penguin, 1985), 525—almost the last thing James says about religion in his concluding chapter. David Wood has stated a contrasting view: David Wood and J. Aaron Simmons, "Moments of Intense Presence: A Conversation with David Wood," *Journal For Cultural and Religious Theory* 10, no. 1 (Winter 2009): 81–101.

59. See, for instance, Edwin Arnold, *The Light of Asia*, http://www.gutenberg.org/cache/epub/8920/pg8920.html, accessed May 7, 2013. The final line is "The Dewdrop Slips into The Shining Sea!"

60. Space does not quite permit a full account of Jane Bennett's recent thinking of "lively" matter through the Thoreavian idea of droplets as the basis of material form. "It Is to the Vegetable that We Always Come Back," paper given at The Secret Life of Plants, Princeton University, May 3, 2013.

61. Friedrich Nietzsche, *The Birth of Tragedy: Out of the Spirit of Music*, trans. Shaun Whiteside, ed. Michael Tanner (London: Penguin, 1994).

62. For instance, see Slavoj Žižek, "Love Beyond Law," http://www.lacan.com/zizlola.htm, accessed May 7, 2013.

63. Glyn Daly and Slavoj Žižek, *Conversations with Žižek* (Malden, MA: Polity, 2004), 96.

64. Theodor Adorno, *Negative Dialectics*, trans. E. B. Ashton (New York: Continuum, 1973), 68.

65. Ibid., 68.

66. *Oxford English Dictionary*, "corny" adj. 1.c, accessed May 4, 2013.

67. Wang Lixiong, "Reflections on Tibet," *New Left Review* 14 (March–April, 2002): 79–111. For a counterargument see Tsering Shakya, "Blood in the Snows: Reply to Wang Lixiong," *New Left Review* 15 (May–June, 2002): 39–60. For a Marxist endorsement of Buddhism see Kevin M.Brien, "Marx and the Spiritual Dimension," *Topoi: An International Review of Philosophy* 15, no. 2 (September 1996): 211–23; Nathan Katz, "Buddhism and Marxism on Alienation and Suffering," *Indian Philosophical Quarterly: Journal of the Department of Philosophy, University of Poona* 10 (April 1983): 255–62.

68. Theodor W. Adorno and Max Horkheimer, *Dialectic of Enlightenment*, trans. John Cumming (London: Verso, 1979), 214.

69. See, for instance, Slavoj Žižek, *The Plague of Fantasies* (London: Verso, 1997), 111–13, 113–16.

70. Monier Monier-Williams, *Buddhism, in Its Connexion with Brahmanism and Hinduism, and in Its Contrast with Christianity* (London: John Murray, 1890), 340–86; Slavoj Žižek, "The Interpassive Subject: Lacan Turns a Prayer Wheel," *How to Read Lacan*, http://www.lacan.com/zizprayer.html, accessed April 3, 2013.

71. Marcus Boon, *In Praise of Copying* (Cambridge, MA: Harvard University Press, 2010).

72. Christopher Hitchens, *God Is Not Great: How Religion Poisons Everything* (New York: Twelve, 2009), 202–4.

73. Slavoj Žižek, *Tarrying with the Negative: Kant, Hegel, and the Critique of Ideology* (Durham, NC: Duke University Press, 1993), 26.

74. Timothy Morton, "Consumption as Performance: The Emergence of the Consumer in the Romantic Period," in *Cultures of Taste / Theories of Appetite*, ed. Timothy Morton (New York: Palgrave, 2004), 1–17.

75. Colin Campbell, *The Romantic Ethic and the Spirit of Modern Consumerism* (Oxford: Basil Blackwell, 1987); "Understanding Traditional and Modern Patterns of Consumption in Eighteenth-Century England," in *Consumption and the World of Goods*, ed. John Brewer and Roy Porter, 40–57 (52–55).

76. Lacan, *Le seminaire, Livre III*, 48.

77. See J. Jeffrey Franklin, "The Counter-Invasion of Britain by Buddhism in Marie Corelli's *A Romance of Two Worlds* and H. Rider Haggard's *Ayesha: the Return of She*," *Victorian Literature and Culture* 31, no. 1 (2003): 19–42. Franklin has recently expanded on this groundbreaking work in *The Lotus and the Lion: Buddhism and the British Empire* (Ithaca, NY: Cornell University Press, 2009), 10–24.

78. For a searching analysis see Donald Lopez, ed., *Curators of the Buddha: The Study of Buddhism under Colonialism* (Chicago: University of Chicago Press, 1995); *Prisoners of Shangri-La: Tibetan Buddhism and the West* (Chicago: University of Chicago Press, 1999).

79. *Oxford English Dictionary* (oed.com), "Buddhism," n.; "Buddhist," n. and adj. See Jonathan A. Silk, "The Victorian Creation of Buddhism," *Journal of Indian Philosophy* 22, no. 2 (June 1994): 171–96.

80. The work of Alphonso Lingis is the current apogee of explorations of overlaps between spirituality and consumerism. See for instance *The Imperative* (Bloomington: Indiana University Press, 1998).

81. Jean-Antheleme Brillat-Savarin, *The Physiology of Taste*,

trans. Anne Drayton (Harmondsworth, UK: Penguin, 1970), 13: "Dis-moi ce que tu manges, je te dirai ce que tu es."

82. Ludwig Feuerbach, *Gesammelte Werke II, Kleinere Schriften*, ed. Werner Schuffenhauer (Berlin: Akadamie-Verlag, 1972), 4.27: "Der Mensch ist, was er ißt."

83. Slavoj Žižek, "Melancholy and the Act," *Critical Inquiry* 26, no. 4 (Summer 2000): 657–81, esp. 674–77; see also *The Fragile Absolute: Or, Why is the Christian Legacy Worth Fighting For?* (London: Verso, 2000), esp. 23, 27–40, 128, 166–67.

84. See Droit, *The Cult of Nothingness*, 93–95 (quotation from p. 95).

85. David E. Cartwright, *Schopenhauer: A Biography* (Cambridge: Cambridge University Press, 2010), 274.

86. Sigmund Freud, *The Diary of Sigmund Freud, 1929–1939: A Record of the Final Decade* (New York: Maxwell Macmillan International, 1992), 10, 107 ("Kannon and Tang Figure bought."). See also xxii ("Earth-touching Buddha."); xxv ("penitent, walking Buddha."); 17, 143 ("Iron Buddha."); 153 ("Buddha head."); 22, 171 ("Ivory Buddha and stone Dog of Fo."); 26, 190 ("Large Kannon.").

87. Freud, *Diary*, 140.

88. Eske Møllgaard, "Slavoj Žižek's Critique of Western Buddhism," *Contemporary Buddhism* 9, no. 2 (2008): 167–80.

89. Elizabeth Lunbeck, *The Americanziation of Narcissism* (Cambridge, MA: Harvard University Press, 2014), 271.

90. Friedrich Nietzsche, *Thus Spoke Zarathustra*, trans. and intro. R. J. Hollingdale (London: Penguin, 2003), 192.

91. Jacques Derrida, "There Is No *One* Narcissism: Autobiophotographies," in *Points: Interviews 1974–1994*, ed. Elisabeth Weber, trans. Peggy Kamuf et al. (Stanford, CA: Stanford University Press, 1995), 196–215 (199).

92. For a discussion of Buddhism and economics see Richard A. Garnett and Natalya Makushkina, "Does Buddhism Really Discourage Economic Development? A Reassessment," *Southern Sociological Society* (2003): n.p.

93. Arthur Schopenhauer, *The World as Will and Representation*,

trans. E. F. J. Payne, 2 vols. (New York: Dover, 1969), 7–8, 8–10, 14–16.

94. Plato, *Ion*, trans. Benjamin Jowett (Cambridge, MA: Harvard University Press), http://classics.mit.edu/Plato/ion.html (accessed April 27, 2013).

95. Marion, *In Excess*, chap. 3 (54–81).

96. Schopenhauer, *Will*, §34 (178–81), §39 (200–207), §52 (255–67).

97. Sigmund Freud, *Beyond the Pleasure Principle* in *The Standard Edition of the Complete Psychological Works of Sigmund Freud*, ed. and trans. James Strachey, 24 vols. (London: Hogarth, 1953), 18.62.

98. John Keats, *The Complete Poems*, ed. Barnard, John, 2nd ed. (London: Penguin, 1987). Jeffrey Cox, *Poetry and Politics in the Cockney School: Keats, Shelley, Hunt and their Circle* (Cambridge: Cambridge University Press, 1998), 146–61. For the Wedgwood facsimile, see http://na.wwrd.com/ae/us/black-jasper/wedgwood+bentley -black-jasper-ls-portl+-vase/invt/091574188225/, accessed May 5, 2013.

99. *The Lalitavistara Sūtra: The Voice of the Buddha, the Beauty of Compassion*, trans. Gwendolyn Bays, 2 vols. (Berkeley: Dharma, 1983), 2:594.

100. See, for instance, Slavoj Žižek, *The Metastases of Enjoyment: Six Essays on Woman and Causality* (London: Verso, 1994), 20.

101. Theodor Adorno, "Sur l'Eau," *Minima Moralia: Reflections from Damaged Life*, trans. E. F. N. Jephcott (New York: Verso, 1978), 155–57 (157).

102. Friedrich Nietzsche, *The Anti-Christ* in *Twilight of the Idols and The Anti-Christ*, trans. R. J. Hollingdale, intro. Michael Tanner (London: Penguin, 2003), §20 (141–42), §21 (142–43), §22 (143–44), §23 (144–45); *Beyond Good and Evil: Prelude to a Philosophy of the Future*, trans. R. J. Hollingdale, intro. Michael Tanner (London: Penguin, 2003), §56 (82). That Buddhism is *"beyond* good and evil" is stated in §20 (141).

103. Heidegger, *Contributions*, 127, 135–36, 150, 189, 259.

104. See, for instance, Nietzsche, *Twilight of the Idols*, §24 (92–93); *The Anti-Christ* §7 (130–31).

105. Harold Ramis, dir., *Groundhog Day* (Columbia Pictures, 1993).

106. Paul Tillich, *Systematic Theology* (Chicago: University of Chicago Press, 1951), 1:188.

107. On the lack of a rigorous proof of LNC, see Graham Priest and Francesco Berto, "Dialetheism," *The Stanford Encyclopedia of Philosophy (Spring 2013 Edition)*, ed. Edward N. Zalta, http://plato .stanford.edu/archives/spr2013/entries/dialetheism/, accessed April 28, 2013.

108. Peter Unger, "The Problem of the Many," *Midwest Studies in Philosophy* 5 (1980): 411–67.

109. The sine qua non of explications is Douglas Hofstadter, *Gödel, Escher, Bach: An Eternal Golden Braid* (New York: Basic Books, 1999).

110. Jacques Lacan, *Écrits: A Selection*, trans. Alan Sheridan (London: Tavistock, 1977), 311.

111. Martin Heidegger, "Language," *Poetry, Language, Thought*, trans. Albert Hofstadter (New York: Harper and Row, 1971), 187–210 (191).

112. Martin Heidegger, *Being and Time*, trans. Joan Stambaugh (Albany: State University of New York Press, 1996), 1.3.17 (71–77; reference 73–74).

113. Heidegger, *Being and Time* 1.5.29 (130); *Phenomenological Interpretations of Aristotle: Initiation into Phenomenological Research*, trans. Richard Rojcewicz (Bloomington: Indiana University Press, 2009); Aristotle, *Rhetoric*, bk. 2 http://classics.mit.edu/Aristotle /rhetoric.2.ii.html, accessed April 29, 2013.

114. Graham Priest, *In Contradiction: A Study of the Transconsistent* (Oxford: Oxford University Press, 2006), 160.

115. Ibid., 170–71.

116. Georg Wilhelm Friedrich Hegel, *Hegel's Phenomenology of Spirit*, trans. A. V. Miller, analysis and foreword by J. N. Findlay (Oxford: Oxford University Press, 1977), §16 (9).

117. Georg Wilhelm Friedrich Hegel, *Hegel's Logic*, trans. William Wallace, foreword by J. N. Findlay, 3rd ed. (Oxford: Oxford University Press, 1975), 119–20, 125, 127.

118. Hegel, *Logic*, 127.

119. See, for instance, Jacques Derrida, "Supplement of Copula: Philosophy before Linguistics," trans. James Creech and Josué Harari, *Georgia Review* 30, no. 3 (Fall 1976): 527–64, esp. 555–64.

120. See Robert Kaplan, *The Nothing That Is: A Natural History of Zero* (Oxford: Oxford University Press, 2000; first published in London by Allen Lane, 1999).

121. Parfit derives much of his Buddhism from Steven Collins, *Selfless Persons: Imagery and Thought in Theravada Buddhism* (Cambridge: Cambridge University Press, 1982). See also Steven Collins, "A Buddhist Debate About the Self; and Remarks on Buddhism in the Work of Derek Parfit and Galen Strawson," *Journal of Indian Philosophy* 25, no. 5 (October 1997): 467–93; Mark Siderits, *Personal Identity and Buddhist Philosophy: Empty Persons* (Aldershot: Ashgate, 2003). For further encounters of analytic philosophy and Buddhism, see Roy W. Perrett, "Personal Identity, Minimalism, and Madhyamaka," *Philosophy East and West* 52, no. 3 (July 2002): 373–85; James D. Sellmann and Hans Julius Schneider, "Liberating Language in Linji and Wittgenstein," *Asian Philosophy* 13, nos. 2–3 (July–November 2003): 103–13; Derek Parfit, "Experiences, Subjects, and Conceptual Schemes," *Philosophical Topics* 26, nos. 1–2 (Spring and Fall 1999): 217–70. Derek Parfit, *Reasons and Persons* (Oxford: Oxford University Press, 1984), 347.

122. Ibid., 281. See Ananyo Basu, "Reducing Concern with Self: Parfit and the Ancient Buddhist Schools," in *Culture and Self*, ed. Douglas Allen (Boulder: Westview, 2007), 83–93; Jim Stone, "Parfit and the Buddha: Why There Are No People," *Philosophy and Phenomenological Research* 48 (March 1988): 519–32.

123. Parfit, *Reasons and Persons*, 347.

124. In Hee-Jin Kim, *Eihei Dōgen, Mystical Realist* (Somerville, MA: Wisdom Publications, 2004), 125.

125. Martin Heidegger, *Being and Time*, §15 (62–67).

126. Edmund Husserl, "Prolegomena to All Logic," *Logical Investigations*, trans. J. N. Findlay, ed. Dermot Moran (London: Routledge, 2006), 1:1–161; *Logical Investigations*, 1:276.

127. Jaroslav Flegr, "Effects of Toxoplasma on Human Behavior," *Schizophrenia Bulletin* 33, no. 3 (2007): 757–60.

128. Slavoj Žižek, *Tarrying with the Negative: Kant, Hegel, and the Critique of Ideology* (Durham, NC: Duke University Press, 1993), 9–18.

129. Lacan, "Agency of the Letter," 166.

130. Douglas Hofstadter, *I Am a Strange Loop* (New York: Basic Books, 2008).

131. Gregory Bateson, "A Theory of Play and Fantasy," *Steps to an Ecology of Mind*, foreword by Mary Catherine Bateson (Chicago: University of Chicago Press, 2000), 177–93.

132. Parfit, *Reasons and Persons*, 81.

133. Reps and Senzaki, eds., *Zen Flesh, Zen Bones*, 95.

134. William Blake, *The Book of Thel*, in *The Complete Poetry and Prose of William Blake*, ed. David V. Erdman (New York: Doubleday, 1988).

135. Theodor Adorno, "Progress," *Philosophical Forum* 15, nos. 1–2 (Fall–Winter 1983–1984), 55–70.

136. Georg Wilhelm Freidrich Hegel, *Phenomenology*, 399.

137. George Friedrich Hegel, *Introductory Lectures on Aesthetics*, trans. Bernard Bosanquet, ed. and intro. Michael Inwood (Harmdondsworth, UK: Penguin, 1993), 83.

138. Ibid., 77.

139. Ibid., 90.

140. Ibid., 73.

141. I take this suggestive term from Gerda Norvig, "Female Subjectivity and the Desire of Reading in(to) Blake's *Book of Thel*," *Studies in Romanticism* 34, no. 2 (1995): 255–71.

142. See, for instance, Slavoj Žižek, *Everything You Always Wanted to Know about Lacan (But Were Afraid to Ask Hitchcock)* (New York: Verso, 1992), 227; *The Parallax View* (New York: Verso, 2005), 4, 29, 83, 122, 152, 213, 320; "Do We Still Live in a World?," http://www.lacan.com/zizrattlesnakeshake.html, accessed April 29, 2013.

143. *Oxford English Dictionary*, "weird" adj.

144. In Walter Benjamin, "Conversations with Brecht," in Un-

derstanding Brecht, trans. Anna Bostock, intro. Stanley Mitchell (London: Verso, 1998), 105–121 (121).

145. See Slavoj Žižek's own contribution to this series, "Neighbors and Other Monsters: A Plea for Ethical Violence," in The Neighbor: Three Inquiries in Political Theology, by Slavoj Žižek, Eric Santner, and Kenneth Reinhard (Chicago: University of Chicago Press, 2006), 134–90.

146. See B. Alan Wallace, Contemplative Science: Where Buddhism and Neuroscience Converge (New York: Columbia University Press, 2009), 65–93.

147. Theodor Adorno, Mahler: A Musical Physiognomy (Chicago: University of Chicago Press, 1996).

148. George Morrison, "The Reawakening of Mysticism," The Weaving of Glory (Grand Rapids, MI: Kregel, 1994), 103–10 (106).

149. See, for example, Keiji Nishitani, On Buddhism, trans. Seisaku Yamamoto and Robert E. Carter (Albany: State University of New York Press, 2006), 79.

150. Theodor Adorno, "Valéry Proust Museum," Prisms, trans. Samuel and Shierry Weber (Cambridge, MA: MIT Press, 1997), 173–186 (180).

GLOSSARY

absolute truth According to *Madhyamaka* philosophy, the truth of *emptiness*, variously defined by different schools. These schools agree that absolute truth is beyond the capacity of the intellect to comprehend, but they differ on the extent to which the ultimate—*emptiness*—should be described as *buddha nature* with its various positive qualities.

Avalokiteśvara The *bodhisattva* or *buddha* of compassion, traditionally depicted as male except in East Asian art. Also the speaker in the *Heart Sūtra*. (*See also* Kannon and Kuan-yin.)

bardo Tibetan term for any period of transition between two major states of mind; commonly used to refer to the period between death and rebirth. In Tibet various *tantric* texts described practices for taking advantage of the opportunity the bardo represents for a practitioner to achieve buddhahood.

bodhisattva According to *Pāli Buddhism*, the bodhisattva is one who has very nearly achieved buddhahood but who vows in front of the *buddha* of her time to forego entering *nirvāṇa* in order to revive the *dharma* once it has been forgotten countless years hence. In *Mahāyāna* Buddhism, the bodhisattva is a practitioner who has vowed to attain buddhahood in order to liberate all beings from suffering.

Buddha A fully awakened one capable of teaching the *dharma*. In *Theravāda Buddhism*, a buddha only appears after the teaching (*dharma*) of the previous buddha has been lost; those who attain full liberation have realization more or less equal to a buddha's.

In *Mahāyāna Buddhism*, countless buddhas exist to help beings, and a practitioner's highest goal is to attain full buddhahood in order to spend countless eons helping others become fully liberated. Prince *Siddhārtha* became the Buddha of the present age (according to traditional accounts) when he fully experienced ultimate reality under the Bodhi ("awakening") Tree. A buddha, from the Indian perspective, is not a god because even the gods are not free from *saṃsāra*, the endless cycle of birth and death, while a buddha is. (Traditional schools of Buddhism do not accept the idea of an all-powerful creator god.)

Buddha nature Emphasized in later *Mahāyāna* scriptures, the inherent identity of each living being as a *buddha*; a fully awakened state as the basis of the ordinary mind.

Buddhadharma The teachings (*dharma*) of the *Buddha*.

Buddhist Wheel of Life Most commonly, a *maṇḍala*-like graphic representation of cyclic existence depicting the three forces driving beings from one lifetime to the next (ignorance, greed, and aversion), the six realms of existence (hell beings, hungry ghosts, animals, humans, demi-gods, and gods, each with a *buddha* to liberate the beings of that realm), and the *Twelve Links of Dependent Origination* as a giant wheel held in the fangs of Yama, the god of death. Outside the wheel are liberated beings who are now free from cyclic existence. (See also *saṃsāra*.)

Candrakīrti/Chandrakīrti (seventh century CE) A commentator, most importantly, on *Nāgārjuna*'s works on *emptiness* who was relatively obscure during his own time but who gained renown later and whose works deeply impacted later *Madhyamaka* thought, particularly in Tibet. Candrakīrti offers some of the most skeptical works in that philosophical tradition, vigorously refuting any notion of phenomena or persons (or even ultimate reality) as existent from their own side in any way. His texts are foundational for what Tibetans call the *Prāsaṅgika-Madhyamaka* view.

channels Pathways through which *energy* (considered a very subtle form of matter) naturally flows in the body. The three major channels are the central, running just in front of the spine from its base to the crown of the head; and the right and left, running parallel to the central channel on both sides from a few inches below the navel at the center of the abdomen to the crown of the head.

Chögyam Trungpa Rinpoche (1939–1987) One of the earliest Tibetan *lamas* to move to the West and teach students in English, (in)famous for his "crazy wisdom" approach that included heavy drinking and sleeping with many of his students; regarded by many of his disciples as highly realized.

D.T. Suzuki (1870–1966) A largely self-taught layman, Suzuki was a key figure in the early dissemination of *Zen Buddhism* in the US in the 1950s and '60s. He wrote about *Mahāyāna* Buddhism as well as *Zen*, lectured at various universities, and inspired many Beats and other early American *Zen* practitioners.

Dalai Lama The spiritual and formerly temporal heads of Tibet since the seventeenth century, the Dalai Lamas are a reincarnating lineage of which the current incarnation is the fourteenth (*see also* lama).

dharma Most significantly, the doctrines or truth taught by the *Buddha*; the term has a wide range of secondary, technical meanings such as "phenomena," "constituents of existence," "rules," etc.

Dōgen Zenji (1200–1253) *Sōtō Zen* master who experienced awakening while he was practicing in China; he emphasized "just sitting" (*shikan taza*) in meditation as the expression of *buddha nature*.

Drepung Monastery One of the three major *Gelukpa* monasteries of Tibet, Drepung is known for its academic rigor. Originally located about five kilometers from Lhasa, Drepung (like the other major teaching monasteries) has been reconstituted in Southern India following the destruction of monastic facilities and other unfavorable conditions in Tibet.

Dzogchen The "Great Perfection" or "Great Completeness," a tradition of Tibetan Buddhism (and Bön) that emphasizes effortless apprehension of the true nature of mind and reality. Dzogchen is the highest practice in the *Nyingmapa* tradition, and its "effortless" meditation typically follows years of dedicated practice.

emptiness The lack of inherent existence of all phenomena and persons. A *Mahāyāna* doctrine with roots in *Pāli Buddhist* texts, emptiness holds that people (and things, etc.) are not only dependent on their own causes (parents, food, their immediately previous lives, etc.); when their causes and constituents are analyzed, no stable elements can be found within those constituents, either. For instance, according to *Mahāyāna* Buddhist philosophers, even what seems like a single moment of awareness can be endlessly subdivided into smaller moments, so there can be no stable, self-existent building blocks of consciousness. Similarly, any physical object is composed of various components, none of which is identical in nature to the object. Emptiness, then, is less a denial that the world exists than a radical critique of the assumption that people and phenomena have their own unchanging essences. (*See also* interdependence.)

energy Subtle currents that run through the body, sustaining life and providing the basis for mind, energy is considered a very subtle form of matter that sustains and influences the mind. Different *tantric* systems enumerate different types of energies associated with various faculties (e.g., "downward voiding wind" causes urination, defecation, etc.), and many traditional Asian medical systems describe maladies that result from blockages in the flow of energy. According to the tantras, the ordinary energies of the body are distorted forms of awakened energies, and *yogic* practice offers the means to effect a transformation from distorted to awakened.

engaged Buddhism A movement in the West and in Asia to bring the values and perspectives of the Buddhist *dharma* into the sphere of social activism, often focused on issues of peace and social justice.

enlightenment Most Buddhist traditions hold that a practitioner experiences moments of enlightenment or awakening, which she then deepens as part of her progress in meditation. Most sects define a state of full enlightenment as a permanent cessation of suffering and delusion that results from a practitioner's realizing the nature of ultimate reality.

five aggregates According to Pāli Buddhism, the actual constituents of the person (with a truly existent self not among them): form (*rūpa*), feelings (*vedanā*), discrimination (*saṃjñā*), conditioning factors (*saṃskāra*), and consciousness (*vijñāna*). See Robert E. Buswell Jr. and Donald S. Lopez Jr., eds., *The Princeton Dictionary of Buddhism* (Princeton, NJ: Princeton University Press, 2014), 828.

formless meditation Highly developed levels of concentration in which a practitioner takes as his object of meditation infinite space, infinite consciousness, infinite nothingness, and neither perception nor non-perception. Successive objects lead to increasingly subtle states of mind.

four noble truths The truth that unawakened life is necessarily unsatisfactory, the truth that dissatisfaction and suffering are caused by grasping at pleasures resulting from mistaken views of the world, the truth that an end to all dissatisfaction and suffering is possible, and the truth of the Noble Eightfold Path leading from unawakened existence to complete *enlightenment*. That path consists of right view, intent, speech, action, livelihood, effort, mindfulness, and concentration. According to traditional accounts of the *Buddha*'s life and teachings, the Four Noble Truths were the topic of his first *dharma* talk.

Gelugpa Founded in the fifteenth century CE by *Tsongkhapa*, the most recent and most scholarly of the four major schools of Tibetan Buddhism.

Heart Sūtra The abbreviated title for the *Heart of the Perfection of Wisdom* [Prajñāpāramitā] *Sūtra*, this short text contains the essence of the *Mahāyāna* teachings on *emptiness*, including the famous maxim that emptiness is form and form is emptiness, as well as a mantra of transcendent wisdom. This sūtra, according to tradition, was taught by *Avalokiteśvara* to *Śāriputra* and approved by the *Buddha*.

Hīnayāna Buddhism The "Lesser Vehicle," *Mahāyāna* Buddhists' pejorative term for *Pāli Buddhism*, this term refers to all the schools of Buddhism that formed before the advent of the Mahāyāna as a separate tradition. Only the *Theravāda* tradition survives out of the eighteen pre-Mahāyāna schools.

hongaku The doctrine that each living being is already a *buddha* (hence "original enlightenment"), it has been contrasted with "actualized enlightenment," a state of complete buddhahood realized through practice. Medieval Japanese internalized and reinterpreted this doctrine to emphasize awakened life as emerging out of daily life rather than being a separate state of existence that frees the practitioner from everyday reality.

Huayan Buddhism Also known as Kegon or Avataṃsaka Buddhism, this school began to take form during the sixth century CE in China. A distinguishing characteristic is its distinctly Chinese outlook that blends Indian Buddhist doctrine with a native emphasis on harmony and the world of appearances. This school profoundly influenced later Chinese Buddhist traditions.

ikebana The Japanese art of flower arranging in which practitioners aim to harmonize the human realm with the natural, drawing attention to the graceful lines of the flower(s) and other elements such as the vase, leaves, twigs, etc.

impermanence At the most subtle level, the moment-by-moment changes of every phenomenon and being, even when they are so minimal that we cannot notice differences from one instant to the next. At coarser levels, the eventual disintegration of persons, situations, structures, etc., that might seem solidly existent and not subject to change. Impermanence is tied to *emptiness* because the very mutability of beings and phenomena results from their lacking a stable, inherent nature of their own. This allows them to disintegrate and new things to arise from their constituents, and it makes possible the transition from unawakened to awakened existence.

interdependence A core Buddhist concept, this can refer to the way phenomena and beings arise in dependence on suitable

conditions (e.g., for a flower to bloom, the plant must have
sprouted, drawn nutrients from the earth, received water, etc.).
It can also refer to the mutual dependence of parts and wholes,
such as a "table leg" being designated as such only in the context
of the whole table. Or in the case of form and formlessness, a
form can only exist because the material from which it is made
was derived from some previous form; *emptiness*, likewise, refers to a form's lack of inherent identity, so neither term makes
sense without the other.

Joshu's Mu A famous *kōan* in which a monk asks the *Zen* master
Joshu whether a dog has *buddha nature*. Although the standard
Mahāyāna answer is yes, Joshu instead proclaims, "Mu!"—that
is, "No." The disciple experiences a moment of awakening.

Kāma Sūtra Probably composed around 400–200 BCE, this sūtra
focuses on pleasure (*kāma*), one of the four main pursuits
considered proper to ancient Hindu men. It is best known in the
West as a sex manual for its list of suggested positions, but it also
offers men advice on other aspects of pleasure as well, such as
finding a lover or wife and making money. (It addresses women
primarily through its discussion of their duties as wives.)

Kamakura period From the late twelfth century CE to 1333, the
period during the shogunate (military dictatorship nominally
subservient to the emperor) began and during which samurai
culture (influenced by *Zen*) flourished.

Kannon Japanese version of Kuan-yin.

Kanzeon (*See* Kannon)

karma Literally, "action." Most simply, karma can refer either,
first, to an intentional action of body, speech, or mind that acts
as a cause or, second, to the result that eventually comes to the
doer of that action. Popular forms of Buddhism often present
karma simply as either positive or negative, with good deeds
similar to deposits to a bank account and harmful deeds similar
to withdrawals. Theories of karma can become quite subtle,
with each event in a being's life functioning as both an effect of
previous causes and the cause for effects yet to come.

Kashmiri Shaivism A tantric tradition originating in Kashmir and focusing on Śiva as the ultimate nature of all that exists. It emphasizes various stages of tantric engagement, from external physical practices to recognizing one's identity with Śiva in a meditation without any method. *Tantric Buddhism* as it was transmitted to Tibet seems to have been deeply influenced by this tradition.

kenshō *Zen* term for a moment of nonconceptual apprehension of reality which must be deepened through practice; when distinguished from *satori*, *kenshō* is the first such moment.

kōan A verbal puzzle, usually pithy, that presents a meditator with a problem the intellect is incapable of solving, thus forcing at least a brief cessation of the conceptual mind and/or transmitting nonconceptual wisdom. (*See also* Joshu's Mu.)

Kuan-yin (Also spelled Guanyin or Quan Yin) Chinese translation of *Avalokiteśvara*, the *bodhisattva* or *buddha* of compassion who looks down on the world with the intent to ease the sufferings of beings. The Indian version of this *buddha* is male, as were original Chinese depictions, but around 1000 CE Chinese images began to show Kuan-yin as female, which has become the standard iconography in East Asia. This *buddha* is said to be able to take on whatever appearance is most useful to help people. (*See also* Avalokiteśvara; Bodhisattva; Buddha.)

kundalini shakti Power ("*shakti*") that, in Hindu traditions, is often pictured as a serpent coiled at the base of the spine. One who practices kundalini *yoga* seeks to arouse this *energy* and lead it up through the central *channel* to the crown chakra to induce awakening or *enlightenment*.

lama Tibetan for "guru," the term can have several different meanings. Sometimes all monks are referred to by this title, but more properly it refers to those (male or female) who have completed at least one three-year retreat or who are recognized when they are young as the reincarnations of deceased masters. This latter category is often also referred to by the title "Rinpoche" ("Precious One").

Lamaist, Lamaism Terms now held to be pejorative by most, used beginning in the eighteenth century by Europeans who encountered Tibetan Buddhism and considered it to be a degradation of the *Buddha*'s original teachings.

Lojong Tibetan techniques of mind training based on slogans designed to help practitioners train spiritual capacities such as mindfulness, compassion, vigor in practice, humility, etc. This type of training was first used by Atiśa (tenth century CE), an Indian teacher who brought Buddhist teachings to Tibet; the slogans most commonly used now were composed by Geshe Chekhawa in the twelfth century.

Madhyamaka The "Middle Way" philosophy systematized by *Nāgārjuna* and developed in various directions by the *Mahāyāna* schools. As its name suggests, this system sees itself as avoiding the extremes of nihilism (nothing inherently exists, so nothing matters) and eternalism (things must exist inherently if they are to exist at all). Instead, it holds that all beings and phenomena exist in dependence on causes, and conditions are *impermanent* and subject to change. Everything an ordinary being perceives seems substantial but is in fact mere appearance; at the same time, the level of *relative truth* is not unreal in that *dependent origination* (*see* Twelve Links of (Inter)dependent Origination) is still operative.

Mahāyāna The "Greater Vehicle," a movement that separated from *Pāli Buddhism* sometime around the beginning of the Common Era and emphasizes training to become a *bodhisattva*; this is the most widespread form of Buddhism in Central and East Asia.

maṇḍala An image representing or instantiating the sacred realm of a *buddha*, usually symmetrically arranged around an image of a *buddha* at the center.

Marpa the translator *Milarepa*'s teacher, a major figure in the Kagyü lineages of Tibetan Buddhism. He inflicted severe hardship on *Milarepa* in order to purify his student's negative *karma* from having murdered dozens of people.

Māyā The world as illusion or dream (i.e., as existent but as profoundly distorted in our perception).

mental aggregates Out of the five aggregates, only one is physical (form, *rūpa*). The other four describe functions of the mind: feelings (*vedanā*), discrimination (*saṃjñā*), conditioning factors (*saṃskāra*), and consciousness (*vijñāna*) (see Buswell and Lopez, *Princeton Dictionary of Buddhism*, 828). These four aggregates, according to Buddhist theories of mind, are so closely interwoven that they seem to present us with a seamless experience of existent phenomena experienced by an existent self. However, many practices aim to tease apart these aspects of experience to leave the practitioner with a vivid experience of finding only processes, not a singular person, behind her experience of herself and her world.

Milarepa (ca. 1052–1135 CE) Among the most revered of Tibetan saints, Milarepa is said to have killed dozens of people with sorcery as a young man, then turned to Buddhist teachings out of fear of the consequences of his actions (*karma*). Following years of austerities under the guidance of his *lama, Marpa the Translator*, Milarepa is said to have awakened fully. He remains an inspirational figure and an archetype of the devoted and an energetic practitioner of *yoga*.

mudrā Most commonly, the hand gesture of a *buddha* depicted in painting or sculpture. Each gesture not only symbolizes a particular state of mind but also (according to some schools) is held to give rise to that state in the practitioner who performs the gesture.

Mūlamadhyamakakārikā *Nāgārjuna's* most influential logical text, it informs all schools of *Madhyamaka* philosophy. Its main thesis is the lack of inherent existence of all phenomena whatsoever—that is, *emptiness*.

Myōan Eisai (1141–1215) A monk and traveler to China, Eisai was the first to bring Ch'an to Japan, thus planting the seeds of the *Zen* traditions and establishing the *Rinzai* school of Zen. He had been trained in *Tendai* Buddhism and its esoteric practices and apparently intended to revitalize that school rather than establish a new one.

Nāgārjuna The systematizer and seminal philosopher of *Mahāyāna Buddhism* whose writings on *emptiness* laid the foundation for *Madhyamaka*. His texts are still widely read and have been variously interpreted by the different Mahāyāna schools. (*See also* Mūlamadhyamakakārikā.)

ngowo A thing or mind's own nature, what it is in itself.

Nichiren (1222–1282) Founder of the various schools that now bear his name, all of which hold the Lotus Sūtra to be the definitive teaching of the *Buddha* and recitation of its title to be the best practice for reaching *enlightenment* in this degenerate age. One extant Nichiren school venerates him as a *buddha*, and members keep the *maṇḍala* he composed of written characters (the *gohonzon*) on shrines in their houses.

nidānas A cause; in the context of the *Twelve Links of Dependent Origination*, each link (or *nidāna*) causes the next.

Nio-i-yin (*See* Kannon)

nirvāṇa The state of cessation of suffering following the full realization of reality (i.e., *enlightenment*); the goal of practitioners in the *Theravada* school.

no-self A core Buddhist doctrine that holds that persons lack a stable and enduring essence, that instead each individual depends on and is shaped by causes and conditions. (*See also* emptiness; impermanence; interdependence.)

Nyingma The oldest order of Tibetan Buddhism, founded in the eighth century CE, it emphasizes the importance of yogic practice. Its highest practice is *Dzogchen*.

original enlightenment (See *hongaku*)

Pāli Buddhism The schools and practice traditions based on the earliest extant Buddhist teachings, usually recorded in Pāli. The *Theravāda* is the only sect of Pāli Buddhism to survive to modern times. This group of schools has also been called Southern Buddhism because of its distribution in Sri Lanka and Southeast

Asia; early Buddhism; or "*Hīnayāna*," meaning "Lesser Vehicle," by some later *Mahāyāna* ("Greater Vehicle") schools.

Prajñāpāramitā Sūtras Often translated as *The Perfection of Wisdom Sūtras*, these constitute a body of texts detailing the key *Mahāyāna* concept of *emptiness*.

Prāsaṅgika Madhyamaka A subset of *Madhyamaka* identified and elaborated on by the Tibetans, this philosophical school is characterized by its refusal to make philosophical assertions of its own and is greatly influenced by the work of *Candrakīrti*. Instead of making claims, Prāsaṅgika proponents simply point to the absurd consequences (*prasaṅga*) of other schools' tenets. Proponents are adamant that *absolute reality* altogether transcends the intellect.

prayer wheel A metal cylinder that spins freely atop the stick that serves as its axis, a prayer wheel can come in different sizes. The cylinder is filled with mantras written on long strips of paper coiled around the stick and is usually imprinted with mantras on its surface. The smallest is handheld, with a small but weighty ball (usually metal or glass) with which the user spins the device. Larger ones can be mounted side by side into a wall along the perimeter of a temple or other sacred place, and the largest can be over six feet tall, supported by the sturdy axis pole, with a railing anchored to the cylinder for the faithful to set it spinning.

relative truth Literally "a truth for an obscured [mind]," the level of reality that we ordinarily apprehend in which beings and phenomena appear to be stable, self-sufficient entities. All such appearances (according to Buddhist *Madhyamaka* philosophy) are mistaken in that they fail to apprehend *absolute truth*, but some schools of *Madhyamaka* divide relative truth into confused vs. "real" relative truth on the basis of whether or not the perceived phenomenon can perform its accustomed function. For instance, a traveler might see a mirage and mistake it for water, but when she reaches the site of the supposed water, she will find nothing to drink.

Rinzai Zen Brought to Japan from China by Myōan Eisai in the twelfth century CE, this school of *Zen* became culturally and politically influential in medieval Japan. It emphasizes awakening to one's true nature and uses both seated meditation and contemplating *kōans* as meditative practices. Rinzai is known for the rigor of its training.

saṃsāra The round of unawakened existence in which a being is reborn, clings to itself and its environment as permanent, seeks for happiness, dies, and is propelled into a new birth by its accumulated *karma*. This cycle is characterized by unsatisfactoriness and suffering and is broken when one attains *nirvāṇa*. (*See also* Buddhist Wheel of Life.)

sangha The community of the *Buddha*'s followers who practice his teachings (*dharma*) together; a specific sangha typically consists of the students of a given teacher or residents and supporters of a particular monastic institution.

Śāriputra A leading disciple of the *Buddha* according to the *Pāli Buddhist* canon, Śāriputra had attained *nirvāṇa* and was renowned for his wisdom.

satori Zen term for a moment of nonconceptual apprehension of reality which must be deepened through practice.

selwa Clarity, the appearance or display of a thing or mind.

sexual union Posture often depicted in *Vajrayāna* or *Tantric Buddhist* art in which a male and a female *buddha* sit or stand while sexually united. The posture symbolizes the blissful union of appearances (male) and *emptiness* (female) or skillful means (male) and wisdom (female), the *ultimate reality* of beings' minds.

shakti Primal creative power in Hindu thought, often associated with the feminine principle.

shikan taza A practice of "just sitting" in meditation introduced to *Zen Buddhism* by *Dōgen Zenji*.

Shinran (1173–1262) Japanese priest who founded the Jōdo Shinshū ("True Pure Land School") that emphasizes devotion to Amitabha and reliance on that *buddha*'s power to guarantee his followers' rebirth in his pure land, Sukhāvatī. Shinran contrasted "self-power" (i.e., a practitioner's efforts to effect his own liberation), to "other-power," reliance on Amitabha's vow to liberate those who call on him.

Siddhārtha Gautama (ca. 500 BCE) According to traditional accounts, the Indian prince who, through *yogic* practice, became the *Buddha* ("the awakened one").

Sōtō Zen The largest school of *Zen* in Japan, Sōtō was introduced from China in the thirteenth century by *Dōgen Zenji*, and his major text, *Shōbōgenzō*, has deeply influenced modern Sōtō schools. Practitioners emphasize silent sitting without an object as the meditator brings awareness to the flow of thoughts and other experiences through the mind; they put less emphasis on *kōans*.

subtle body The *channels*, *energies*, and "essential drops" (extremely subtle energies) of the body that are all considered the very subtle matter that provides support for the mind. Much of *tantric* practice is explicitly formulated to transform the ordinary subtle body to an awakened state, and even practices that are neither tantric nor explicitly involved with the subtle body typically involve shifts in the energetic state of the subtle body.

Tantric Buddhism The latest of the major branches of Buddhism to develop in India, this form emphasizes working directly with the body's *energy* system to quiet the ordinary mind, identifying oneself as being in the actual presence of or as indivisible with a given *buddha*, and transcending dualistic categories such as good and bad, pure and impure, etc. Some tantric practices called for significant social transgressions. (*See also* Vajrayāna Buddhism.)

Tendai school Originating around the ninth century CE, this school was inspired by the Chinese Tiantai tradition and focused on original enlightenment (*hongaku*). Also, this school transmitted Chinese masters' esoteric traditions, making it attractive to Japanese rulers.

Theosophical Society An early popularizer of Asian religions in the US, the Theosophical Society was founded in 1875 by

Madame Helena Blavatsky and a few colleagues. Although the organization was avowedly nonsectarian, it was heavily influenced by Blavatsky's "channeled" teachings that established an elaborate cosmology of Hindu- and Buddhist-influenced esoteric themes, "root races" of beings that became human, "astral" bodies and planes of existence, etc.

Theravāda The only remaining sect of the eighteen *Pāli Buddhist* groups that crystallized in the centuries after the historical *Buddha*; it survives now in Southeast Asia and Sri Lanka.

transmission In the context of Ch'an Buddhism (the Chinese model for Japanese *Zen*), *dharma* transmission referred to an illustrious teacher's approval of a student's realization of the truths of his lineage and that teacher's permission for the student to succeed him as the primary teacher of the lineage. Ch'an and *Zen* texts refer to "mind to mind transmissions" of nonconceptual wisdom from the *Buddha* or a patriarch of their school to particularly gifted students. Most schools of Buddhism have some sense that the most important truths are communicated from the contemplative virtuosi of one generation to those of the next through some form of transmission.

Tsongkhapa Lobsang Drakpa (1375–1419) Posthumously regarded as the founder of the *Gelukpa* tradition, Tsongkhapa was one of Tibet's most brilliant logicians. He emphasized monastic discipline and academic study, and his order is associated with those two pursuits, but he also wrote extensively on *tantric Buddhism*.

Twelve Links of (Inter)dependent Origination A foundational concept, this describes the way beings perpetuate *saṃsāric* existence; more generally, the concept of dependent origination explains that everything arises in dependence on its causes and subsides when those causes dissipate. This description thus underpins the entire Buddhist path to *nirvāṇa*: to break the links of this chain is to free oneself from cyclic existence. The links of the chain are: (1) ignorance (Skt. *avidyā*, Pāli *avijjā*), (2) predispositions (S. *saṃskāra*, P. *saṅkhāra*), (3) consciousness (S. *vijñana*, P. *viññana*), (4) name and form (*nāmarūpa*), (5) the six internal sense-bases (*āyatana*), (6) sensory contact (S. *sparśa*,

P. *phassa*), (7) feeling (*vedanā*), (8) attachnemt (S. *tṛṣṇā*, P. *taṇha*), (9) grasping (*upādāna*), (10) becoming (*bhava*), (11) birth (*jāti*), and (12) old age and death (*jarāmaraṇa*). (Buswell and Lopez, *Princeton Dictionary of Buddhism*, 669).

Vajrayāna Buddhism The "Lightning Bolt" or "Diamond" (vajra) vehicle (yāna), this branch of the *Mahāyāna* was the final development of Buddhism in India and emphasized *buddha nature* and techniques for realizing that nature in a single lifetime (i.e., relatively speaking, with the speed of lightning). Vajrayāna traditions became dominant in Tibet, Nepal, and other Himalayan regions and also flourished in Japan. (*See also* Tantric Buddhism.)

valid cognition In conversation with non-Buddhist Indian epistemological systems, the Buddhist logicians Dignāga and Dharmakīrti established that valid inferential cognition, valid direct sensory perception, or yogic direct perception were all epistemologically sound ways of establishing information (unlike scriptural authorities, which some non-Buddhist traditions accepted as a source of valid cognition). In the *Gelukpa* tradition (particularly by the time of Gendun Chopel), the study of these topics and of the logic that undergirds valid inferential cognition had become major topics in monastic curricula and were often taught in a formulaic way.

yab-yum (*See* sexual union)

Yeshe Tsogyal According to traditional accounts, Yeshe Tsogyal was one of the wives of King Trisong Detsen of Tibet, who invited the realized *yoga* practitioner Guru Rinpoche to teach the Buddhist *dharma* in Tibet. Yeshe Tsogyal became Guru Rinpoche's consort and is held, particularly by the *Nyingma* school, to have achieved full buddhahood. Together and separately, these two founders of that order practiced in remote mountain areas.

yoga As a spiritual practice, yoga typically refers to a discipline or set of methods by means of which a practitioner trains to realize the truths of her tradition.

zazen, zuochan Seated meditation emphasized in Chinese Ch'an and passed on to Japanese *Zen* traditions. Different schools emphasize various aspects of practice within *zazen*, such as *samādhi* (concentration), contemplating *kōans*, or simply sitting and observing the thoughts, sensations, etc., that flow through the mind without reacting to any of them.

Zen A set of *Mahāyāna* (Greater Vehicle) schools that emphasizes meditation as the means to realize one's *buddha nature*; derived from Chinese Ch'an, Zen developed in Japan and has now spread globally. (*See also* Mahāyāna; Rinzai Zen; and Sōtō Zen.)

Claire Villareal
Rice University

Lightning Source UK Ltd.
Milton Keynes UK
UKOW06f1850240616

277021UK00003B/13/P